Praise for Jennifer Lauck's *New York Times* bestseller

BLACKBIRD

"The unblinking look of one child at a hard world. Written gloriously and movingly."
—Frank McCourt, author of *Angela's Ashes* and *'Tis*

"A beautifully written memoir—utterly absorbing, alternately heartbreaking and inspiring."

—Hope Edelman, author of *Motherless Daughters*

"A standout debut."

—*Newsweek*

"Riveting. . . . [*Blackbird*] fills me with an admiration for which I cannot find words. . . . Read this book and be humbled, as I was, by the story of this lovely child, and her ultimate triumph over events and experiences that seem impossible to overcome."

—*The London Times* (U.K.)

"A novelistic vision of a life with both hope and heartache to spare."

—*Harper's Bazaar*

"Heart-wrenching, vividly remembered, and shockingly real."

—*The Denver Post*

"A searing, soaring memoir of one girl's complicated and almost unbelievable childhood. . . . Lauck's literary achievements . . . are as extraordinary as those of Frank McCourt and Dave Eggers."

—*Kirkus Reviews* (starred review)

"Gives hope to those who have weathered the loss of a parent, particularly a mom."

—*People*

"Magnificently written . . . will move even the most cynical of readers."

—*The Sunday Tribune* (Ireland)

"Riveting. . . . [Lauck] succeed[s] brilliantly in portraying the innocence and intuition of a child, the vulnerability and strength, and the moral clarity and will to survive. . . . A brutal coming-of-age document[ed] with remarkable lucidity and forgiveness."

—*Booklist* (starred review)

"*Blackbird* reads like a modern Grimm's fairy tale. . . . Lauck is a fine storyteller . . . [who] has accomplished something remarkable: she has taken the remnants of a nasty and heartbreaking girlhood and arranged them in a literary mosaic that is as stirring as it is therapeutic."

—Chelsea Cain (author of *Dharma Girl*) in *The Oregonian*

"The writing is vivid and beautiful. The story is poignant and remarkable. . . . This riveting, unforgettable book deserves many, many readers."

—*The Denver Post*

"Lauck takes us into the mind of a child in all its terrible clarity, helplessness, fury, and incomprehension."

—*The Sunday Times* (U.K.)

"This heartbreaking memoir . . . remains true to the child's eye and keeps the reader sympathetic and engaged."

—*Publishers Weekly*

"Riveting. . . . Jennifer Lauck dissects childhood helplessness, lays it bare. . . . Her improbable triumph is everywhere in this remarkable book."

—*The Plain Dealer* (Cleveland)

"Direct, evocative, and emotionally honest, *Blackbird* will haunt readers with its startling story and its vibrant narration."

—Diana Abu-Jaber, author of *Arabian Jazz*

"*Blackbird* is Lauck's stunning testament to the inborn ability children have to survive. By the book's bittersweet final pages, you're on your feet cheering for her."

—Gregg Kleiner, author of *Where River Turns to Sky*

"Lauck's beautifully rendered memoir about the dismantling of her young life . . . [is] powerful and engaging. . . . Perhaps Lauck's greatest talent is her ability to articulate the boundless alienation and loneliness that Jenny lives with."

—*Newsday* (New York)

"A gripping memoir. . . . Lauck's account of courage in the face of cruelty gives new meaning to the word *survival*."

—*Glamour*

"A tender and delicately rendered tale of a young girl's survival."

—Laura Cunningham, author of *A Place in the Country*

"An affecting, well-rendered memoir."

—*Seattle Post-Intelligencer*

"A beautiful tale. . . . Lauck captures the spirited, scratchy resilience of a child managing to shine through trauma. Heartbreakingly moving yet totally unsentimental."

—*Elle* (U.K.)

ALSO BY JENNIFER LAUCK

Blackbird: A Childhood Lost and Found

STILL WATERS

JENNIFER LAUCK

WASHINGTON SQUARE PRESS
New York London Toronto Sydney Singapore

A Washington Square Press Publication
1230 Avenue of the Americas, New York, NY 10020

Originally published in hardcover in 2001 by Pocket books

ISBN: 0-7434-3966-X

First Washington Square press trade paperback printing October 2002

10 9 8 7 6 5 4 3 2 1

For information regarding special discounts for bulk purchases, please contact Simon & Schuster Special Sales at 1-800-456-6798 or business@simonandschuster.com

Printed in the U.S.A.

For Bryan

ACKNOWLEDGMENTS

Father Albert, a teacher at Conception Seminary, taught me that a prime pillar of spirituality is reverence.

Reverence defined is respect and devotion.

With these feelings in my heart, I must send all my devotion to Steve Dorsey, husband, friend, restorer of trust and faith.

In my home community, gratitude goes to Kamala Bremer, Susan Hall, Rhonda Hughes, Larry Colton, and Peter Sears, who read early drafts and gave equal parts of much-needed advice and encouragement; Tom Spanbauer, whose words of writing wisdom were always in my heart, even when I wasn't at the table; Carol Ferris, Howard Waskow, and Kate Finn, who healed me time and time again. And you too, Jay Yarnell.

For those in the business of publishing, I am indebted to Pocket Books and Judith Curr, who didn't hesitate to invest in me and my story; Rosemary Ahern for her early read and advice; Kim Kanner, who continued to be a tireless advocate, a good friend, and a first-rate editor; and Molly Friedrich, a formidable agent who, beyond the call of duty, pushed me to the highest level of excellence.

On the path of investigation, I must thank Steve, Jeffrey, Megan, and Kari—you know why; Father Samuel, Father Albert, Brother Thomas, Brother Jude, the Sisters of Clyde, and, of course, Father Christopher Hellstrom for all your wisdom; Martin Louis, Jeffrey Harp at the University of Oklahoma, Joann Kolsted, Martha Finely, and Dale Gooch, all stepping-stones to the truth.

To Georgia and Charles Ferrel, all my thanks for your open door and open hearts.

Back home again, my devotion goes to you as well, sweet Spencer. I'm blessed you chose me to be your mother; your spirit gives more joy than one heart can hold.

You can't change the past but, with understanding,
you can sometimes draw the poison out of it.

CARLOS GEBLER—*FATHER AND I*

University of Oklahoma Police Department
Case no: 03-84-0884

CODE: 2811 **CRIME:** LOST/MISSING **CLASS:** PERSON
DATE REPORTED: 03/26/84 **VICTIM:** Lauck, Bryan Joseph
OCCUPATION: Student **RACE/SEX:** C/M

DESCRIBE: Reported that victim was missing; further investigation showed that victim had taken a firearm from the room.

NARRATIVE: Reported that victim had not come to work and could not be located. Victim's roommate stated he had not seen victim since Wed., 3/21, or Thurs., 3/22. He also stated that victim's bicycle, a red 10-speed, was missing from the room, but none of the victim's personal possessions had been taken, including clothes, checkbook, etc. Victim's roommate also reports a Smith & Wesson revolver was missing from the bottom drawer of the roommate's dresser. The weapon was kept, against OU student code regulations, in a shoulder holster rig in a drawer. Weapon was not loaded. Roommate stated that only the victim and a subject across the hall knew of the weapon. Roommate is certain that the victim took the weapon but not the ammunition, which roommate still has stored in a metal Band-Aid box.

Victim was planning to enter the U.S. Army as a warrant officer to begin helicopter flight training.

Further, it was found that both the victim's natural parents were deceased and that the victim previously lived with an uncle.

Spoke with a Father Thomas Briller of the Church of the Magdalene in Tulsa, OK. Father Briller stated the victim is a pleasant person but moody at times.

Spoke with a subject known as "Angie," in California, and she identifies herself as a cousin of the victim. She says victim is known for severe episodes of depression.

Excerpt, police report, University of Oklahoma

PART ONE

RENO

ONE

RENO, NEVADA ⁂ MAY 1975

The bus pulls into the Reno terminal and I hold the dirty duffel bag in my lap. People stand on the sidewalk and all the faces are just faces with eyes that don't look for me.

Inside my chest is a heavy alone feeling. Maybe no one will be here for me. I get off the bus and look around and my eyes stop on Grandpa Ed, Daddy's daddy.

"There she is," Grandpa yells.

I squeeze my fingers around the bag strap and walk until we are face to face, me small, him tall. Grandpa has his hands fisted on his hips like he has something to say but he just looks at me and shakes his head.

"Well, give your old Grandpa a hug," he says, kneeling down, arms wide.

I drop my bag and hug around his neck, the smell of coffee mixed with peppermint. He's just like I remember—round cheeks, wide nose, white hair, and bushy white eyebrows. Grandpa laughs deep and warm against my face and stops hugging first.

"My goodness," he says, hands on the top of my shoulders, holding me back, "you're a young lady now."

My throat hurts, a lumpy kind of hurt and I smile and nod since I don't know what else to do. My arms and body still feel Grandpa's hug. I wish I was still hugging him.

I look at my tennis shoes with the hole worn through that shows my big toe and the silver key for the pink trunk is tucked safe under the laces.

Grandpa picks up my duffel bag and stands up then. "Is this all you brought with you?"

"No," I say. "My trunk is under the bus."

"Under the bus?"

A man unloads suitcases and boxes on the sidewalk.

"There," I say.

My trunk is pink and silver with flecks of gray and inside is everything I could fit. There are the wedding photos of Momma and Daddy, her pearls and wedding ring, stuff from my princess bedroom and my books.

I run up the sidewalk, pat the side of the trunk and it makes the solid sound of something packed tight. I put my hands on the black handle and lift, cool metal against my legs. The trunk is heavy but it's not too heavy to carry.

"Hey now," Grandpa says, "don't go and break your back."

"I can do it," I say. "I've done it a hundred times."

Grandpa moves his golf hat around on his head.

"That may be so, Jennifer Lauck," Grandpa says, "but you put that darn thing down and let me get it for you."

It's funny how he says my whole name, all serious, and I roll my lips together to keep from smiling. Grandpa bends, puts his hand on the black trunk handle and lifts like it's going to be easy.

"Be careful," I say. "It's heavy."

He makes a deep grunt sound and lets go of the trunk,

stands straight, hands pushed into the low part of his back. He looks at me, at the trunk, and then laughs out loud.

"You're right," Grandpa says. "It is heavy."

Maybe it's the way he says those words, so surprised, maybe it's how he looks at me like I'm crazy for trying to carry the trunk myself or maybe it's how long it's been since I've seen him and how good it is to know he's here. I can't help but laugh at Grandpa and the two of us laugh so hard right there in the Reno bus terminal, I think I am going to cry.

Reno air is so hot, it's like being slapped across the face and it is this dusty color, not brown, not gray, but in-between with the lightest shade of green from the sagebrush bushes that grow everywhere.

Grandpa and me ride in his big car called a Toronado. Grandpa says he just had it painted to match his golf cart back home. He calls the color metallic green.

The air conditioner is on full blast and the smell of the air is wet and cold.

I look out the window at everything, the wide blue of the sky, the sagebrush, the flasher signs with the names of casinos in bright lights. COME TO THE MAPES, WIN AT THE NUGGET.

I know I'm here, but I can still feel L.A. in my body, dirty pavement under my feet, homeless people holding up their cups and asking for a nickel and in my stomach, that hungry feeling that never goes away.

I can still see Deb with her green cat eyes and her angles and edges and I can still hear her kids laughing and calling me names, happy I was finally leaving.

I rub my hand over the goose bumps on my arm and look over at where Grandpa sits. He wears wrap-around dark glasses that go over his regular glasses and they make him look like a superhero. While he drives out of the bus station, he asks about the bus ride, did I meet anyone, if I ate. I tell him the bus ride was boring, no one sat next to me, and I ate a whole roll of hard cherry candies I bought when we stopped in Fresno.

Grandpa laughs when I say that about the hard cherry candies and it's nice to make him laugh. He drives under this big arch that says RENO in big letters and under reads THE BIGGEST LITTLE CITY IN THE WORLD. Grandpa stops at a red light and then looks over at me again, a funny tilt to his head.

"I'm just trying to remember the last time I saw you," he says. "Was it '71?"

In the reflection of his wrap-around shades, I can see myself shrug my shoulders.

"It couldn't have been that long ago," he says, rubbing his hand over his face and then pinching his wide nose. "Maybe '73?"

"I don't know," I say, tucking a bit of hair behind my ear.

"Hmm," he says, both hands on the steering wheel, lower lip pushed out, face set to thinking.

This is something grown-ups do, using the years to remember, but I don't think about time that way.

Time is the last big thing that happened, how it was L.A. this morning, one-way ticket and twenty bucks in my hand, good luck and good-bye.

"No, no," Grandpa says, "I think it was '74."

How I rode from L.A. to Fresno without anyone sitting in the seat next to me. In Fresno, I got off the bus, looked over the desert, and thought I could just walk down the road and disappear into that empty wavy space of heat on asphalt.

" '72?" Grandpa says, talking to the windshield.

How I got on the bus instead, hard cherry candies in my hand, nineteen dollars and some change in my back pocket.

"It had to be '72," Grandpa says. "The year your dad married Deb."

I kick my foot up and down on the floor mat.

"What?"

"The last time I saw you," Grandpa says. "1972, the house in Fountain Valley."

The light changes from red to green and Grandpa makes a left onto the freeway.

"That's it," Grandpa says, "I'm sure of it."

The only sound is the fan blowing cold air and out the window, Reno slips by at sixty miles an hour, sagebrush and blue sky. The air in the car is cold and I squeeze my arms around myself.

Grandpa's seat is adjusted so he sits straight up and close to the steering wheel, those funny glasses on his face. He looks down my way, smile on his face, and I see myself bite my lip.

"Something on your mind?" he says.

"I was just wondering," I say.

"What, honey?" he says, leaning toward me like he can't hear.

I sit up in the seat and clear my throat.

"What's going to happen now?"

"Oh," he says, leaning back to normal sitting, eyes out on the road.

"I'm going to take you home to Grandma," he says, "and then, well, we'll just have to see."

"See about what?" I say.

"Oh, this and that," he says, head side to side, "complicated things you don't have to worry about."

"Is Bryan there?" I say.

"At the trailer? No, no, he's over in Carson with Georgia and Chuck for a bit, but not for long."

"Why not for long?" I say.

Grandpa smiles then, something about that smile that makes me think of Daddy. He puts his hand on my leg, pat-pat the way grown-ups do.

"I forgot that about you," he says.

"What?"

"You like to ask questions," he says.

I bite the edge of my thumb, that soft spot past the nail, and look out at Reno again. It's true about the questions; Deb used to say I ask too many questions but I can't help it. Questions are like air, always there, even when you don't stop to notice.

Grandpa gets off the freeway, drives up a long road and ahead of us are rows and rows of mobile homes, metal siding shining under the sun. We go past the sign that says WELCOME and then up another hill past a pool so blue compared to all the dusty brown. Grandpa says the pool is for residents and their families, says I can swim whenever I want.

"You do know how to swim, don't you?" he says.

I watch out the window until I can't see the pool anymore and then shift in my seat.

"I can hold my breath under water for three whole minutes," I say.

Grandpa nods like that makes sense.

"That could come in handy," he says.

He makes a hand-over-hand tight turn, goes past one, two, three trailers. At number four, he makes another hand-over-hand turn, moves his big car in a narrow spot next to his golf cart painted metallic green.

He turns the Toronado off, says he'll bring in my trunk later, says to be careful getting out.

"Don't want to ding the paint," Grandpa says.

I twist to the side, slip myself between car and golf cart, shut the door extra careful.

"Is that my little girl?" a voice says. When I look up, Grandma stands on their porch wearing a long dress, fabric like I imagine Hawaii, flowers of pink and green and purple. She reaches out, loose skin trembling under her arms, and one hand holds a thin brown cigarette.

"Come here and give Grandma a big hug," she says.

I scoot sideways between the car and cart until I reach the chain-link fence and the gate. I push the latch up and swing the chain-link gate open.

She's older than I remember, shoulders more sloped, more lines on her face, but the rest of her is about the same, white hair cut short like a man's, glasses on her face, bright blue eyes.

Grandma puts her arms around me and presses her cheek to mine. Her body feels so soft it's like hugging too hard would hug her apart so I keep myself to myself, my hands patting through her dress to the softness of her body.

She sets me back then and holds my face between her hands. The skin on her fingers is dry rice paper and I can feel the cigarette filter on my cheek.

"After all these years," she says, "as pretty as a picture."

"Doesn't she look great?" Grandpa says.

"She looks great," Grandma says.

"Hasn't she gotten tall?" Grandpa says.

"She is *so* tall," Grandma says. "What are you, eleven now?"

"Twelve," I say.

"You can't be twelve," Grandma says.

"It's true," I say.

She laughs a deep laugh that sounds rough, lets go of my face and puts the thin brown cigarette between her lips.

Grandpa comes up the steps, holds my bag out to me.

"We were just trying to figure out when we last saw this one," Grandpa says, winking like we have a secret. "Got it down to '72."

"That can't be," Grandma says, head back to blow a line of smoke up.

I take my bag from Grandpa, put it over my shoulder. He pulls open the screen and then pushes open the front door, the two of them debating the whole thing again.

"They were in that Fountain Valley house," Grandpa says. "We had a barbeque."

"I don't remember any barbeque, Ed," she says, going in first, one hand holding up her dress, bare feet under.

Grandpa waves me in and inside is a cool green world—green plaid sofa, two green Barcaloungers, and a shiny green globe lamp on a table between. It's green carpet, green paneling and green plastic plants in green pots.

"It was the year he married that Deb," Grandpa says, closing the door on the hot Reno day. "I'm sure of it."

"Deb!" Grandma says, hand waving over her head, cigarette ash floating off the end of her cigarette and down to the carpet. "Worst mistake he ever made."

"Now, Maggie," Grandpa says, one hand to my shoulder, shaking his head on something.

She picks up an ashtray, jabs out her cigarette, mouth set up mad, pink color from her lipstick in the lines around her mouth.

"Your grandma is a little peeved at Deb right now," Grandpa says.

I look at Grandpa, at Grandma.

"It's okay," I say, "I'm always mad at her."

They both look at me, no expressions on their faces, and past that is surprise in their eyes like I'm not quite what they expected.

Grandma sets her ashtray down.

"Let me get a better look at you," she says and reaches one hand out, palm under my chin and fingers on the bones of my jaw to my ears. She moves my face side to side and her hand smells like cigarettes, coffee, and some kind of medicine.

Anyone else tried to touch me this way, I'd kick them in the leg, but she's held my face before; I can feel the memory of it under my skin. It's the memory of people who've known you always, even though you haven't seen them in a long time.

I hold my breath, arms against my sides, and wait.

"Well, one thing is clear," she says, letting go of my face just as quick as she got ahold of it. "You are too skinny, you need a bath, and your hair needs a trim."

I touch my fingers to the side of my face, just under my ear, the feel of her hand still on my skin, and I almost laugh out loud since technically, those are three things.

Grandpa puts his hand on my back, pats one time, and winks.

"See," he says, "Grandma is going to have you shipshape in no time."

After that, Grandma goes off to the kitchen to fix martinis for them, ginger ale for me, and Grandpa shows me to the guest room, where the fold-out sofa is already made into a bed.

"Just make yourself comfortable," Grandpa says.

The end of the fold-out bed is against a green desk and on top of the desk is a bunch of golf stuff. There are a handful of white wooden tees, white golf balls, and a tiny gold trophy with the words HOLE IN ONE on the metal tag.

I come all the way into the guest room and set my bag on the floor.

"What's that mean?" I say. " 'Hole in one'?"

Grandpa takes off his golf cap, bald on top with some white hair around his ears and the back of his head.

"In golf," he says, "you get so many hits to put your ball in the hole—usually takes three or four—but a hole in one means you did it in just one."

Grandpa sits down on the edge of the fold-out and tosses his cap next to the trophy.

"It's an accomplishment," he says, "like bowling a perfect match or winning a race."

"Wow," I say, hand cupped over the gold ball on top of the trophy, the cool metal against my hand, "congratulations."

"It was a while back, but thanks," he says. "I understand you have a few trophies yourself, for running, right?"

I sit down on the edge of the bed, close to Grandpa, my hands on the end of the fold-out mattress and there's a strange feeling of how I know him but don't know him at the same time.

"Sure," I say, "but I never won first place or anything."

"Your dad told us you were a good runner," he says. "Olympic quality."

I laugh out loud in the quiet room.

"I don't think so," I say. "Maybe Deb's kids, but not me."

"Hmm," Grandpa says.

"Daddy was probably just being nice," I say.

Grandpa is quiet for a second and then puts his arm around my back, hand squeezing my shoulder.

"But you did go out there and run?" he says.

"Sure," I say.

"So you did your best?" Grandpa says.

I look up at his face, wide smile, wide nose, glasses with these gold metal frames.

I'm not sure I get what he means, "did my best." I did what I was told but the whole time I hated it and when no one was watching, sometimes I even walked. I'd think doing your best would be doing something with your whole heart and soul but I don't think that's what Grandpa means.

He watches me, waiting, and I can see Daddy in the cinnamon spice color of his eyes.

"I guess I did my best," I say, looking away from him.

Grandpa squeezes my shoulder again.

"That's what counts," he says.

Down the hall is the sound of ice against glass, and Grandpa's eyes search past me.

"Cocktails," Grandma calls to us.

Grandpa clears his throat, fist to his mouth.

"Well," he says, "I could use a drink. How about you?"

"Sure," I say. "Why not?"

Cocktail hour is really an hour and a half that starts at four with Merv Griffin and ends at five-thirty after the news.

Merv Griffin interviews a hoochie-coochie singer named Charo and she shakes her shoulders and laughs with her head way back so you can see all of her neck.

Grandma sits in her chair, a glass full of ice and two olives on a toothpick balanced on her lap.

"She's a wild one," Grandma says.

Grandpa sits in his chair too and reads a golf magazine. He looks around the side of the magazine to see the television.

My ginger ale is in a tall glass with a bunch of yellow stripes and I tilt the glass side to side, ice clink sound against glass. Grandma has a plate of crackers and cheese set between her and Grandpa. I have my own plate, and it's on the long coffee table in front of the green plaid sofa.

I act like I know all about cocktail hour and crackers with cheese and Merv Griffin. I sip my ginger ale and on the TV is a commercial for Pepto-Bismol, pink stuff in a see-through stomach.

Grandma rattles the ice cubes in her glass.

"Refills!" Grandpa says.

My glass is still half full of soda and I hold it in both hands, the cool through my fingers.

"Need more ginger ale?" Grandpa says.

"No," I say. "Thanks."

"So polite," Grandma says.

"Very polite," Grandpa says.

Grandma looks at me and the light from the green globe lamp shines off her glasses. She claps her hands and the sound snaps me to sit straight on the sofa.

"So," Grandma says. "Tell me about you. Tell me everything."

"Everything?" I say.

Grandpa comes back with the glasses filled again and two new olives in each glass.

"I think your grandma means," he says, "tell us how you are doing, what you've been up to."

He sets the martinis on the table between their big green chairs. On the TV is a commercial for crescent rolls, that puffy white guy with the little-kid voice.

Grandma sips her drink, Grandpa sits back down in his Barcalounger, and I don't know if I should laugh or cry or what since all of this is so different than what I've been up to.

I set my ginger ale on the special coaster Grandma put down just for my drink.

"Well, there's been a lot going on," I say.

Grandma watches me, Grandpa too, and I look down at my own hands as if they hold the version of things I want to talk about.

"Yep, there's been a lot going on," I say.

I look at her, at him, and tuck my hair behind my ears, clearing my throat.

"I'm just pretty tired right now, you know?" I say.

Grandma sets her drink down on the big table that separates their chairs and puts her hand over her heart.

"Of course you're tired," she says.

"Well sure," Grandpa says. "You've had a heck of a day."

The two of them look so serious and worried, and it's been a long time since anyone has looked at me that way.

"You just set back and relax," Grandma says, reaching for her cigarettes, shaking out a long brown one from her pack that says MORE on the outside. "We'll have a nice dinner, get you off to bed and there will be plenty of time for chitchat later."

"That's a good idea, Maggie," Grandpa says.

Merv Griffin comes on again and some singer is on the stage with a microphone in her hand singing, "My Eyes Adore You."

"I love this song," Grandma says, eyes going soft behind her glasses. Grandpa shoves back in his Barcalounger with a grunt and opens his golf magazine.

That night, after dinner, I'm tired but I can't sleep, new place, new sounds, new smells. I lay in the back room on the fold-out bed and the sheets are cool and soft and smell like flowers. Grandma made me take a shower, told me to wash my hair two times and scrub everywhere else good with a washcloth.

My skin tingles from being so clean and my hair is softer than I knew it could be.

The curtains are open over the bed and moonlight is around the corners of the room, over the desk with its Hole in One trophy, the cushions from the sofa balanced in one corner and my pink trunk on its side in the other corner.

Grandpa brought that in after dinner, shouldering it down

the narrow hallway to the back bedroom, knocking over pictures on the wall and scraping against the door frame on the way and Grandma warning him to be careful of his heart. He finally got the trunk into the room but had to push it upright and back into a corner, saying it was such a tight fit that it might be a while before I could get inside.

"That's okay," I said. "I don't need to open it."

"Aren't your clothes in there?" Grandma said.

"No, no," I said. "My stuff is in my bag, that trunk has other things in it, stuff from my bedroom—you know, lamps and books and my bedspread."

Then, Grandma made me dump out all the clothes I did bring which added up to a couple of pairs of shorts, my long velvet skirt, and a few T-shirts, holes and stains and rips. That made Grandma angry with Deb all over again, asking what kind of mother sends a child off with no clothes.

I almost laughed out loud at the idea of Deb as my mother.

Deb was never my mother. She was mean to the core even back when she first married Daddy, just after Momma died. Deb just acted all sweet to Bryan and me in front of Daddy. After Daddy died, she was 100 percent mean. Deb told us Daddy's death was his own fault, bad energy he brought on himself.

Not much later, she dumped me in a commune house—said it's called survival; figure it out—and didn't come back for what seemed like a year.

One month ago, my fingers dirty from checking phone booths for extra change, Aunt Georgia and Uncle Charles, family from Momma's side, showed up from Nevada and took both Bryan and me to their hotel. On that day, Deb showed up, screaming, "What the fuck is going on," accusing Aunt Georgia and Uncle Charles of kidnapping even though technically that's not what happened.

Bryan says Deb only kept us with her in California for the money that came every month, Social Security death benefits, and maybe the money ran out or it just wasn't enough anymore. One thing I learned about Deb, there was never enough of anything for her.

She sent Bryan off first, and then it was me—pack your bags, one-way ticket and good-bye.

Far off, I hear the TV and the sound of Grandma and Grandpa's voices talking quiet in the living room. Here in Reno, safe and clean and in the fold-out bed, Deb's starting to fade away like a story you can close the book on, turn off the light, and, finally, go to sleep.

Each day with Grandma and Grandpa is about the same.

In the morning, Grandpa makes coffee in the Mr. Coffee machine and Grandma makes sourdough toast. Grandpa, Grandma and me sit in the living room, eat toast, and watch the *Today Show.* Every half hour, the local weatherman cuts in to talk about Reno weather, saying it's going to be hot and windy, which makes Grandpa happy. Hot and windy are perfect for a round of golf.

Grandpa plays golf every day.

On Tuesdays, I go with him, driving his cart up and down the path that runs along the course and after, we go to the grocery store to get eggs, milk, orange juice, and real butter. Grandpa always stops in the cookie aisle, lets me get whatever I want, and I always get the angel chocolate-chip cookies in the pink-and-white package.

After shopping, we drive to the liquor store and Grandpa buys one bottle of vodka and one jug of red wine and then we drive back to the mobile home for cocktail hour that's really an hour and a half.

On Thursday, he plays golf and after, takes Grandma and me to the library. She turns in her old books, soft-cover romance novels, and then checks out a bunch of new ones, enough to fill a grocery bag. I help pick a few based on the covers I like, mostly the ones where the lady and man are wrapped in each other's arms so close you can't tell where one begins and the other ends.

On the other days of the week, I stay at the mobile home with Grandma. In the mornings, she reads soft-cover romance novels and I watch television. At noon, it's lunch, and after we eat, Grandma says I can have a couple of the angel chocolate-chip cookies. When she isn't looking, I end up taking more than two and push them into my pocket for later. In the afternoon, she reads some more and that's when I walk down to the swimming pool.

Most days, it's just me, the pool and the faraway sound of cars on the flat line of freeway in and out of Reno. I never swim, just sit on the pool edge, kick my feet in the water and eat my chocolate-chip cookies.

On Sundays, Grandma, Grandpa, and me spend the day together, going to the Catholic church where the pews are made of dark wood and there's a pad you pull out for kneeling. I sit between Grandma and Grandpa with a prayer book on my lap and Grandpa points out what page we are on and what prayer we're supposed to say. I keep my finger on the page, follow along, stand up, kneel, and sit down just the way everyone else does.

There's lots of talk about God that I don't understand but the music is nice and there is a time every Sunday when you get to ask God to forgive your sins. In my head, I always ask God to forgive me for taking the cookies but I wonder if He hears, if He's up there at all.

I have all new clothes now, matching shorts and T-shirts, a great bathing suit that's yellow and a lime green color, white buckle sandals, and a pair of tennis shoes without any holes in the toes that actually fit my feet. My long hair was cut at a beauty parlor, all one length to my chin, and since being in the sun by the pool every day, it's even a lighter color of brown. I've been eating all the time too, breakfast, lunch, dinner, and then a bowl of ice cream after dinner. Grandpa says I eat like a horse; Grandma says I'm filling in.

It's normal and it's boring, but I like being here with them. Each day fades away what was before and when I close my eyes, Deb is finally gone. I can't even remember what she looks like or the sound of her voice.

Instead, there's a quiet and a calm in me, a slowing down, and I'm tired all the time. I fall asleep by the pool, take a nap in the afternoon, and always fall asleep on the sofa after dinner. Grandpa says I sleep like the dead, but Grandma says I must be catching up.

When it's time for dinner, Grandpa always turns off the television and plugs in the electric fireplace, which is this hunk of white plastic molded to look like a mantel and bricks. Where there's supposed to be a real fire, it's a plastic log with a light behind, and the log squeaks as it turns around and around. After she puts the food on the table, Grandma always pulls open the sheers that hang over the big dining-room window and out that window is a pretty view of Reno that changes from day to night as we eat.

The three of us sit in the dining room with bowls of Grandma's homemade chicken noodle soup. Grandpa sits at the head of the table, Grandma next to him, her back to the big window, and I sit across from her.

Grandpa puts his face over his bowl, steam on his glasses.

"Smells delicious, Maggie," he says.

"You can't get this out of a can," she says.

The soup has celery, carrots, and chicken, and it does smell good, even if it's strange to eat soup in the summer.

Grandma sips at her soup, eyes up to the ceiling.

"Needs more salt," she says. "Hand me the salt, Ed."

"I don't think it needs more salt," Grandpa says.

She sips again and moves it around in her mouth.

"No," she says, "it definitely needs more salt."

Grandpa moves like he's going to get up but I get up first.

"I got it," I say. "I'm closest to the kitchen."

Grandpa nods at Grandma, she nods back at him, and I can feel them watch me. In the kitchen, the salt is over the stove. I take the shaker back to the dining room.

"Why, thank you, honey," Grandma says.

"Sure," I say.

"Jenny was a big help today," Grandpa says. "She steers that old golf cart like a pro."

Grandma shakes salt over her soup and puts the shaker down on the table.

"She did all the breakfast dishes for me this morning too," Grandma says.

They say how I did this and did that, and I sip soup and listen, as if they are talking about someone else.

The sun goes behind the mountains, sends a pink color up to the bottom of the white clouds, and a few lights of the city start to sparkle.

Grandma sets her spoon in her bowl, and just like that, it's quiet except the squeak of the log in the fake fireplace.

They look at me and I look at them, and all the quiet sends a bad feeling up the back of my neck.

"We thought you might like to see your brother," Grandpa says. "What do you think of that?"

I hold extra still, spoon in my hand and over my soup.

I should have thought about Bryan before, but the truth is, I haven't. Bryan is behind the tired feeling that's in me all the time now, the memory of him not much better than Deb and her kids.

I put my spoon down in the soup, sit back in my chair, hands in my lap to the cloth napkin spread out over my legs.

Grandpa leans his elbows on the table and adjusts his glasses higher on his wide nose. "You haven't said much about your brother since you got here," Grandpa says. "Aren't you kids very good friends?"

"Friends?" I say.

"Didn't you do things together in California?" Grandma says. "Weren't you close?"

Grandma's dress has the kind of neck that shows part of her shoulders and her collarbones and I look at where her dress collar ends and her pale skin begins.

Up until now, they haven't asked much about before and what I've told them is very little. I even made up a few things so they'd think everything was normal. They don't need to know how I dropped out of school or begged on the streets for money or saw a homeless man jump in front of a bus. No one needs to know that stuff. They sure don't need to know about Bryan and me, how he ended up siding with Deb's kids and tormented me into crying more times than I can count.

Right now, I wish I could make up something nice to say about him, but I can't.

I bite my lips together and look at my soup, just the soup.

"You haven't really told us much about your time in California with Deb and her children," Grandpa says.

Grandma nods and frowns.

"We know some things," Grandma says, "but you've told a very different story than what we heard from Georgia and Chuck, not that they are the most reliable people in the world."

"Of course, Deb has her own version of things," Grandpa says.

"Oh, Ed," Grandma says, hand flat on the table between them, "we both know that woman is certifiable."

Grandpa shakes his head at Grandma, *Not now* in his eyes.

I look at Grandma, at Grandpa.

"You've been talking to Deb?" I say.

Grandma opens her mouth to say something and closes it again.

"Just a couple times, really," Grandpa says. "She's not the easiest person to talk to."

All the calm and quiet of being here is gone, and in their place is a mess of the real past and the one I made up. I never thought about Aunt Georgia and Uncle Charles telling a different version of the story, I never thought about Deb having her story too.

I feel backed up in a corner, trapped and mixed up, the sting of tears in my eyes.

Grandma reaches across the table, squeezes her hand over mine.

"We know it's hard, honey," she says, "but if you tell us a few things, we can decide what to do."

"Do what?" I say.

Grandpa takes his napkin off his lap, sets it on the table next to his bowl.

"Let's put it this way," he says. "We want to help you have a normal life."

Grandma takes her hand off my hand and pushes her bowl of soup away.

"As normal as you can, considering," she says.

"What Grandma is trying to say, honey," Grandpa says, "is it's up to us to find a home for you."

"I don't understand," I say.

"What?" Grandma says.

"I don't know," I say. "I just thought, you know . . . Can't I stay here?"

Grandma shakes her head, sad and slow.

"That's what we were afraid of," she says. "That you'd get the wrong idea."

"Did I do something wrong?" I say.

Grandpa laughs, but the sound of his laugh isn't right. "No," he says, "you didn't do anything wrong."

"It's just you need a family," Grandma says, "you need young people."

The log in the fake fireplace squeaks, and what's left of the pink sunset is almost all gone now, a dark gray about to turn to night. Grandma and Grandpa talk then about the future, about stability, about options. Grandpa says Bryan and me might be better off apart since we're not that close anyway. Grandma says I could go live with Auntie Carol except she's getting a divorce from Uncle Bob. Grandpa says there's Aunt Peggy and Uncle Dick and since they have a two-year-old daughter, I'd have a brand-new little sister to look after and grow up with. Grandpa says Bryan gets to decide since he's 15 years old, but they have to decide for me since I'm so young.

The sound of their voices is just sound and I know the truth. All this was just pretend, too good to be true, and they don't want me—they probably never did, not like I thought they did anyway.

I want to tell them I'll try harder, do better, only I can't through the tears that come up and out of me.

Grandma comes to my side of the table and puts her soft

arm around my shoulders. I put my face into my hands and my shoulders shake under her arm.

"We know this is hard," Grandma says. "You go ahead and cry."

She pats my head, and Grandpa clears his throat.

"Maybe this wasn't such a good idea," Grandma says.

"We had to tell her," Grandpa says.

They talk like I'm not here at all and I take a deep breath and wipe my hands down my face. Grandma moves her hand into the pocket of her Hawaiian dress and pulls out a ball of tissue. She presses the tissue into my hand and I hold it in my fist.

Grandma and Grandpa look at me, eyes wide and worried.

"I'm sorry," I say, sniffing.

"No, we're sorry," Grandma says, hands into her dress, wadding up the Hawaiian material and then letting it go again. I look up at her face, at her bright blue eyes.

"I don't want to go anywhere else," I say, new tears in my voice.

"We know," Grandma says, patting my shoulder, and she looks over at Grandpa, tears in her eyes too. "We know, honey."

"You've got to understand, Jenny," Grandpa says, pressing his hand flat on the table, "we're just trying to do what's best for you."

"That's right," Grandma says.

Grandpa waves his hand for her to sit down, but instead, she goes back to her chair, standing behind it with her hands on the back.

Out the window, Reno is dark now. The sunset is long gone and the white lights of the strip are like stars that have fallen to the ground.

"It's hard now," Grandpa says, "we know that, but you'll see it's going to be the best in the long run."

"You're going to be just fine," Grandma says.

"That's right," Grandpa says, "you're going to be just fine."

PART TWO

BLACK SPARKS

TWO
BLACK SPARKS, NEVADA

Aunt Peggy and Uncle Dick live in Black Sparks. Grandpa says Black Sparks is military housing.

"Is Uncle Dick in the military?"

"No," Grandpa says. "He works for Sears."

It's quiet the way it gets when nothing makes sense, and out the window is Reno's strange color of brown, sagebrush growing low over the open spaces of land. Cold air from the air conditioner blows in my face and my nose tingles like a sneeze.

Next to being with Deb again, if there is one place I do not want to be, it's Aunt Peggy and Uncle Dick's.

It's not really Aunt Peggy who is the problem, it's Uncle Dick.

Back, way back was a time I visited them with my cousins Tracy and Faith Ann. I don't know if Aunt Peggy and Uncle Dick were married then, but we stayed with them a couple of days, and it seemed like Uncle Dick was about 10 feet tall with a loud voice and eyes that couldn't see kids at all. He threatened to spank all of us with his belt if we got out of line and even though he didn't do it, I was so glad to get away from him.

I didn't see Uncle Dick again after that and only saw Aunt Peggy one other time, when she as was at Daddy's funeral, her stomach huge since she was about to have a baby.

It figures I don't get a choice and out of all the choices, I get the worst possible one. It figures Bryan gets a choice.

Grandpa takes the Black Sparks exit off the freeway, turns right to a winding road and then we're in a neighborhood of small houses built close together. There are no trees here, no real bushes either, not even real lawns. It's like a concrete world, yards filled with gray gravel, and if people have lawns, the grass is burned up a dry yellow.

"That's their place on the right," Grandpa says. "See?"

I lean against the seat belt to get a better look.

Army green.

Grandpa parks in the driveway behind a white van, the words SEARS AND ROEBUCK written on the back door.

The front door of their house opens and a poodle jumps off the porch and runs to the Toronado, like a bullet out of a gun.

"There's Peg and Kimmy," Grandpa says, hand wave, happy smile.

Aunt Peggy is out of the house, little kid on her hip and behind her Uncle Dick stays by the door, tall with dark hair.

Grandpa stops waving, stops smiling. "And there's Dick."

Grandpa parks in their driveway and I lean back in my seat.

"Well, Kiddo," Grandpa says, "ready?"

I cross my arms over myself and tuck my chin to my chest. I'm on the wrong side of a fit, part of me about to beg him not to leave. I can see it too; I would cry and scream and bang my fists on the leather seats of the Toronado, and if that didn't work, I could hold on to something and they'd have to drag me out.

"I don't want to go here," I say, voice low.

Grandpa takes a deep breath in and leans down to me.

"Now, we've talked all about this," he says.

"I know," I say.

"Just give them a chance," he says. "They're good people, young but good, and I know you're going to like them a lot."

I've already heard all about Aunt Peggy and Uncle Dick, all the good things, of course. Grandma says they are young people, in their twenties, just right for a fresh start. Grandpa says they are just thrilled to have me at their place, how they can't wait for me to help around the house and with Kimmy, and blah, blah, blah.

"Come on—tell me you'll try."

Grandpa's eyes, so much like my father's, that color of spices all ground up. How I can I throw a fit when he looks at me with those eyes?

"Okay?" he says.

I nod okay, no words to say what I want to say.

"That's my girl," he says.

The dog jumps up against the car, wet nose on the outside of the window.

"That damn dog is going to scratch my paint," Grandpa says.

He opens his door.

"Peg, watch the paint," he yells.

"Sorry, Daddy," Aunt Peggy says. "RC, get down right now. Bad dog, bad!"

From where I sit in the car, I just watch them together, Grandpa with a worried look on his face, rubbing his hand over the door of the Toronado, Aunt Peggy watching him, worried on her face too, and then Uncle Dick coming over to say the paint job looks good on the old car.

I take a deep breath, an idea that I could sink down and hide in here, but then door pulls open.

"She's right here," Grandpa says. "Come on out and say hi."

Hot air rushes into the car and over my skin, and I look at all of them looking at me.

I get out of the car, the backs of my legs stuck to the green leather of the seat. I stick a smile on my face and say hello.

Aunt Peggy says hi, and Uncle Dick says hi too, looking me over at the same time.

The dog jumps inside the car and over the back seat.

"Darn it, Peg!" Grandpa says.

"Sorry, Daddy," Aunt Peggy says. "RC, get out of there right now."

The dog jumps out of the car and circles around my legs. It jumps up, paws on my legs.

"RC," Aunt Peggy says, "down."

"That's okay," I say.

Kneeling down, I pet the little gray dog between the ears.

"Why do you call her RC?" I say.

"For the cola," Aunt Peggy says. "You know, RC cola?"

"Does she drink soda?" I say.

"Of course not," Aunt Peggy says.

I look at the dog again, gray curly fur, pink stomach.

"RC is brown," I say.

Aunt Peggy moves her head a little, maybe impatient.

"Uncle Dick likes to drink RC," she says.

"Oh," I say.

Grandpa juggles his keys around and clears his throat, says he has my things in the trunk of the Toronado, and Uncle Dick says he'll come help get them out.

I stand up again. RC jumps up, wet nose into my leg.

Grandpa says he hates to leave but he's got a one o'clock tee time; Uncle Dick says he understands.

"Kimmy," Aunt Peggy says, "this is your cousin Jenny."

Aunt Peggy puts Kimmy down, and Kimmy stands with her

bare feet on the dead grass. "Can you say 'Jenny'?" Aunt Peggy says. "Can you say, 'Hi, cousin Jenny'?"

Kimmy opens her blue eyes so wide they look like they might pop out of her head and I laugh. Aunt Peggy looks at me like she doesn't know why I'm laughing and I stop.

Kimmy steps away from Aunt Peggy and reaches to my hand. Her fingers are round and soft, a whisper of a touch on the back of my hand.

"Jen-ny," Kimmy says.

Uncle Dick shoulders my trunk and Grandpa takes out my duffel bag, slams the trunk of the Toronado.

"Did you hear her say 'Jenny'?" Aunt Peggy says.

"Sure did," Grandpa says. He hands me my duffel bag and I put it over my shoulder.

"Did you hear that, Dick?" she says.

"Yeah, yeah," he says. "This is heavy. Where do you want it?"

Aunt Peggy scoops up Kimmy, stands up again.

"Back bedroom," she says.

Uncle Dick goes into the house with my trunk and Aunt Peggy kisses Kimmy and bounces her up and down. "What a smart girl with your words. Isn't she smart, Daddy?"

Grandpa adjusts his golf cap on his head and nods.

"Sure is," he says.

"You guys need to come out and have dinner sometime," Aunt Peggy says.

"Yep, we should do that," Grandpa says, rubbing his hand over his face, "but you know how busy we get."

"Oh sure," Aunt Peggy says.

It gets quiet between them, Grandpa looking at the ground, Aunt Peggy fussing with Kimmy on her hip.

When Uncle Dick comes back out, Grandpa acts like he's in

a big hurry to get going, looking at his watch, talking about his tee-off time. He kisses Aunt Peggy's cheek, pats Kimmy, shakes Uncle Dick's hand, and then tells me to be good.

Aunt Peggy, Kimmy, and Uncle Dick go up to their army green house, but I don't. I stand on their dead lawn, my legs under me but not under me at the same time.

Grandpa pulls out of the driveway and shifts the gears around.

In my stomach I know I shouldn't be here in Black Sparks with Aunt Peggy and Uncle Dick, I should be in the metallic green Toronado. It's Tuesday, golf, the grocery store and then home for cocktail hour, dinner and ice cream while we watch TV.

Grandpa drives slow up the road, looking my way, his hand up in a wave.

I can't smile or even wave back. From the middle of my chest is a pull where I'm running after him, arms waving and calling out, "please, don't leave me here."

"Come on, Jenny," Aunt Peggy calls from the front door of their house. "Come on in."

I look her way, all three of them on the porch, Kimmy on Aunt Peggy's hip. I bite my lip and look after Grandpa again, but he's gone.

Aunt Peggy and Uncle Dick's house is a living room, dining room, kitchen, and a long hall to rooms I can't see. The place is filled with frog decorations, ceramic frogs on the coffee table, frog place mats on the dining-room table, a frog face painted on the backrest of Kimmy's high chair.

I back up until I'm against a space between the wall and the front door. My leg presses against a pot with a green vine plant that grows up a tall stick, held in place with a wire trash-bag tie. In the dirt at the bottom of the plant is a glass frog with black eyes.

"Frog," Kimmy says and points at her high chair.

Aunt Peggy slides Kimmy into the frog high chair, and on the tray is a cut-up sandwich.

Uncle Dick shuts the front door with a slam.

"I gotta get a move on, Peg," Uncle Dick says.

He walks past me and goes into the kitchen. Aunt Peggy picks up a piece of sandwich and shoves it into Kimmy's wide-open mouth.

"Daddy is such a grouch when he is hungry," she says.

Uncle Dick stands in the doorway between the dining room and the kitchen, a handful of chips in one hand and an RC cola in the other. He's a big person but has a small head and small eyes set close in his face. I'm not sure what color his eyes are, maybe blue, like a gray blue. Uncle Dick blinks past me as if I'm not here at all.

"Peg," Uncle Dick says, "I gotta fix a washer at one o'clock. Make me a sandwich."

Aunt Peggy tips a Mickey Mouse Sippy cup to Kimmy.

"All right, Dick," Aunt Peggy says. "Keep your pants on."

Uncle Dick stuffs all the chips into his mouth and wipes his hand on the front of his pants.

"Chips," Kimmy says, reaching out toward Uncle Dick.

"All gone," Uncle Dick says through a mouthful.

"Chips, Momma," Kimmy says, "chips."

"Don't tease, Dick," Aunt Peggy says, "give her some chips."

Uncle Dick laughs and drinks his soda. He looks at Kimmy and holds up his empty hand.

"All gone," Uncle Dick says.

Kimmy screams so loud it's the only sound, and when she stops, my ears still hear it.

"God damn it, Dick," Aunt Peggy yells. "You really tick me off."

A red stain of anger lifts up from Aunt Peggy's neck, and without another word, she goes past Uncle Dick, gets chips for Kimmy, and makes a sandwich for him. Finally, the red is gone from her face and she remembers about me.

"Well, come on," she says. "You can come in."

I step from my spot against the wall, best behavior stiff, and adjust my bag on my shoulder.

"Are you hungry?" she says.

"No, I ate at Grandma's," I say. "Thank you."

Uncle Dick sits in the living room with his lunch, chews his food and watches the television at the same time. He looks my way for a second, looks back at the television.

Aunt Peggy tugs her T-shirt down so it's smoothed out and puts her arm in my direction.

"Want to see your room?" she says.

I bite my lip, looking at Uncle Dick over there on the sofa, at Aunt Peggy who is waiting.

"Sure," I say.

"Okay," Aunt Peggy says, big smile.

She leads the way and I follow up the narrow hall where she has some framed photos hung on one side. There's a shot with Kimmy, bald head and a red dress, Uncle Dick in a military uniform and a hat way too big for his head, and then Aunt Peggy looking happy with long brown hair down her back like you'd see in a Breck shampoo advertisement.

Aunt Peggy walks ahead of me, hair in a ponytail now and she opens a door at the end of the hall.

"It's not a big house," she says, "but we have three bedrooms."

Inside the room are bunk beds, a dresser, and a desk, all painted avocado green. My pink trunk is in the corner and the color of it is all wrong compared with the green.

Aunt Peggy goes to the window, pulls a string for the shades, a view of burned-up grass outside.

"You have a couple windows too," Aunt Peggy says, "so you can see outside."

I stand at the door and she goes to the closet, slides open the double door.

"There's lots of space for clothes," she says, "and anything else you want to put here."

She slides the other closet door open, talks about extra pillows and blankets.

Grandma says that all of her daughters, Auntie Carol, Aunt Elizabeth, and Aunt Peggy, are girls with big bones and up close, it's true. Aunt Peggy has wide shoulders, wide hips and her head is shaped almost like a man's, wide at her jaw and forehead. It's not like she's fat or anything, she looks solid and steady and big. Big boned.

"You can just unpack your trunk whenever you want," she says. "Put your things in the closet or even the dresser."

I shift the duffel bag over my shoulder, come the rest of the way in the room to where my pink trunk is in the corner. I lean my hip against it, the cool of the metal on my leg.

"This stuff isn't really unpacking stuff," I say, "it's more like books and photos."

"Oh," she says, "what kind of photos?"

"Just family things," I say.

"Well," she says, "maybe you'll show me sometime."

"Maybe," I say, polite smile.

On her face are a pair of thick glasses and Aunt Peggy adjusts them, looking around.

"Well, that's really about it," she says. "Not much, but at least it's private and quiet."

"Thanks," I say.

Aunt Peggy hugs herself tighter, one hand up and down on her arm, and then she tilts her head at me.

"You know," she says, "you remind me of your mother."

"I do?"

She nods, lips together.

No one has said that to me, not ever, and even though it's probably the nicest thing a person could say, I know it's not true. My mother was beautiful, perfect white skin, dark eyes, curly dark hair.

I lick my lips and clear my throat.

"You know I'm adopted," I say.

"Oh sure," Aunt Peggy says, waving her hand like flicking away a fly and tucking her arms over herself again. "Everyone knows that, but it doesn't change how you were hers, does it?"

I stay extra still, the weight of my bag between my shoulders.

"We were good friends, you know," Aunt Peggy says.

"Really?" I say.

"Oh sure," she says, rolling one shoulder forward, like a shrug but not a shrug. "Well, I mean, she was quite a bit older, but I like to think she was my friend. She was such a good person."

The look on Aunt Peggy's face, the idea of my mother around us, and an old sadness lifts from the center of my body.

"Maybe you and I can be friends too," Aunt Peggy says, "I hope so anyway."

I look at Aunt Peggy, really look. I don't want to like her, I don't, but there's something kind of nice about her, and maybe Grandpa is right, maybe I should at least give her a chance.

"Sure," I say, "we can be friends. Why not?"

Black Sparks is on the edge of Reno, and out here, the wind blows dry, the sun burns hot, and if you were a bird flying over, you would not stop. There's a park with a couple of wood picnic tables and some swings, but you won't find a lot of trees, and there sure isn't any shade.

Aunt Peggy says she's a housewife and I guess that means she stays home all day.

In the morning, she makes breakfast for Uncle Dick and packs him a lunch in his black lunch box.

After he leaves, Aunt Peggy takes care of Kimmy, cleans the house, and talks about whatever she's going to make for dinner.

"Tonight is taco night. Dick just loves tacos."

"Tonight is Salisbury steak night. Dick just loves Salisbury steak."

"Tonight is rigatoni night. Dick just loves rigatoni."

You don't have to be a rocket scientist to figure out Aunt Peggy is crazy about Uncle Dick—I mean head over heels. Dick this, Dick that. Whatever she sees in him, I sure can't see.

When he comes home at night, Uncle Dick looks through me, and if he does put his attention my way, it's to make me do something.

"Get me an ashtray."

"Fill up my coffee cup."

"Get me a new pack of cigarettes."

Uncle Dick never says thank you and he calls me a no-neck.

"Get me my cigarettes, no-neck."

"Wash the dishes, no-neck."

"What are you looking at, no-neck?"

It's like a nickname or something but it doesn't make any sense. I do have a neck. And even if it is a joke, it's just stupid.

Aunt Peggy says Uncle Dick is not as bad as he seems, that he's really a big teddy bear down deep and that's what she loves about him, his soft side, but when he's around, I keep my distance.

When he's gone, I stay close to Aunt Peggy and do what she

does. If she's in the kitchen, I'm in the kitchen. If she watches TV, I watch TV. If she does housework, I help.

When we're together like that, all day, every day, Aunt Peggy goes about her business of being a housewife and at the same time tells me her stories. Some are simple, stories like how she cut her leg real bad when she was skiing, how she was in a sorority called Tri-Delta in college and how she used to drive this little car called a Corvair. Her other stories aren't so simple though, like the one about how she dropped out of college just shy of graduating to elope with Uncle Dick and that made Grandma and Grandpa so mad they didn't talk to her for a whole year.

"Why?" I say.

"He was divorced," she says, "and a Mormon."

It turns out Uncle Dick has a bunch of kids from another marriage, kids he never sees since his first wife took off with them, and apparently, he didn't graduate high school but has something called a GED. Grandma and Grandpa didn't think Uncle Dick was good enough for Aunt Peggy, and when she talks about it, Aunt Peggy gets herself all fired up, angry even, a surprising kind of anger that slips out quick and then gets tucked away just as fast.

She tells more stories about herself after that, says she was something called a change-of-life baby, born at a time when there weren't supposed to be any more babies.

"Your dad was 15 when I was born," she says, "the same age I was when you were born."

"Wow," I say.

"Grandma and Grandpa were all done raising their kids," she says, "and here I come."

The angry edge to Aunt Peggy slips out with this story too, and she tells me how hard it was to grow up, all her sisters and brothers gone, her parents so much older, how sometimes she felt like she had more in common with the cleaning girl than anyone in her own family.

"Plus, I went through an awkward phase," Aunt Peggy says.

"Awkward?"

"I was the chubby kid, bad skin, the works," she says, an embarrassed look on her face and in her brown eyes.

"That's why I loved your mom so much," Aunt Peggy says. "She was interested in me, helped me with my clothes and hair, gave me advice."

When we get to this part of the story, the part about her awkward age and my mother, we are outside in the afternoon sun, working on our tans.

Uncle Dick is at work.

Kimmy is down for her nap.

RC is off in the yard sniffing at the edge of the fence.

Aunt Peggy wears a blue-and-green-plaid bikini, lies stomach down on a white sheet she laid over the dead grass. I'm in my yellow-and-lime-green swimsuit, and I lie stomach down too. I can feel the dead grass poke my skin through the sheet.

The suntanning spot is between the house and the garage, back door open so Aunt Peggy can hear Kimmy if she wakes up. There is a chain-link fence a little way off, and through the links is a view of the driveway, the front yard, and then the street.

Aunt Peggy says my mother gave the best advice on clothes that would slim her figure.

"Janet was so easy to talk to," Aunt Peggy says, words against her arm. "I could just tell her anything."

I lie like she does, arms crossed in front, my face against them. I kick my foot up and down, heel on my behind.

"She even threw me a sweet-sixteen birthday party."

"What's that?" I say.

"Oh, just this special party," she says.

The afternoon wind blows hot and dry, and a shadow from the garage moves over the grass toward where we are.

Aunt Peggy talks about how she used to come over to the house on Mary Street to baby-sit Bryan when Momma was too sick to get out of bed.

I stop kicking my leg on my butt.

"When your mom got better and they adopted you, Janet was so excited," Aunt Peggy says. "She sewed these little matching outfits for the two of you. I don't think she even knew how to sew."

She leans up on her elbow, takes off her sunglasses. Aunt Peggy without any glasses on her face looks different, pretty.

"You were a funny baby," she says, "strong willed and always into everything, but sweet."

She reaches across the sheet, taps her finger on the side of my leg, just at the edge of my bathing suit, and it tickles.

"You had this big birthmark on your behind," she says, "it was shaped just like a strawberry."

I twist myself a little, look down at that part of my leg.

"Really?"

"Yep," she says, pulling her hand back, "and your mom loved to show your butt off to anyone who would look."

My face gets hot all the way to my ears.

"Aunt Peggy!"

She rolls on her side then and the sound of her laugh is deep.

"Oh, that's not all," she says, shaking her head, ponytail bobbing around. "I'll never forget this one time when you were two years old—I think two—and your mom had you in the bathroom on the potty chair, the kind that has a tray to hold you in."

She moves her hands around in front of her in a circle.

"Like a high chair?" I say.

"Right," she says.

RC sniffs over to the sheet and settles herself in front of Aunt Peggy, who starts to pet her curly gray fur.

"So your mom and I were chatting away in the living room, and she forgot about you in there," Aunt Peggy says, and then she imitates my mother's voice; " 'Oh my gosh,' Janet says, 'Jenny is still on the potty,' and then we went in there, you were fast asleep with your head down on the tray."

Aunt Peggy's stomach moves with her laugh, tears in her eyes.

"Janet even took a photograph of you like that, she thought it was so funny."

Aunt Peggy sniffs and wipes a tear out of the corner of her eye. The tip of her nose is red from the laughing, her eyes moist, and she gets very quiet, looking down at the dog. Aunt Peggy pets RC for a while and then shoves her over, rolling flat on her stomach again.

The Nevada wind blows in a gust between the house and the garage, blows up a corner of the sheet and Aunt Peggy smoothes it flat again, lays her face down against her arms.

"It was terrible how she died," Aunt Peggy says then. "Unbelievable, really. I had no idea she was so sick."

The shadow from the garage moves over her ankles and the back corner of the sheet. It should be hot out here in the sun, but it's not.

I lie with my face against my arms like Aunt Peggy does and hold so still.

No one ever talks about my mother, not ever.

Grandma and Grandpa didn't.

Bryan never did.

Daddy never did.

Deb and her kids never did. Why would they?

It seems like all I've ever had are questions about my mother and all I've wanted to do is talk about her but now, I'm just confused. I can't believe she died either. It's just unreal, this thing that can't make sense and past that, is this feeling like she's so close but on the other edge of the world, too far away to reach. In the space between where I am and she is, there is so much sadness and loneliness I can barely think about it, so I don't.

Another gust of wind pushes through the sun tanning spot and makes the white sheet ripple at the edges.

Aunt Peggy closes her eyes and I close mine too.

When you talk about the thing no one talks about, everything changes. Aunt Peggy and me are different now, like sisters, and in this new place, I tell her everything there is to tell, one story flowing into the other.

I tell about Deb's cat eyes, her angles and edges, Deb's kids always ganging up on me, one of them knocking out my teeth with a broom during a particularly bad fight, and the Freedom Community Church, this creepy place where you are supposed to contemplate life differently.

I tell her how Deb dumped me off in the big house one day, who knows why, just left me there with my princess bedroom set and 10 bucks.

" 'It's called survival,' Deb said. 'Figure it out.' "

"You are kidding me!" Aunt Peggy says.

"I'm serious," I say. "The woman was certifiable."

Aunt Peggy laughs when I say certifiable but I keep right on talking.

I tell how I saw twins being born that day at the big house, about my best friend Zoë who had white blond hair, about dropping out of Hoover Street Elementary since no one was watching me anyway, and how I used to jump on cracks in the sidewalks because that's how bad I hated Deb.

"You know, 'Jump on a crack, break your mother's back,' " I say.

"My goodness," Aunt Peggy says.

It must take a whole week to get out stories that go from now to as far back as I remember, stories about Huntington Beach and getting my examination, and Daddy driving up, heart attack right there on the front lawn, and how Deb said it was his own fault, that he died because he wished a heart attack on his business partner. How Deb had us in Palo Alto going to some Freedom Community school that wasn't a school at all, how she had us running 1.5 miles on Mondays and Fridays, 3 miles on Tuesdays and Thursdays, 5 miles on Wednesdays, and how every day she made us take a mountain of vitamin pills, except I flushed mine down the toilet.

We cook dinners and I talk.

We fold laundry and I talk.

We give Kimmy a bath and I talk and talk and it feels so good, like letting go of a heavy load I've been carrying around.

We are in the back bedroom with my pink trunk wide open for the last story, the most important one, about how Daddy gave me the princess bedroom set for my birthday. I sit cross-legged in front of my trunk, Aunt Peggy is on her knees, and RC is between us, sniffing around the trunk I pulled out of the corner.

Kimmy is with us too, thumb in her mouth, hand holding her blanket.

"All this stuff goes with the set," I say. "There's the bedspread, the curtains, the canopy."

I kick off my shoe, open my trunk with the key and don't even think about how Aunt Peggy watches me; none of that matters now.

RC sticks her poodle face over the stuff in the trunk.

I dig my hand down past the pink bedspread and curtains and pull out an old stuffed animal.

"Looky, Kimmy," I say, dancing this white stuffed lamb side to side.

Kimmy takes her thumb out of her mouth, the shine of her spit on her skin.

"Baby," she says.

"That's right," Aunt Peggy says. "It's a baby sheep."

Kimmy drops her blanket on the floor and reaches both hands out.

"No, no," Aunt Peggy says. "That's Jenny's."

"That's okay," I say handing the lamb over. "She can play with it."

Kimmy takes it into her arms and hugs it to her chest like it's the most wonderful thing ever.

"You might not get it back," Aunt Peggy says, laughing.

"That's fine," I say.

Kimmy drops down to the floor and wraps the lamb in her blanket, and RC plops her dog self down on the floor too. Aunt Peggy reaches out, rubs the pink material of the bedspread between her fingers.

"So, Bud got this for you?" Aunt Peggy says, "this princess bedroom set?"

"He picked it out himself," I say, nodding, "and then came home from work and set it up for a surprise, and when I came home from school, there it was."

Aunt Peggy puts her hand back on her lap, quiet, like she is thinking.

"I didn't know your dad that well," she says. "Like I said, he was already gone when I was growing up."

She looks over at Kimmy, who is still playing with the lamb. "He never even met Kimmy," Aunt Peggy says.

"I know," I say.

She looks at me then, eyes behind her thick glasses.

"I saw you at the funeral, remember?" I say. "Kimmy was still in your tummy."

Kimmy looks at me, at Aunt Peggy, and goes back to playing, this little cooing noise as she talks to herself, and RC sniffs at the air, nose up.

Aunt Peggy nods, adjusting her glasses on her face. "That's right."

"It was a strange funeral, wasn't it?" Aunt Peggy says. "That guy with the guitar, playing what? Cat Stevens songs?"

"Daddy really liked Cat Stevens."

"He did?" she says.

"Sure," I say.

I can't help think it's not right not to know your own brother, especially someone like Daddy, and that makes me want to tell Aunt Peggy everything about him. I pet RC, her soft gray fur against my fingers, and I tell about Daddy's laugh, deep and rich, his smile that made me think of sunshine, and how he always tried to act like things were fine, even when they weren't.

"He worked all the time," I say, "but he still took me to Disneyland for my birthday every year and even picked me once for this sailing trip to Catalina."

It hurts to talk about him, and at the same time, it seems important, more for her than me.

"He was great," I say, "not just handsome either, but more like . . . I don't know . . . perfect, I guess."

Kimmy watches us, her big blue eyes on me and Aunt

Peggy, as if she's listening to me talk about Daddy too. Aunt Peggy smiles at her.

"Every little girl thinks her daddy is perfect," Aunt Peggy says.

Kimmy smiles at Aunt Peggy then.

"But he was," I say.

Aunt Peggy shakes her head like she doesn't get it.

I dig my hand into my trunk again, down past the layer of stuffed animals, and pull out this small square of a book with photos in plastic covers, gold letters on the front, their wedding album.

"Just look at him," I say.

Aunt Peggy takes the album, turns it side to side, and Kimmy pushes up off the floor and comes to Aunt Peggy's side.

"Where did you get this?"

"Auntie Carol gave it to me," I say, "just after Momma died."

Aunt Peggy frowns, her dark eyebrows pulled together as she flips the book open and then turns quick through the photos.

Kimmy leans in to look too, and I reach over, stop Aunt Peggy from turning so quick, and stop at the page where Daddy and Momma stand between two baskets of white flowers.

"See," I say, pointing at his picture with my finger.

"I know what he looked like, Jenny," Aunt Peggy says.

"Daddy?" Kimmy says.

"No," Aunt Peggy says, "that's Uncle Bud."

"That's my daddy," I say.

Kimmy doesn't get it, I can see it in her blue eyes, and that's not a surprise—she's just a little kid—but Aunt Peggy doesn't get it either, and I wish I could explain, except I'm all out of words.

Aunt Peggy flips through the photos again and at the last page, she finally stops.

"Hey," she says, moving the book closer to her face, "that's me!"

"Where?" I say.

She points her finger on the plastic that protects the photos.

"Right there," she says.

"Mommy?" Kimmy says.

"Yes, Mommy," Aunt Peggy says.

I take the book from Aunt Peggy then, turn it around to look closer. Aunt Peggy pulls Kimmy on her lap, holds her with one arm.

In the photo she is eight or nine years old with light-colored hair.

"Oh, I remember that dress and those shoes," she says. "It was such a cute outfit."

All the times I've looked at these pictures, I would have never recognized her, not in a million years. Aunt Peggy grown up doesn't look a thing like Aunt Peggy as a kid.

"Isn't that neat?" she says, all happy about the picture of herself in my book, bouncing Kimmy on her lap. RC is up too, excited by Aunt Peggy's voice, and she walks in tight circles close to Aunt Peggy's legs.

It's great to see a picture of Aunt Peggy, I guess, but it really bugs me she didn't even look at the photos of Momma and Daddy, not the way she should, not the way I do. It's like I've been talking all this time but she isn't listening.

It's quiet in the room, too quiet, and I try to figure out where we were in the story to begin with. I push the wedding album back into its place in my pink trunk and pull the lid closed over all my things, the sound of the metal lid banging down.

"Well, anyway," I say, "he gave me the bedroom set for my birthday."

"Oh, right," Aunt Peggy says, sliding Kimmy off her lap and on to the floor again, handing her the stuffed lamb.

"Deb says she is going to send the rest later, but I doubt it," I say.

"She might," Aunt Peggy says, dancing the stuffed lamb for Kimmy.

Pulling on my tennis shoe, I don't say anything, just tie the laces quick, hiding the key under the way I do.

"I met Deb at the funeral and she seemed very nice," Aunt Peggy says.

The beginning of a laugh comes out of me, not ha ha but like I can't believe what she's saying, especially after all the things I've told her.

"Trust me, Aunt Peggy," I say, "Deb is lots of things; nice is not one of them."

Aunt Peggy puts her full attention on me again, lips set tight together.

"Your dad must have loved her," she says.

I look at her whole face, the square shape of her jaw, thick glasses over her face.

"Did you ever really meet Deb?" I say. "I mean, spend any time with her?"

"Well, no," she says, one hand adjusting her glasses on her face, "just at the funeral, but Mom and Dad have told me some things, and Leonard thought she was pretty nice."

I take a deep breath, looking at my hands for the right words.

"You know about the evil stepmother in those fairy tales you read about?" I say. "Not those Disney stories. The *Grimm's Fairy Tale* stories?"

"I've never read those," Aunt Peggy says, blank expression on her face.

"Well, the stepmothers are these evil women," I say. "They marry men with children and make them do terrible things; they are, like, two-faced. You know, acting one way with the husband and then different with the kids?"

I clear my throat and look at her, at both her eyes. "Deb had a way of being nice on the surface," I say. "She was that way with Daddy too, but down deep, she wasn't like that. I know—I lived with her, and if you don't believe me, call up Bryan, and he'll tell you the same thing."

Aunt Peggy raises her eyebrows a little behind her glasses.

"You might be a little more generous to Deb," Aunt Peggy says. "I'm sure she did her best."

Kimmy has her blanket in her hands again, thumb in her mouth, blue eyes going back and forth between Aunt Peggy and me.

"If that was her best," I say, "I'd hate to see her worst."

Aunt Peggy looks away from me first and clears her throat.

"Well, anyway," Aunt Peggy says, reaching her hands out to Kimmy, "I guess we should get dinner started."

Aunt Peggy shifts herself up then, pushes off the floor with a grunt, and says something about how she got a cramp from sitting on the floor.

"I think tonight we'll have rigatoni," she says then, going up the hall, RC following behind her. "Dick just loves rigatoni."

I sit there on the floor, trying to put it all together, but the pieces just don't fit. It's like I don't know what I know, and I wonder if I'm remembering things wrong, if Deb was this nice person, only I got it mixed up somehow.

Off in the kitchen, Aunt Peggy talks in a baby voice to Kimmy and there is the bang of pots and pans.

In me is doubt, as if I might have made a mistake about Deb, as if I am making it all up, even though in my heart I know she was horrible, a witch, a nightmare you couldn't wake up from.

All the weight I talked off is back again, a heaviness on my shoulders and I know I've made a mistake, a big mistake telling Aunt Peggy all I did.

I put my hand on the lock of my trunk then and shut it tight with a click.

On a Friday, Uncle Leonard brings Bryan to the Black Sparks house for what everyone calls "a visit."

Bryan picked Uncle Leonard to live with, and he's moving to Oklahoma. I've never been to Oklahoma, but it sounds flat and dusty and dried up. Bryan loves Nevada and Lake Tahoe, and his next favorite place is anywhere close to the ocean. Why would he pick Uncle Leonard, and why Oklahoma?

From the window of the living room, I watch Uncle Dick and Aunt Peggy stand on the dead grass lawn and talk to Uncle Leonard, who has thick glasses on his face, just like Aunt Peggy but is bottom-heavy and bald on top.

Kimmy runs around on the grass with RC, the grown-ups talk, and Bryan stands apart from everyone looking at a jet that's high in the sky, just a silver speck up there. He has on a pair of cutoffs, a white T-shirt that's too big for him, and he's tall and dark, that serious expression on his face.

I don't even know the last time I saw him, face-to-face, anyway. We were living with Deb in L.A., and then one day, he was just gone. I asked Deb where he went, and she said on vacation; when I asked where, she told me to mind my own business.

Aunt Peggy waves toward the house from the front lawn, hand up to her eyes, and I wonder if she sees me here.

I step back from the curtain, arms crossed over myself,

and I guess I should go out there too, even though I don't want to.

"What are you doing back there?" Bryan says, his voice a shock, and he stands right there at the front door.

"Nothing," I say, uncrossing my arms and then crossing them again the other way.

"You look like you're hiding," he says.

I take another step from the window.

"Well, I'm not," I say.

Bryan is like always, black hair, black eyes, mole over the top of his lip. He watches me and I watch him, and then he rolls his eyes like I am such an idiot.

"So this is where you are staying," he says, looking around.

"Duh," I say.

Ignoring me, he comes the rest of the way in and does this quick shake of his head so his bangs angle over his forehead.

"Check out all the frogs," he says.

"I know," I say.

"Frogs meet the Old West," he says.

I stay where I am by the curtains, the sofa between us.

"So?" I say, crossing my arms tighter.

At the dining-room table, he picks up a frog saltshaker and puts it down again.

"So it's bad taste," he says.

I look around the room then, frog décor, avocado green furniture, and then the rest of Aunt Peggy and Uncle Dick's stuff. The sofa and loveseat are covered in this black and brown fabric that looks like a cross between zebra and tiger print, the coffee table is made from wrought iron and slabs of wood, and on top of the television is garage-sale junk—cast-iron waffle pan, horseshoes, and another ceramic frog.

Even though he's right, it is serious bad taste, I want to say something smart aleck about Oklahoma and how I'll take frogs any day over a place named Oklahoma, but I don't. I just shrug my shoulders.

"It could be worse," I say.

Bryan laughs again, eyes around the room one more time. "I doubt that," he says.

Uncle Leonard says he has some things to do, and he leaves Bryan with us for a couple hours. Aunt Peggy puts Kimmy down for a nap, and the four of us play a game of Monopoly at the dining-room table.

"You owe me two hundred dollars, Uncle Dick," Bryan says.

Bryan holds his hand open, palm out, and Uncle Dick counts up two hundred dollars of fake money.

"Thank you very much," Bryan says, all dramatic.

Aunt Peggy laughs at Bryan, takes the dice, and rolls a five. Uncle Dick half sits, half slouches, arm over the back of his chair, watches Aunt Peggy move her dog piece to a railroad.

"I'll buy it," she says.

While we play, Bryan talks about how great Carson City was, how he learned how to snow-ski and rode these cool dirt bikes up on the trails behind Aunt Georgia and Uncle Charles's house.

"Your turn, Jenny," Aunt Peggy says.

"And it's going to be even more cool with Uncle Leonard," Bryan says, looking over at me, making some kind of point, "we're going to travel all over the place, ski in the winter, go camping."

I shake the dice, and it's a five and a three, and I knew Bryan was having a great time, knew he would get to make the good choice, and it figures.

"I hate to tell you this, old man," Uncle Dick says, shifting in his chair, "but there ain't a lot of snow in Okey-la-homa." Uncle Dick laughs at his joke, "Ha, ha, ha," and Aunt Peggy laughs too.

Bryan stays still, a look on his face I know so well that says Uncle Dick is an idiot and I almost laugh out loud.

"Jenny," Aunt Peggy says, pointing across the board to me, "you have to move your piece eight spaces."

"Oh yeah," I say, rolling my lips together.

I move my top hat piece to Go, and Aunt Peggy gives me two hundred dollars. I lay my money in neat piles, and when I look up, Bryan watches me with the same look he just gave Uncle Dick.

"What?" I say.

"Good job," Bryan says, all sarcastic.

"Screw you," I say.

"Hey, you two," Aunt Peggy says, sitting up straight, "that's no way to talk."

Uncle Dick looks at Aunt Peggy and she looks at him, this smug look between them as if they know something about Bryan and me.

It's quiet in the room then. I don't even know whose turn it is, and Bryan reaches into his pocket and pulls out an old golf ball.

"What's that?" Uncle Dick says.

Bryan holds the ball between his fingers and shows the whole table like it's the most interesting thing in the world.

"I cut the cover part in half," Bryan says. "I'm going to see what's in the middle."

Bryan holds it in his lap, picks at the white cover of the ball with his fingernail.

Uncle Dick yawns and stretches his arms over his head, T-shirt up so high you can see his stomach pushing out over the waistband of his pants. He shakes his head like he's trying to stay awake and readjusts himself on his chair.

"Your turn, Dick," Aunt Peggy says.

Uncle Dick reaches long over the Monopoly board and takes up the dice. He shakes a six, moves his car piece down the board to a utility Aunt Peggy owns. She adds what he owes her on a little pad.

"Eighty-five dollars," she says.

Bryan peels off the other half of the golf ball and inside it's a wound tight wad of rubber bands that unravel with a hissing sound.

"Look at that," Bryan says.

"Okay B.J.," Aunt Peggy says, "your move."

Bryan moves his whole hand over his ruined golf ball and stops the rubber bands from unraveling. He puts his dark eyes on the Monopoly board, red stain on his cheeks all the way to his ears.

I reach over the Monopoly board, then tap my finger on Aunt Peggy's side, my head shaking.

"Don't call him that," I say.

Aunt Peggy's face goes from smiling to serious. She looks at me and then at Bryan. "Why not?" she says.

"You just don't," I say.

Uncle Dick nudges her arm with his hand. "Don't you get it?" he says.

"No." Aunt Peggy says. "What's to get?"

"Forget it," Uncle Dick says, rolling his eyes. "I'll explain later."

Bryan looks my way, a change in his face and he even smiles. I make my face all screwed up at him, like *Up yours.* He laughs a little snorting laugh and looks down at the golf ball in his hand.

Aunt Peggy clears her throat.

"Well, does anyone want a soda?" she says, "I've got Crush and RC."

"I'll have an RC, Peg," Uncle Dick says.

"Jenny?" Aunt Peggy says.

"No thanks," I say.

"Bryan?" Aunt Peggy says.

Bryan leans back in his chair. "Crush," he says.

"Okeydokey," Aunt Peggy says. She scoots back from the table, stands up, and pulls her T-shirt down around her hips.

Bryan goes back to his golf ball, peels rubber bands off, and piles them on the end of the table. After all the rubber bands, there's a small black ball in the center, and Bryan rolls it around in his hand, shakes it a little, and holds it close to his ear.

"Sounds like some kind of liquid," Bryan says.

"Water," Uncle Dick says.

"Maybe some chemical," Bryan says.

"Probably water," Uncle Dick says.

I put my elbow on the table, chin in my hand, and my head hurts behind my eyes.

Aunt Peggy comes back to the table, two cans of soda.

"Here we go," she says.

Bryan presses the ball with his fingers, juggles it from one hand to the other and then mashes it hard between his flat palms, shooting some liquid right into my eye.

I press my palm against my eye, a burn past the eyelid. "My eye!" I yell.

"Shit," Uncle Dick says.

"What happened?" Bryan says.

"My eye," I yell.

"Get her to the bathroom," Aunt Peggy yells.

It gets crazy in the house then, the rush of me being pulled down the hall by Uncle Dick, Bryan screaming something, Aunt Peggy saying something else, and RC barking the way she does when she's excited.

In the bathroom, Uncle Dick pushes my head down, turns on some water, and tells me to splash my eye, hurry up and I do like he says.

It's probably the first time I've been this close to Uncle Dick, his hand on my shoulder, gentle words out of him about how it's going to be okay.

"Better?" Uncle Dick says.

"I think so," I say.

In the mirror, my eye is red and my face is wet. Uncle Dick hands me a towel, then pats me on the shoulder again.

Out in the hall, Bryan screams, his voice strange and wrong. "I blinded my sister," he screams.

Kimmy calls from her room, Aunt Peggy says something to Bryan, and it sounds like Bryan is crying.

Uncle Dick opens the bathroom door, and Aunt Peggy comes up the hall with Kimmy on her hip. Kimmy's face is all sleepy, thumb in her mouth, blanket in her arms.

"Is Jenny all right?" Aunt Peggy says.

"She's fine," Uncle Dick says. "What's wrong with him?"

Aunt Peggy adjusts Kimmy on her hip. "I don't know," she says. "He just snapped."

"What a nut case," Uncle Dick says.

Aunt Peggy shakes her head at Uncle Dick.

"What?" he says.

"Not now," she says.

Aunt Peggy pushes into the bathroom, all four of us in there a tight fit.

"Jenny," Aunt Peggy says down to me, "go show Bryan you're okay."

I hate how they act like they know about Bryan, I hate that smug look on Uncle Dick's face and the secrets in Aunt Peggy's eyes. I want to tell them both that they are wrong about Bryan, that they don't know anything. I want to tell him he's just different sometimes, moody and that he can be a jerk, but then he can be okay too.

I put the towel down on the toilet seat, scoot my way out of the bathroom.

In the dining room, the Monopoly board is all messed up and Bryan is pressed into a corner like he's trying to back out of this place. His dark eyes are wide open and he looks raw and undone. I can't believe he'd get so upset about something as silly as a golf ball squirting in my eye. He's done a lot worse to me on purpose, and he never got that upset. I want to say, *What about the time you sat on my stomach and pounded my chest with your finger? What about the time you chased me through the house and twisted my arm with an Indian burn?*

I hold my hands out. "I'm okay," I say.

Bryan hits his hand upside of his head, just over his ear. "I'm so stupid," he says, "stupid, stupid, stupid."

"It was an accident," I say.

"I don't know what I was thinking," he says.

"Bryan," I say, "forget it. I'm okay."

He crosses his arms tight over himself, back still pressed into the corner, and then looks at the floor, through the floor, into a place I can't see.

When Uncle Leonard gets back, there's a whispering hush over everything, Aunt Peggy whispering to Uncle Leonard, Uncle Leonard looking over his shoulder at me, at Bryan, at me again.

Through it all, Uncle Dick keeps his mouth shut, but he has that same smart-aleck expression on his face like he still thinks Bryan is a head case.

I don't know what to think of any of it.

I've seen Bryan upset, I've seen him angry, but I've never seen him this upset about anything to do with me.

When he leaves, it's a stiff good-bye, and Uncle Leonard says Bryan will call on my birthday and Christmas and that there will be vacations so we can visit.

Deep down, I know I'm not going to see Bryan for a long time, and it's sad somehow, him going all the way to Oklahoma and me staying here, like we're not brother and sister anymore.

Bryan's always been my brother. He's not my best friend or anything, but I know just about everything about him. I know his favorite color is blue, his favorite meal is double cheeseburgers with onion rings, and his favorite music is Led Zeppelin, that album with a blimp on the cover. I know he acts all tough and moody, but you just keep clear of him when he's like that and he snaps out of it after a while.

Bryan isn't the best brother in the world, but he is my brother—at least he was—and I feel like I should say or do something before he leaves for good.

"See ya," Bryan says as he goes past me and out the door, one hand up in a half wave.

"Yeah," I say, "see ya."

He goes with Uncle Leonard, and the two of them climb into the motor home.

Out the front window is the view of the dead grass, the mailbox, the street, and I watch them drive away. In the back of the motor home is a long rectangle of a window, and even though that window is covered with dirt on the outside, what looks like handprints on the inside, I think I can see Bryan, at least the outline of him, and maybe he's looking at me right now.

I wave my hand, just in case, only Bryan doesn't wave back, and I guess he wasn't looking at me after all.

A couple weeks later, Aunt Peggy, Uncle Dick, and me are at the green dining-room table, Kimmy is in her frog high chair, and the television is turned to some Western show. Uncle Dick sits sideways in his chair so he can see the TV while he eats.

"Pass the salt," Uncle Dick says.

Aunt Peggy picks up a frog saltshaker and sets it by Uncle Dick's plate. She talks about how this lady, a long-lost cousin she just found out about, lives in San Francisco and how I'm going to stay with her for a while.

"Why?" I say.

"It's a terrific opportunity to meet some new family," Aunt Peggy says, voice high and happy, too happy. "Sharon has a five-year-old daughter you can play with and she's a single mother."

I sit extra still in my chair.

"Think of it as a little vacation in California," Aunt Peggy says.

"Which is where you're from anyway," Uncle Dick says, looking my way but through me, like I'm nothing.

"I'm not from California," I say, looking right at him. "I'm from Nevada."

"But you lived in California for a lot of your life," Aunt Peggy says.

"Yeah," Uncle Dick says, "don't you miss all them hippies?"

"What?" I say.

"Come on, Dick, not now."

"I don't understand," I say.

Uncle Dick pushes his plate away. "What's to understand?"

he says. "It's supposed to be fun, you're going, so just go and don't ask so many questions."

I put my hands wide. "I haven't asked any questions," I say.

Uncle Dick shifts around in his seat and puts his elbow on the table, one finger pointing my way. "Don't give me lip, girl," he says. "Just do like we tell you."

Both Kimmy's hands are in the potatoes, and she holds them up in the air.

"Messy," she says.

"Oh, honey," Aunt Peggy says, "no, no, no."

Aunt Peggy leans over and wipes Kimmy's hands.

Off in the living room is the sound of commercials on the television, some local car dealer who screams that his low prices are making him insane.

"Great meal, Peg," Uncle Dick says.

"Why, thank you, honey," she says, all smiles at him.

Uncle Dick tugs his work shirt out of his pants and undoes his belt. "Why don't you get these dishes done for your Aunt Peggy," Uncle Dick says, "and then bring me a cup of coffee." Uncle Dick tosses his belt over the back of his chair, buckle clanking against the wood, and goes into the living room.

Aunt Peggy picks up her fork and looks at her food like she's figuring out what to eat next.

I wait for a long time, like maybe Aunt Peggy will look up at me, explain what this really is, but she doesn't.

I stand up and pick up my plate, pick up Uncle Dick's plate, and take them into the kitchen.

Sharon is a short person, not much taller than me, and she has brown curly hair.

Sharon's little girl is Kelly, and Kelly has straight blond hair.

Sharon is divorced, but she has a boyfriend named Gary who talks all about meditation and massage and likes to quote some guru of his with this name I can't even pronounce.

"Peg says you're a real girl's girl," Sharon says, "that you love bubble baths and things like that."

I want to tell Sharon I don't know what she's talking about since I never took a single bubble bath at the Black Sparks house. I don't say anything, though, just smile and nod and follow along like it's completely normal to be staying at the house of a person I've never met, hanging out with her daughter, long-lost cousins or whatever.

After a week at her house, Sharon says we're taking a trip to the woods.

"Why?" I say.

"It's a little vacation," Sharon says.

"I thought this was the vacation," I say.

"It's another vacation," she says, "only it's for all of us, you know, to be together."

"Okeydokey," I say, copying the way Aunt Peggy talks.

The four of us stay at this old cabin in the woods with the smell of dirt and pine trees and off a ways is a creek that runs through the trees.

During the day, we hang out together, mostly listen to Gary go on and on about free love and letting go of our hang-ups, and then he looks off at the trees and quotes his guru.

"You gotta get back to basics, man, let it all go."

Gary likes to touch too, always has his hands all over Sharon and Kelly. He has this squirt-bottle of oil and massages them for a long time, talking about how beautiful the human body is, how natural and free children are, how groovy it is to be one with nature and your body, blah, blah, blah.

I guess Gary is an okay-looking person, not counting that beard and mustache that cover his face but he's a total goofball, a fake, and I've seen dopey guys like him in L.A.

I keep my distance from all of them, just watching and listening, but part of me misses being touched like that, and maybe that's what bothers me. Gary and Sharon and Kelly are part of something; they can just let it all hang out and be free. Maybe I'm the one with the problem, the one who is uptight.

At night, Sharon and Gary sleep downstairs. Kelly and me share a bed upstairs, and I don't like it up there since it's all open unfinished attic with spider webs in the eaves.

I sleep with the covers over my head to hide from the spiders. In my dreams Gary is under the covers too. His hands move on my back and legs, and his voice is this far-off sound saying, "Take it easy; let it go."

In the dream, part of me fights but another part of me gives, and I don't know how many dreams I have like that—seems like a few, the same thing every night. I don't want to have that dream anymore. I don't want him to touch me or say take it easy, but when I try to pull myself out of the dream, I can't and it turns out it's not a dream at all.

Gary is really here and he has his hairy face between my legs, his hands holding me open, holding me down.

I try to kick him off, try to bring my legs together, but I can't. Gary's fingers push hard into my skin, hurting me.

"Take it easy," he whispers.

Kelly is on the other side of the bed, curled up in sleep, and I don't want to wake her up or scare her.

Gary's whiskers scratch on my legs, his fingers moving over me, this warm liquid feeling in my legs and stomach.

I twist myself away, pushing harder at his shoulders.

"Easy," Gary whispers.

"No," I say. "Stop it."

Gary finally stops then and moves from under the covers.

I roll on my side, curl up in a tight ball closer to Kelly, and hold my breath.

I still feel his hands on my skin, his face on my legs, and I curl myself even tighter from that terrible feeling.

I don't know if he's still standing there or if he left, and finally, I turn my head to check. The room is empty now, no evidence of him here at all.

I pull my nightgown between my legs and my heart beats so hard, I can feel it in my ears.

I don't know what happened to me, don't know what he was doing to make that thing happen, but deep in my stomach is a feeling like I might throw up. I lie there for a long time, waiting to see if I will, except I don't, and finally, I go back to sleep.

The sick feeling is still in me the next morning.

I get up and the house is quiet, Kelly still sleeping.

In the kitchen, Sharon is at the table in her bathrobe and she drinks a mug of something.

"Where's Gary?" I say.

"He's out," she says, smiling. "Probably meditating or something." She has her feet up on the seat of her chair, knees to her chest, mug between both hands.

I sit in a chair directly across, and between us is a rough wood table.

"Where's Kelly?" Sharon says.

"Still asleep," I say.

Sharon nods and sips her tea, eyes looking away and out the window.

I haven't been with her long enough to say I like her or not; I guess she's okay. She isn't a mean person, I do know that. She's more like an all-business person, someone you can be straight with.

My hands hold tight to the seat of the chair and I stay extra still until she looks at me.

"Something is going on with Gary," I say.

Sharon has a small face with these narrow-line eyebrows. She lifts those eyebrows up.

"What do you mean?" she says.

"Last night, he was in the attic," I say.

She keeps her eyes on me, and I do the same, eye to eye.

"So?" she says.

I clear my throat then and take in a deep breath. I search for the words to describe what it was Gary was doing but can't find them.

"He's doing things he shouldn't be doing," I say, looking at Sharon and then down at my hands in my lap.

"He was touching me, down there, you know, with his mouth."

That sick feeling is up the back of my throat and I can't say anything else. I cross my arms over my stomach and wait.

Sharon looks at me for so long I wonder if she even sees me anymore. She blinks and blinks and then slams her mug on the table with a hard bang. The sound of the mug on the table goes through me to the bone, a jump from the inside out.

"God damn it," she says.

Sharon stands up then, adjusting her robe tighter and she walks from the table to the door and then back to the table again, her hand pushing through her hair. It's like what happened to me actually happened to her. "Here's what we're going to do," she says, voice down-to-business serious. "We'll call Peggy right now, this morning," she says, "and they can come get you." She pushes her hand through her hair again, tightens the belt on her robe again too. "We'll just tell them you were homesick."

"Homesick?" I say.

Sharon nods and puts both hands on the edge of the table, leaning her weight on them. "I won't tell them about Gary, and maybe you shouldn't either; maybe it should be our secret."

The idea of a secret makes me feel worse, as if what happened up there was my fault and now I have to hide.

"So we have a deal?" she says. "This is our secret, right?"

I keep my arms crossed over my stomach and look at her looking at me. I want to say, *No way—I'm not going to lie for him or for you,* but then, I don't know what else to do. I can't stay here.

I nod, just a quick nod, and Sharon smiles, but it's not happy at all.

Aunt Peggy and Uncle Dick show up that night, and I didn't know the cabin in the woods was so close to Reno.

I'm relieved to see them, and Kimmy and Aunt Peggy act happy to see me.

Kimmy runs at me with one of her big hugs that hits around my legs, and Aunt Peggy does a strange pat at my arm and then stops.

"You got homesick, huh?" she says, smiling at me.

"Yeah," I say.

Uncle Dick stays in their car with his elbow leaned out the open window, cigarette between his lips, bored expression on his face. He still has on his Sears uniform, grease splatters on his collar, his sleeve.

I say good-bye to Sharon, and she says it was great having me, see you later, and then I climb into the backseat. Kimmy gets into the back behind me, and Aunt Peggy gets in up front.

"Hi, Uncle Dick," I say.

Uncle Dick looks at me in the rearview mirror, cigarette hanging from his mouth, and in his eyes is that look like I'm nothing.

"There's just no getting rid of you," he says.

"Dick!" Aunt Peggy says.

"Just kidding, Peg," Uncle Dick says. Uncle Dick turns his back to me, then shifts himself in his seat, cigarette still hanging between his lips. I know he's not kidding and I wish there was a way to make him look at me like I am a real person instead of a nothing.

Gary isn't around anywhere, and Sharon and Kelly wave good-bye from the front door of the old cabin. Sharon doesn't smile, just waves like *Go away,* and she has her other arm tight around Kelly.

I wave back to her, Aunt Peggy waves too, and Kimmy snuggles closer against my side, her arm on my arm. I put my arm around Kimmy's shoulders then, let her lean against my side, and she puts her thumb into her mouth.

It's a Tuesday afternoon when a man comes from the VA and asks a bunch of questions about living with Aunt Peggy and Uncle Dick. Uncle Dick is at work, and it's just Aunt Peggy, Kimmy, and me with the VA man.

Aunt Peggy is dressed nicer than I've ever seen her, makeup on her face, and she laughs a lot.

The VA man asks if I'm going to go to college. I tell him, yes, I am going to go to college.

He asks Aunt Peggy for personal references, and she writes a few names on a sheet of paper and hands them over.

At the very end of the interview, Aunt Peggy says all my VA money will be saved for my college, and then out of the blue, she says they are planning on adopting me.

After the VA man leaves Aunt Peggy explains how they didn't want to tell me about the adoption until it was official, something about my Social Security and VA benefits.

"We had to make sure you kept your benefits," she says.

"I don't understand," I say.

Aunt Peggy has changed out of her nice clothes and we are in the kitchen making tacos for taco night.

I grate a yellow brick of cheese while Aunt Peggy cooks hamburger at the stove.

"It's a lot of money," she says, looking over her shoulder at me. "It would be foolish to give it up."

Kimmy is on the floor between us, plays pretend cooking with some of Aunt Peggy's Tupperware containers. RC sits on her back legs, face up, alert in case Aunt Peggy drops food on the ground.

"It will be just terrific," Aunt Peggy says. "You can even call me Mom."

I stop grating the cheese.

"Is that what you want?" I say. "For me to call you Mom?"

Aunt Peggy looks over her shoulder at me and smiles.

"Well, sure," she says.

I bite my lip and look down at Kimmy and RC, such a strange feeling in me, like I'm trapped in a way. If I say I don't want to be adopted, it might hurt her feelings, but if I say yes, then that is strange too.

I watch Kimmy stir nothing in her plastic container.

"Does that mean I have to call Uncle Dick Dad?" I say.

"Well, of course," she says.

My hand slips on the cheese, knuckle against the grater. I put my knuckle into my mouth quick.

"Are you okay?" she says.

I take my finger out of my mouth, look at where I cut myself, but it's just a scrape. "Yeah," I say, "it's fine."

Kimmy bangs her wooden spoon on the plastic bowl, a drum sound, and the kitchen smells like hamburger and spices.

"So?" Aunt Peggy says. "What do you think?"

It's quiet in the kitchen, the sound of the hamburger sizzling on the stove, Kimmy talking to herself in baby talk.

"I don't know," I say.

Aunt Peggy puts her fist on her hip and turns to me. "What?" she says. "What don't you know?"

Kimmy looks at Aunt Peggy, at me. Even RC looks at me.

"Well, it's really nice and everything."

"But?" Aunt Peggy says, a high rise of red color up her neck.

She's never been mad at me before and I get the feeling I should just be quiet and not say anything, even though it's too late for that. I bite my lip and look down at the pile of cheese I grated, yellow in a white bowl.

"I don't think Uncle Dick likes me very much," I say.

"Of course he likes you," she says, hand up in the air between us and then back, fisted, on her hip. "He loves you."

"He does?" I say, a laughing sound in my voice.

"Well, of course he does," she says. "Why else would he want to adopt you?"

Aunt Peggy turns to the stove then, digs at the meat in the pan with hard, sharp movements. I go back to grating cheese and I wonder if I'm wrong about Uncle Dick. Does he love me only he doesn't know how to show it? Is love looking through a person as if they aren't there, is it calling them a no-neck and bossing them around without a please or a thank-you?

"Maybe you don't think he's good enough for you," Aunt Peggy says.

I stop with the cheese again.

"Just because he didn't go to college and fixes appliances for a living, well, that doesn't mean he's not a good man."

"I never said that," I say.

Aunt Peggy talks to the pan of meat, shoves it around, her voice louder and louder, like I'm not right here in the kitchen. "I don't know why people can't see the good in him," she says. "If you just tried to see it from his point of view, see who he really is deep down, you wouldn't be so high and mighty about him."

"Aunt Peggy, that's not what I said," I say.

She goes to the refrigerator, takes out a couple of tomatoes, puts them on the cutting board, and slices with big moves of her arm.

"I'm sorry, Aunt Peggy," I say.

"You should be," she says, no give in her voice.

Her anger is everywhere, as big as an elephant in the middle of the kitchen, no room to move or even sneak by.

Kimmy puts her spoon down on the floor, picks up her blanket, and pops her thumb in her mouth, and RC lowers her head and goes into the dining room.

I stay extra still, waiting for something, but that's it. Aunt Peggy stays angry and quiet, going through the motions of making dinner and ignoring me.

I do like she does, going along as if everything is normal. I set the table, fold the napkins in triangles and put out four plates, four cups, and four sets of silverware.

At five-thirty, the dinner is done, Uncle Dick comes in the door like he always does—"I'm home," and finally Aunt Peggy breaks her silence by going past me and over to Uncle Dick.

Her anger is still there, but she pretends it's not, kissing him hello and asking, "How was your day?"

✦ ✦ ✦

Aunt Peggy can stay angry for a long time.

You can see it in every expression on her face and hear it in the tone of her voice, which is sharp with sarcasm.

I try to find a way to talk about it with her, but she just won't, saying, "I don't know what you mean" when I bring it up. Then she pretends she's not mad, even though I know she is.

That fall, Aunt Peggy, still mad, takes me school shopping for a couple pairs of jeans and sweaters and then enrolls me in middle school.

It's nice to be away from Aunt Peggy and in school again. The work is easy, the teachers are friendly, and I make a few friends, Toni, Melinda, and Wendy. At lunch, a few of us girls get together with a tape player of Motown music and make up dance routines to pass the time.

Every day, after school, I ride the bus back to Black Sparks, get dropped at a stop a couple blocks from the house and walk as slowly as I can, kicking my way along.

After I've been in school about a month, out in front of the house is a moving truck, the word MAYFLOWER written on the side.

RC is outside too sniffing the edge of the truck tires and when I go into the house, everything is different.

The entryway and dining room are crowded with a couple moving boxes open, with paper pulled out and new things that aren't new at all. It's the hutch, buffet, dining table, and six chairs that were my mother's dining-room set, tulips and vines painted on for decoration. I'm so surprised to see it here that I just stand there for a long time, blinking at everything.

I've known this dining-room set since we lived at our first house on Mary Street. It's been moved from the house in Carson City, into storage at the apartment in Hermosa, then into Deb's place in L.A., the house in Fountain Valley, the house in Huntington, the house in Palo Alto, and then back to L.A.

I put my hand on the back of a chair, the ladder-back shape familiar and the wood is cool on my skin.

Down the long hall is the sound of voices, Aunt Peggy's and the deeper voice of a man.

"Aunt Peggy?" I say.

"You're home," she says. "Come on back and see this."

I walk down the hall and she's in the back bedroom with a man who holds a clipboard.

My princess bedroom set is there too, pieces of white furniture trimmed in gold, and they fill the room completely.

I put my hands over my mouth, and Aunt Peggy laughs out loud, no sign of her anger for the first time in a long time.

"Surprise," she says.

"Where did it come from?" I say.

"Deb sent it," Aunt Peggy says.

"No way," I say.

"It's true," she says. "She sent all this stuff."

I touch over everything, making sure it's real—dresser, desk, chair, bookcases.

Kimmy is at one of the bookcases, opening a drawer and then closing it again.

She looks up at me, blue eyes round. "Pretty," she says.

"Yeah," I say.

Aunt Peggy is all busy with the moving guy, signs a bunch of papers, walks him to the front door.

The story of my father giving this set to me on my birthday and living in California aren't just stories anymore, they are more real now the princess furniture is here. It's like I'm more real too.

When Aunt Peggy comes back, she leans one shoulder on the doorframe. "This is all very pretty, Jenny," she says.

I sit down on the bottom bunk bed, nodding.

RC runs in the room, weaves her dog body around the furniture, and comes to me pushing her nose against my hand for a pet.

"Maybe you were wrong about Deb," Aunt Peggy says.

I pet RC's head and look at Aunt Peggy across the room.

"What?" I say.

"Maybe she wasn't as bad as you thought."

On her face is a strange expression, that old anger mixed with a new look, as if she knows something I don't and she's going to set me straight.

I take my hand off RC and hold both hands on my lap.

Aunt Peggy tucks a bit of hair behind her ear and adjusts her glasses on her face. "What do you think?" she says.

"About what?" I say.

"About Deb," she says, "especially now that she sent your things."

I look around the room, and it's very nice that my things are here, but it doesn't change anything about Deb or what I know. "I'm not going to lie to you, Aunt Peggy," I say.

"I'm not asking you to lie," she says, her voice sharp.

"What are you asking?" I say.

Aunt Peggy's eyes shift, flat behind her glasses.

"I'm asking if you misjudged her," she says.

"No," I say.

Kimmy stands between us, blue eyes wide, and then she goes to Aunt Peggy, arms up. Aunt Peggy scoops up Kimmy, the red stain of her anger slipping up from the collar of her shirt.

"You have a lot to learn about people, Jenny," she says. "You aren't as good as you think you are, and other people aren't as bad."

She lifts her chin with that, going out of the room with Kimmy on her hip.

It's like a slap without being slapped.

I don't think I'm better than Aunt Peggy or even better than Deb—saying someone is a mean person means *I'm telling the truth.* But maybe you aren't supposed to tell the truth at all. Maybe you are supposed to be like Aunt Peggy and hold how you really feel deep inside.

My princess bedroom set is around me like building blocks waiting to be set right, and that trapped feeling is in me again, the same as when Aunt Peggy told me about being adopted. I didn't have a choice about where I'm going to live, and now I don't have a choice about who I am supposed to be or how I'm supposed to feel.

It's a terrible thing to feel this trapped, like you are being choked to death very slowly.

I get up then, close the door, and stand with my back against it until Aunt Peggy calls me to help with dinner.

That night, Uncle Dick and Aunt Peggy move their avocado furniture out of my room and then they go into the dining room and move that furniture around. While they work, I put my room together by myself.

Uncle Dick says there's no way I can do it, that smug look on his face and Aunt Peggy is mad again and so, fighting against that trapped feeling and Uncle Dick's smug look and Aunt Peggy's words, I make myself busy with work.

I drag my bed here, my dresser there, my desk under the window, and piece by piece, my room goes together the way it always has.

What does that mean, *not as good as you think you are*? Does she mean I'm being a snob, snooty and unfriendly, with my nose in the air?

I push a pillow into a pink pillow sham, punch it three times so it's nice and fluffy, and put it at the head of the bed.

If that's what she means, that makes me mad.

I take all my stuff out of the pink trunk, stuffed animals for the bed, books on shelves, jewelry box on the dresser in the center of the mirror and Sleeping Beauty lamp on the desk.

I'm not that way. I know I'm not.

I snap on the lamp and go to the doorway, switching off the overhead light that is way too bright.

It's a perfect room, canopy bed, bookcases on each side, dresser with the mirror over, desk with the chair that has its own gold seat to match the trim. My father said it was a room fit for a princess, and he was right, even if I'm nowhere near a princess.

There's a knock, and I open the door to Aunt Peggy on the other side.

"How's it going in here?" she says, the sound of her voice like she's tucked her anger back a little bit.

I almost say, "What do you care?" but I shove it down and do like she does. "Great," I say, voice different, loud. "Come on in."

She is still for a second, eyes behind thick glasses and I arrange my face all casual. Aunt Peggy takes in air through her nose and walks past me.

"Well," she says, coughing into her fist, "it's not even the same room."

I want to say, "No duh—it's not the same room; what do you think I am, an idiot?" but I hold to the fake smile instead.

Uncle Dick comes up the hall then, ducks his head a little when he comes into the room, and snaps on the overhead.

"What are you doing in the dark?" he says. He stops then, a look of surprise as if he's just crossed into a new world. "Look at this."

Aunt Peggy laughs at his surprise and adjusts her glasses. "Doesn't it look nice?" she says.

"It does," he says, "not bad at all."

"She said she would do it," Aunt Peggy says.

"She did say that," Uncle Dick says, rubbing his hand over his face and looking my way like he can finally see.

I reach over from where I stand by the door and snap off the overhead light again so it's the warm circle of light from the Sleeping Beauty lamp.

"Don't you think it looks better this way?" I say.

Aunt Peggy looks at Uncle Dick and he looks at her, that thing they do between them, talk without talk. "Yes, I suppose it does," Aunt Peggy says.

Uncle Dick tugs at the back of his pants to bring them up on his hips. "I guess we're not needed here after all," Uncle Dick says.

"I guess not," Aunt Peggy says.

She goes out of the room then, says good night as she leaves, and when Uncle Dick goes out, he nudges a fist against my arm.

"Good work, kid," he says.

"Thanks," I say.

I watch them until they are gone in the living room and from here can see the dining room set up with my mother's old stuff now, the green of their table gone.

\+ + +

That winter, on a Sunday afternoon, Uncle Dick, Aunt Peggy, and me clean the kitchen together. My job is the refrigerator, Aunt Peggy wipes down all the shelves where they keep plates and glasses, and Uncle Dick scrapes out the oven.

Kimmy is down for her nap and RC is curled up asleep at the entry of the kitchen. From the living room, music plays, "Afternoon Delight," by the Starland Vocal Band.

I've heard this song only a couple of times, but already I know all the words. It's a thing I like to do, holding the words in my head, one line running to the next like a map that helps pass the time.

"I think we've really outgrown this place," Aunt Peggy says.

"We could get a great deal on a place in Reno Park," Uncle Dick says.

"It's nice out there," Aunt Peggy says.

There's a bucket of warm water at my feet and I dip my washcloth in and wring the extra water out.

"You could even go to the same school," Aunt Peggy says.

"Where?" I say.

"Reno Park," she says, "where Dick says we might get a new place."

Uncle Dick leans back, head out of the oven, and he has on a pair of Aunt Peggy's yellow rubber gloves, which is just about the funniest thing I've ever seen.

"It's just a few miles north," he says. "Wide open spaces, lots of kids."

Since Deb sent my stuff, there's been more and more talk of adoption, and he's been different with me. Uncle Dick still teases and bosses me around, but it's not as bad, or maybe I'm just getting used to him.

"What in the world did you get stuck in here, Peg?" Uncle Dick says, scraping at the oven again.

"That silly apple pie," she says. "It spilled over."

Aunt Peggy tugs on her T-shirt, white with blue around the arms and neck. Whatever anger she had at me ran out too, and she's back to being almost normal again, even saying how excited she is about the adoption.

She wipes her face with the back of her wrist and smiles my way. "How's it going over there?"

"Almost done," I say.

"Good work," she says.

I wipe down the last shelf of the refrigerator and maybe it's having the princess bedroom set here again, maybe it's the change in them or maybe it's how they are going to be my parents now. I'm not sure why I feel like I have to be myself, my whole self and talk about Gary, I just do, as if talking about it will pull it out of the shadows and make sense of what happened.

Aunt Peggy dumps a tub of dirty water in the sink, rinses it out with hot water.

"Aunt Peggy?" I say, closing the door of the refrigerator.

"What?" she says over her shoulder.

"If someone told you to keep a secret," I say, "even if it's a bad secret, should you do it?"

"What kind of secret?" Aunt Peggy says, turning off the water.

Uncle Dick sits back on his heels again, spatula in his hand, those yellow gloves still on.

"Who told you to keep a secret?" Uncle Dick says.

I put my washcloth down on the counter and stand up straight.

"Sharon," I say.

Aunt Peggy looks at Uncle Dick and he looks at her.

Uncle Dick sets the spatula down on the door of the open oven and pushes himself to standing.

"Sharon has no business telling you to keep a secret," Aunt Peggy says, one hand fisted on her hip.

Uncle Dick nudges the back of his rubber gloved hand over the side of his mouth.

"Let's hear it," he says.

Don't tell them is in my head, *Don't do it* but I don't know how to back out now, the two of them looking down at me.

I look down then too, at my hands, and tell the whole story of Gary, how he messed with me in the middle of the night and how I told Sharon about it and she called them and said I was homesick. In my head, it was a clear story, but out of my mouth, it's all messed up with other things, how it feels like it might have been my fault and how I hate that I lied to them for so long except I didn't know what else to do.

Time stops in the kitchen, the Starland Vocal Band singing "Falling in a Deep Hole."

"I just thought I should tell you," I say, "since you are adopting me and everything, I just want to be honest." I look back and forth from her to him.

Uncle Dick pulls off the yellow gloves with a snap, takes his cigarettes out of his shirt pocket and shakes one up.

Aunt Peggy nods her chin up at him. "I could use one of those," she says.

Uncle Dick hands her the pack and they both light up. He leans on the counter on one side of the kitchen and Aunt Peggy leans on the counter on the other side, looking at each other through the cigarette smoke.

"We should talk about this," Uncle Dick says.

Aunt Peggy takes a hard pull on her cigarette, cheeks in, holds the smoke in her body, and then blows the smoke toward the dining room.

"Yes," Aunt Peggy says, "we will talk about this."

She looks my way, crossing one arm over and holding her elbow in the other hand while she smokes.

"Maybe you can just go to your room for a while," Aunt Peggy says, "and we'll talk about this."

I don't go, though, I just stand there watching them, a terrible feeling in my stomach.

I don't know what I expected from them, but now it's out there, I want them to tell me it wasn't my fault, that it's going to be okay or even that they are going to call Sharon to get to the bottom of it. That's what parents do, right? They look out for you and they explain what you can't understand. But they don't do that.

I made a mistake, this whole thing is a mistake but now it's out there and it's too late. Turning myself to the side, I squeeze past them and step over RC.

As I go down the hall, I listen for words between them but there is nothing now, not even music.

We don't talk about Gary ever again, as if I never said it, as if it never happened. Everything goes on like normal, days in school, weekends around the house, and then in the middle of the week in February, I go from being Jennifer Lauck to Jennifer Duemore.

There is a courtroom, a lawyer, a judge, and a lady who types on a tiny typing machine.

Aunt Peggy is dressed in a brown-and-green wool skirt that's shaped like the letter A and a white blouse that ties at the neck with a big bow. Uncle Dick wears cowboy boots and jeans, a brown corduroy jacket, and a clean white T-shirt. Kimmy has on a red dress and white tights. I'm wearing a purple-and-orange cotton dress Aunt Peggy got for me as a surprise. The dress is practically see through and is too small for me, short skirt and elastic that pinches around the armholes. Aunt Peggy says it was an Easter seasonal on sale and she can't take it back.

I'm tugging my dress down another time when the judge calls out my name, tells me to stand up, and then asks if I am making this decision of my own free will.

Free will? I don't know what he means, the idea around and around in my head, the pinch of the dress around my arms.

Uncle Dick and Aunt Peggy look down at me, Aunt Peggy saying something like "Answer the man."

"I do," I say, my voice too loud, and I don't know why those are the words that came into my head.

Aunt Peggy looks over at Uncle Dick, the two of them laughing, and even the judge up at the bench smiles.

After that, there are a few more questions, a few signatures, and a man who came in with us says he'll send the paperwork over as soon as it's processed.

After the adoption, we go to lunch at this place that smells like french fries and hamburgers, the floor slick with grease.

All of us get arranged in a big corner booth, Kimmy crawling to the deep corner, me next to her, adjusting the skirt of my dress over my legs.

Before today, there's been plenty of talk about how things are going to be, mostly from Uncle Dick. He says they are going to parent me differently than Kimmy, that I need something called "tough love," which may seem harsh sometimes even though it's going to be for my own good.

Aunt Peggy scoots in at one end, body up and down as she moves over the plastic seat. Uncle Dick sits heavy on the end closest to me and nudges me with his hand.

"How's it feel to be a Duemore?" he says.

I shift myself under the too-tight dress and pick up a menu. "Just great," I say, fake happy smile to go with my fake happy voice.

The waitress comes to our table then, setting out four sweaty glasses of water, her own version of a fake smile with a bright pink lipstick on her front teeth.

"How we doing today?" she says.

I look outside to a view of a parking lot, a four-lane road, and a shopping center. In the window is a reflection of all of us in here. Aunt Peggy's wide shoulders and that silly bow around her neck, Uncle Dick's slope shoulders, even in a jacket, Kimmy in red with her soft round face and her blond wispy hair that Aunt Peggy pulled into a top ponytail and tied with a red ribbon.

I have no idea what tough love actually means, but a girl at school was caught shoplifting and her parents sent her off to juvenile detention for a whole month. Maybe that's tough love—screw up and you go right to jail.

My face is just an outline in the window, thin and narrow, eyes dark with dark circles. Duemore, Jenny Duemore.

Aunt Peggy says she's on a diet today, orders an iced tea and a chef salad, and wants to know all the different kinds of salad dressing available.

Uncle Dick orders a triple bacon cheeseburger and fries, "And I think I'll get a milkshake," he says.

"What flavor?" the waitress says.

"You surprise me, sweetheart," Uncle Dick says.

"Jenny?" Aunt Peggy says, "do you know what you want?"

In the reflection of the window, everyone watches me.

"Grilled cheese," I say, tugging at my sleeve.

The waitress writes on her pad, eyebrows up.

"No fries?" Aunt Peggy says.

"Nope," I say.

"Nothing to drink?" Uncle Dick says.

"I'll just have water," I say.

The waitress takes my menu.

"What's wrong with you?" Aunt Peggy says.

"Nothing," I say.

Aunt Peggy watches my face, and I can't look at her anymore. I search the tabletop for something, anything. In the middle is a kids' menu and a cup of crayons.

"Looky Kimmy," I say, my voice high and happy, "crayons!"

Kimmy sits up on her knees, reaching for the crayons.

After that, Aunt Peggy and Uncle Dick share an ashtray, smoking their cigarettes and talking about what, I don't know, just words about something.

"Want to color?" Kimmy says, holding a green crayon to me.

"Sure," I say. "Why not."

The menu has flowers on one side, and I use the green to color in the stems extra careful while Kimmy uses her red crayon to draw great big circles all over the rest of the menu.

When we get home, I say I'm tired and go to my room.

All during lunch and then on the ride home, every time I said "Aunt Peggy" or "Uncle Dick," they would correct me.

"That's Mom, now," Aunt Peggy would say.

"I'm your father now," Uncle Dick said. "Just call me Dad."

In my own room where I can just be myself again, I take off the stupid dress and kick it into the corner of my closet. Around my arms are indents from the elastic, and I try to rub them away.

I pull on a pair of jeans and a T-shirt and then sit on my canopy bed.

It's a lot of work pretending the way they do around here, like lying about everything and trying to remember where you are in the lie so you don't get caught.

Outside is dead grass, the chain-link fence around the yard, and the square shadow of the garage. RC is out there too, and she sniffs around the edge of the yard, her little gray head down.

I look over at the door of my room, closed, me in here, them out there.

One thing I know for sure, Aunt Peggy and Uncle Dick do not come into my room and they never mess with my stuff. Aunt Peggy says a girl needs private space and if I respect their space, they will respect mine.

So far, it's been true, and I even took my key off my shoelace, and stored it in my jewelry box for when I need it.

I push off the bed then, cross the room to my dresser and take out the silver key for my pink trunk.

Kneeling down, I unlock the silver lock and push the lid of my trunk open. It's practically empty now, just a few trophies and medals for running, the black velvet bag with my mother's jewelry inside, wedding ring and pearls, the Our Wedding album and that painting Daddy had done of me at Disneyland.

I reach in and take up the velvet bag and the Our Wedding book, holding them in my lap.

A long time ago, Auntie Carol gave me this stuff and told me to keep it safe.

"You are Janet's daughter," Auntie Carol said. "It's your job to hold her treasures and remember her life."

Part of me didn't believe her that day. I knew I was adopted, Bryan told me all about it but then after Momma died and Auntie Carol gave me these things, I felt different, important, as if my mother was gone but that I could still do something that could make a difference.

What do I do now? Do I keep this stuff, throw it away, or maybe send it to Bryan?

As I look at the ceiling, tears roll down my cheeks and fall on the black velvet bag and the cover of the Our Wedding book.

Far off is the sound of the television and Aunt Peggy talks in a low voice.

I wipe my tears off the cover of the book and turn it open to them on the page, my parents. So much has happened since they died, one storm after another, and now, it's almost like a dream they were alive at all.

Still, I feel them in my heart, I ache for them, and how do you stop that? How do you stop being one daughter and become another?

There's a knock at the door, and in a second, without waiting at all, Aunt Peggy opens the door and looks in.

"What are you doing?" she says.

I should close the book and put it away, I should say *This is nothing—don't worry about it,* but I can't shift into the lie that fast. In fact, for a wide-open second, I imagine Aunt Peggy seeing the truth about the way things are and maybe becoming a different person who can understand and even help.

Aunt Peggy comes in then and stands over me, no expression on her face. "What the hell is the matter with you?" she says, fists on her wide hips, the flare of her skirt stiff to each side of her body.

"What would Dick think if he saw you with that?" Aunt Peggy says, pointing down at my book of photos. "How do you think this makes me feel?"

The red color lifts up her neck and cheeks, her voice loud

in the small room. She says my tears make her sick, that I'm selfish and self-absorbed and if I stopped feeling sorry for myself for one minute, I'd appreciate the sacrifices they are making for me.

My tears dry to crust as she yells and I look at a spot on the wall.

"I want you to cut this out right now. Put that thing away, and if I see it again, I'll throw it in the goddamned trash," she says.

I shift my eyes to her face then.

"Dick is your father now," she says, putting her hand on her chest, "and if you can't at least show some respect for me, show some respect for him."

The most real thing to do would be to stand up and scream that I don't give a shit about Dick, that he will never be my father and that there's no way she will ever touch my wedding book or anything else of mine.

I keep extra still, the book on my lap over the velvet bag with my mother's pearls and wedding ring.

I do what she says, closing the book on my parents and, in a way, on the person I used to be.

Good-bye, Jennifer Lauck.

Hello, Jenny Duemore.

Without faking how much I hate her right now, I look up.

"Happy?" I say.

Aunt Peggy shifts her jaw side to side, no more words to say. She looks like she could hit me right now—I'd probably even deserve it—but she doesn't. Instead, she goes out of the room as fast as she came in, slamming the door shut so loud it shakes the walls.

PART THREE

ST. HELENS

THREE

ST. HELENS, WASHINGTON ☙ 1978

The band plays the school fight song, cheerleaders wave maroon pom-poms, and around us other kids clap with the music or just look around with bored expressions on their faces.

"Right there," Megan says, pointing through the crowd.

On the gym floor is a row of guys, shoulder to shoulder. Football guys. They wear matching jerseys and expressions—so serious.

"See," she says, "Number 80."

I clap my hands in time with the music, but I can't see that far away, not unless I squint my eyes and tip my chin up. I see the great big 80 on the jersey, see it's a guy, but the rest is a blur.

"Isn't he cute?" she says.

"It's possible, but I can't really see him," I say.

Megan rolls her eyes, disgusted with me.

"I'm sorry," I say, still clapping my hands. "I can't see him—sue me."

"You need glasses," she says. "You are blind."

Megan has a face shaped like a heart, brown curly hair and blue eyes with a brightness that's charged from a deep place inside. There's something bouncy about her too, a happy-to-be-alive quality and we are best friends. My nickname for her is Moog.

That guy out there is her cousin, and a couple of rows down from where we stand, she has another cousin. Her brother is up in the stands behind us, and she has a couple of sisters who are down by the floor.

That's one thing about St. Helens—everyone is related or is neighbors or goes to the same church. The whole town is like a big family, practically linked from birth.

Last year, when we moved here from Nevada, I didn't have a link. I was the new girl, curious looks and raised eyebrows, but then I made friends with Megan and a few other girls, and now, it's like I've always been here. I'm part of the family.

I squint at Number 80 again and I put my hand up to shade my eyes like that's going to help.

"All right," I say, "he's adorable, a total knockout—so what?"

Megan puts her hands on her hips, all attitude. "He wants to meet you," she says.

"Ha, ha," I say.

"It's true," she says. "He told me."

The band stops then and everyone sits but me. I stand there, mouth open.

"Don't be a dork," she says, laughing and tugging me down. "Everyone's looking at you."

I want to ask Megan a hundred questions—When did Number 80 tell her that? How did he say it? What does it mean exactly?—but the principal of the school walks across the gym floor with a microphone in his hand. He's new here, a cheesy guy who is always smiling and saying things like "I want to be your pal first and principal second."

Holding the microphone close to his mouth, he talks way

too loud about how 1978 is going to be a great year and how this football team is going to make us proud.

"Oh, great," I say, rolling my eyes. "Mr. Spirit."

"What a goofball," Megan says.

"We are the Mighty Bulldogs," the principal yells, voice swinging into high gear. "Let's show our school spirit. Let's carry ourselves proud. Let's bark like a big dog."

I lean over to Megan. "Is that embarrassing?" I say, "A grown man barking into a microphone?"

"*Woof Woof,*" the principal barks, his face turning red.

"I'm embarrassed for him and I'm all the way up here," Moog says.

Moog and me together for ten minutes always ends like this, smart-aleck jokes about anything, everything, and then running that joke into the ground just to hold on to that perfect laughter that makes everything good.

"He is supposed to be a role model," I say.

"What must his wife think?"

"And his kids?"

We are too funny, hilarious, laughing until our sides hurt.

"I want to see everyone out tonight to support our Dogs," he yells. "Go-oooo, Dogs!"

The band starts up, everyone clapping again and we get it together, standing up too.

"That man loves the microphone," Megan says, wiping her eyes.

"Woof, woof," I say, the two of us laughing all over again.

Our laughter makes me brave enough to stand tiptoe and look over everyone's head at Number 80 just one more time but he's still just a blur.

St. Helens is a soaking wet town in the evergreen trees with a heavy sky of gray clouds that weave in and out of the pine trees.

They call it St. Helens since on a clear day you can see Mount St. Helens in the distance.

Downtown has one blinking yellow light, a main street, a few businesses and railroad tracks that arch in from somewhere and make a straight line out of town. On the west side of the railroad tracks is this massive tree stump with a plaque nailed on top. WORLDS BIGGEST TREE, it says, but I doubt it's true. How do you prove a thing like that? It's more like a claim to fame since St. Helens used to be a big logging town.

We don't live near The Stump. We live just off the interstate at the dead-end turnaround of a road and that's what you notice most about our place, how people drive to the end and when they get to the dead end, they pull into our driveway, back up and then drive away. Our place is where you turn around and go back the way you came.

The house is painted white and looks just like one of those houses in a little kid's drawing: triangle top, square bottom, one window, a door.

Behind the house is an old barn that's about to fall down, and past the barn is a rectangle of wild land with hip-high grass, fierce blackberry bushes, and a stand of white paper-bark trees drowning in the overgrowth. Those trees don't belong here; they don't fit. I've looked around for others like them but haven't seen any. I wonder who planted them, what they were thinking or hoping at the time.

Deep down, I think about how nice it would be to hack away all the dead grass and the blackberry bushes, just to see all of those trees, from the trunks to the tops, a little grove of perfection.

When we first moved in, there was a bunch of wild cats down there, a mother and her kittens, and one day, while Dad was at work, Mom got the idea to round them up. One of the kittens bit her on the hand, so the whole litter had to be taken to the pound and killed since Mom thought they might have rabies.

Now, Kimmy and me aren't allowed to go down there, just in case there are more wild cats.

Kimmy and me aren't allowed to cross over the barbed-wire fence that separates our house from an open spread of farmland either. Dad says it's private land and the owner might shoot us.

From our side of the barbed-wire fence, you can look out over the flat farmland to the shadows of thick pine trees and I wonder if some old guy is in those shadows with a gun on his knees. Maybe he just waits for a kid to walk on his land so he can pick up that gun, pull the trigger, and take a life.

Dad says whoever owns that land wouldn't even get in trouble for shooting.

"Why not?" I said.

"You're breaking the law," Dad said. "It's trespassing."

Inside, the house is small and you can walk a full circle, living room to the dining room to the kitchen to the bathroom and then through the bedroom that leads back to the living room.

In the living room is a big metal oil heater bolted to the floor and it's painted a dark brown color.

Every wall of the house is paneling with this dark brown wavy wood grain, only it's not real wood—it's just painted to look like wood. The carpet is dark green felt, and it makes me think of the stuff on pool tables.

When you go from the dining room to the kitchen, there's a narrow run of stairs, a pipe screwed to the wall for a banister, and up there is attic space with more paneling nailed to the slope of the roof.

That's where Kimmy and me sleep.

Kimmy's room is small like a closet, but her stuff fits pretty good in there—toy box, bed, dresser.

My room isn't a room. It's a wide-open space marked on one side by a column of brick that goes up and through the roof and on the other side by the steep stairs with the pipe handrail. The ceiling is too low for a canopy bed, even without the canopy. It's too low for the bookcases, too low for the princess mirror, too low to even sit at the desk when it's pushed to the wall.

My room is one of those nothing-special spaces you use for storage or a rainy-day playroom or your hobby train set. Mom says I am lucky to have so much space.

I hate my room.

I sleep on one of Kimmy's old bunk beds and almost all my princess bedroom set is stored away now in the attic crawl space. Rats and mice live in that crawl space.

Every night, I fall asleep to the sound of the rats and the mice, the scratch of their feet on the other side of the paneling in the attic, a rodent freeway of them sniffing and chewing and clawing at our things shoved away in storage. I even hear that sound in my dreams. It's the kind of thing you can never get out of your head once you've heard it.

It's a week after the big football rally, right before lunch period, when Number 80 walks right up to me in the hall. Moog warned he was going to introduce himself one day and that I should be ready.

Of course, I'm not ready. I have too many books and folders and I wish I was already at my locker so I didn't look so confused.

He cuts his way through the crowd of kids who rush through the breezeway on their way to lunch or another class.

Kids yell, "Hey" and "What are you doing later?" and "Save me a spot." He stops right in front of me, this look on his face like I'm the one he wants to talk to.

"Hey," he says, voice slow and warm and a little bit lazy.

Up close, he is so tall, I actually have to tilt my head back and he is very thin. His face is a nice face and his eyes are a warm light brown, the color of honey in a jar when you hold it up to the light. I've seen him only from far away but up close, there's something about him. Boy next door, but serious too.

I adjust my books to one arm and put out my hand like a total idiot.

"I'm Jenny," I say, "Jenny Duemore."

He looks at my hand for a second, not sure, and I almost put it down. He smiles then and takes my hand with a firm hold.

"I know who you are," he says. "I'm Luke."

Goose bumps run a race over my skin, up my arms, and meet between my shoulder blades.

"I know," I say, laughing then, so stupid, and I make myself knock it off.

Luke laughs too, and puts his hand back in his pocket. When he laughs, the Adam's apple on his throat moves up and down, and on the left side of his neck are two scars that run side by side, whiter than his normal skin.

"Which way are you going?" he says.

I look away from his neck, the idea of the scars in my head.

"Going?" I say.

"Is this your lunch, or are you going to another class?" he says.

"Oh yeah," I say. "Right, no, this is my lunch right now, but I'm going to put my stuff up first."

The bell rings, the breezeway clears out, and there are just a few kids running now. Luke looks around, maybe searching for someone he knows, maybe about to say " 'Bye" or "See you." He looks at me again, and my eyes go to those lines on his neck for just a second, and then I make myself look at his face.

"I'll walk with you," he says.

"Oh, okay," I say.

I am nervous and wrong, the words out of my mouth all mixed up, and I bet he thinks I am so stupid.

Luke puts his hand at the low part of my back—no one has ever done that. There's something so familiar about it. I swallow hard and walk like it's totally normal to have this guy with his hand flat on my back.

We go to the lockers for the freshman students, and it's strange how one minute you don't know someone and the next they are walking you to your locker, hand on your back, other hand reaching to open the door for you and wait until you go in first. It's so strange, like I am a different girl completely.

Megan is at the lockers with some of the other girls and she sees us.

"Hey, you two," she says, that singsong in her voice, and I scrunch my whole face at her.

"Hey," Luke says.

Megan winks at me, shuts her locker. Some of the other girls look at me then, all of them smiling like they know what's going on, and I roll my lips together, more nervous than I can remember.

Luke offers to hold my things while I unlock my locker. This close, he smells nice, some kind of spicy woody cologne.

My locker is painted a dark brown, like all the other lockers, and inside I keep it neat and tidy, books arranged by class, all my papers on the top shelf next to my lunch, my coat on the hook. The inside of the door is decorated with stuff I stuck up with Scotch tape. There's a fuzzy red foot sticker, a rainbow sticker, my class ID from last year, photos of Megan and Cathy and Sandy and everyone.

"I'd hate for you to see my locker," he says.

Luke stands there with my stuff in his arms, letterman jacket with LUKE on the left side, the scars on his long neck. I make myself not look, just take my folders and put them on the top shelf.

"What's wrong with your locker?" I say.

"It's a total mess," he says.

He laughs then, and I laugh too, even though it's not that funny to be a slob.

I take my books, slide them in order with the spine facing out, take my pencils and put them into the special box for holding pencils. Luke watches me, one hand holding open my locker door, and then he clears his throat and points at my face in last year's school ID.

"I remember you from last year," Luke says. "I saw you in the hall a few times. I wanted to meet you then."

I look at him and he looks at me and it's quiet in the hall, all the other kids gone now.

Sometimes you just get a feeling about a person, an instant connection. It's in the beat that's between you, an unspoken charge that runs deeper than words. I felt that with Megan right away, could see it in her eyes, and it was in the easy way we laughed at the same things. I knew right off we would be friends, probably forever. Luke is just the same; it's right there, obvious and yet still hidden in a way.

I lick my lips then and smile.

"Well," I say, "why didn't you?"

Luke takes his hand off my locker, a lost look about him.

"I'm kidding," I say, touching the sleeve of his jacket as if we've known each other a long time.

"Oh, right," he says, laughing then and nodding at the same time. "Megan said you've got a great sense of humor."

"Obviously not," I say.

He laughs then, really laughs.

"No," he says, "you just caught me off guard."

I reach to the locker door then, take out my lunch, and swing the door shut with a metal-on-metal sound.

"Better watch yourself," I say, "I have a way of doing that."

Luke stands up taller, as if that's possible, and in his light brown eyes, I can see what I already know: I'm not what he expected at all, and it's a good thing.

"I will," he says.

We've been at this family thing for three years now, and I still have to stop and think to make myself call them Mom and Dad, like a hiccup in my brain. I've gotten used to the idea that she's Mom, but Dad just doesn't work. He'll always be Dick in my heart.

He's always sending me away. First it was San Francisco with Sharon, then with some friend of his in Reno where I cleaned house and looked after their kids and then he sent me to stay with his brother and his wife for more than three months. It's like I'm garbage he always wants to dump.

I don't look at photos of my own father or mother anymore, not since the day I was adopted, but it turns out I don't have to. All I have to do is get very still and they are there, like a permanent layer of who I am. She's more shadowy and black and white, but I can see my father in full color. He smiles one of his big smiles, wears a maroon V-neck sweater, and sits in his red sports car with one hand on the steering wheel and the other hand on the gear shifter.

I even dreamed about him that way. We were together in his

car, and he said something about this old cat I had. Natasha. He said the cat got lost, and he kept looking down at where I was sitting in the passenger seat, like he was checking on me. In the dream, it was such a surprise to see him, boy-next-door drop-dead handsome, the sound of his voice, the length of his arm reaching to the shifter knob as he drove. I wanted to ask if he was real or dead, or if I was real or dead, only I couldn't speak.

It must have been the dream that gave him back to me, like a sign from the other side. That I can't see my mother is maybe a sign too, as if I'm supposed to try harder with Peggy.

She's not the greatest mother, she's still moody and hard to figure out, and when Dad's around, forget it—she will barely speak to me. Still, she has nice moments, and if I keep my room clean, fold towels the way she likes, do the dishes without being asked, set the table at dinnertime, she seems happy.

Dad got a Sears transfer from Nevada to Washington just after the bicentennial. Washington State is home to the whole Duemore clan, brothers, sisters, nieces, nephews, aunts, and uncles. Mom says they are a colorful bunch, some on welfare, others who square-dance, and a few high school dropouts. One of them is doing time for writing bad checks, another grows marijuana in the backyard, one had a baby born with only one tube to his heart, a couple of kids had to be put into foster care since the mother went to prison. There are wives who aren't allowed to get driver's licenses or hold jobs, sisters who were nine months' pregnant at their high school graduation, and grandmothers who chew tobacco and spit the juice 10 feet in the air.

When we first moved here, Mom and me got to be best friends, us against them, because she thinks the Duemore clan is a little strange, especially Dad's mother, Grandma Duemore.

Mom hates Grandma Duemore.

That first summer, Mom went through a big slim-down

makeover, 10 pounds off with the Calorie Counter Diet and a perm for her hair. She taught me how to play card games, hearts and rummy, and during our games, Mom went on and on about Grandma Duemore, how she had a heart of stone, was mean and cold and just bitter.

I agreed about Grandma Duemore and even made jokes about her just to make Mom laugh.

When I started back to school that fall, things shifted between us. I was all wrapped up in being the new girl, something I hate and Mom put on weight again, her perm growing out of her hair and everything about St. Helens driving her crazy. It rained too much, the people in St. Helens weren't friendly enough to her, the house was too small, and then one day, she just snapped.

It was a school day and I was coming home with a girl who lived up the street, a new friend I wanted Mom to meet.

We were walking down to the dead end of our road when, far off, we heard something deep and hollow, a beating drum sound.

Closer to the house, it was pounding and screaming, Mom's voice loud and wrong and full of obscenities she never says. Nothing else in that house could make a sound like that pounding, and I knew right away she was beating the oil heater.

My thoughts went right to Kimmy. Was she home and holed up in her little square of a room, thumb in her mouth? Was she taking her nap, and how could she sleep with all that noise? Was she somewhere else, maybe playing with her cousins at Grandma Duemore's place?

How I hoped Kimmy was out of the house.

It's funny how you act at a time like that, so calm and practical even though inside, you're scared beyond feeling.

Cathy and I talked about all the things we could do, go to

the house, call for help, or just wait. I thought we should do something, but Cathy didn't think it was so strange for a mother to be in her house going crazy. It was her idea to just sit and wait a while.

"She's probably letting off steam," Cathy said, matter-of-fact.

We went to the edge of the property line, sat where the road meets the grass, and listened to Mom's storm.

She could have ended her life that day or she could have hurt Kimmy or maybe my friend was right—maybe it was just the thing she needed to let off steam.

After the banging finally stopped, Cathy went home and I went to the front door.

The air in the house was thick the way it gets when doors and windows stay shut. RC met me at the door, jumping up and down like she was happy to see me and then wiggling herself out of that house. I found Kimmy next, curled on the sofa, thumb in her mouth, eyes on *Sesame Street,* where all the puppets were singing that song, "Who Are the People in Your Neighborhood?"

Kimmy looked at me, blue eyes wide open and round, nothing in them, and then she looked at the television again.

I expected the place to be a real mess—tables overturned, sofa cushions thrown here and there, broken glass on the floor—but there was no mess. The oil heater was just like always, this big brown thing in the middle of the living room, not even a dent in the metal. The rest of the house was the same too, neat and tidy, not one sign of pounding and screaming, as if it never happened.

I took slow steps, expecting some explosion from around the corner. In the dining room, Mom sat at the table and smoked a cigarette, her skin blotchy white and pink, puffy around the eyes. Her hair, still a little wavy from her perm, was all messed up, going this way and that way, and at the roots, I could see the beginning of gray hair I hadn't noticed before, as if in this afternoon, she had aged into an old woman.

She looked at me, dark eyes behind her thick glasses.

"Are you okay?" I asked.

She nodded then, eyes off somewhere past me. She looked lost, miserable, broken down by something, and even though I didn't know exactly how she felt, I had seen that look in the mirror a million times.

Pulling out a chair on the other side of the table, I sat down. "Do you want me to get you a cup of coffee?"

Mom, still looking off at the drapes, cigarette burning down between her fingers, nodded again.

I poured her a cup of coffee, black the way she likes, and brought it to the table. "Do you want to play a game of cards?"

She nodded again.

I went to the buffet and found a deck of playing cards called KEM, which are her favorite since they shuffle so easy.

"Hearts or gin rummy?" I said, sitting down across from her again, splitting the deck of cards.

Mom looked over at me then and her mouth trembled a little, as if she might start to cry.

I had never seen her cry before. Mom isn't that way; she doesn't show how she feels, doesn't say, "I love you," doesn't like you to touch her or to be touched, and she never cusses. Her way is to harden and go silent, the dirty looks on her face and the slice of her voice the only signs of what's really going on.

"You have been my best friend," she said, voice far away. "I don't know what I would have done without you."

"Come on, Mom," I said. "You've been fine. You are fine. Don't worry about it." I cut the deck of cards and shuffled them together the way she taught me last summer, bending the cards so they make a bridge as they come together as one deck again, like a big-time card dealer in Vegas.

"No," she said, hand flat on the dining table between us. "I've been going crazy in this place with these people and Dick's mother and all this rain, and I'm so thankful to have had you here to keep me company."

She looked at me and I looked at her, and for one moment, we stopped playing the game of being "mother" and "daughter," and were just two people caught together.

I knew it was hard on her being in St. Helens with the Duemore clan and Grandma Duemore as her only company. I knew she missed Reno and her family and even the sunshine.

We played cards that afternoon, Mom different than I've ever seen her before and probably will ever see again. We didn't talk about what happened or why. How do you talk about something like that anyway?

A few weeks later, Dad took out the oil heater and put in a new furnace, Mom took a full-time job in Longview, they found a day care for Kimmy, and we all joined the Catholic church.

Luke is a junior. He has lots of friends and comes from a good family, a normal family—mother, father, brother. He even grew up here in St. Helens.

He is the most polite person I have ever met, smells wonderful, and he dresses nicer than anyone in high school should dress: slacks, sweaters, button-down shirts, loafer shoes.

Before I came to St. Helens, there was a boy in another town and another school, and I liked him a lot until one day, he howled at me with one of his friends, just because I was singing along to a Barbra Streisand song on the record player.

Luke is ten times better than that other guy but why he's interested in me at all is a mystery.

Of course, he doesn't really know anything about me. I haven't told him my real story. Too serious. Too sad. Too weird. Besides, where do you begin to tell a story like mine?

That's what I think when Luke asks me to come to his house for dinner.

"Dinner?" I say.

"Sure," he says, "you know, chicken, potatoes, maybe some pie."

Luke and me are in the lunchroom, and we usually sit with all the other kids, except today, Luke wanted to sit off at the end of the last table, alone even though we're not alone.

"You do eat dinner, don't you?" he says.

"Ha, ha," I say.

Across the lunchroom, Megan's at a table crowded with all the girls—Posie, Cheryl, Gail, Sandy. I wish she would look up and wave, except they are busy talking.

Luke sits with his elbows on the table, chin resting on his hands.

"I'm serious," he says. "I'd like you to come."

I look at him again and he is serious—so serious it makes me nervous.

"I don't know if I can," I say, looking down at the table. "My dad says no dating until I'm sixteen."

"This isn't really a date," he says, smiling. "It's just dinner with my folks."

Luke is quick, doesn't miss a beat, and I like that about him, usually, but there's something to how intent he is right now, like he's looking into me and not just at me.

I get busy gathering up my lunch stuff, empty chip bag, sandwich bag, napkin. "Let's go outside," I say.

"Sure, why not."

I stand up then, and Luke gets up too, takes his tray to the counter. We go through the lunchroom, all the kids hanging out, laughing, some saying hi to Luke and he knows everyone, waving and smiling.

When we pass her table, Megan looks up, a little wave of her hand, and I shake my head like *You are not going to believe this*. Her bright blue eyes get all round and exaggerated like she can't wait to hear everything.

The clock says twelve-thirty, just 15 minutes left in lunch break, and Luke puts his hand at the low part of my back, holds the door open that leads to the parking lot.

It's one of those days you don't see a lot of in St. Helens. The sky is blue and the air is warm and off in the distance is the mountain, a round bowl of a top that's white with snow, even at the end of summer.

"I told my mom about you," Luke says. "She really wants to meet you."

"She does?" I say.

"Sure," he says, "of course."

I take a deep breath, act all calm and normal, since calm and normal are always good. I don't really know him that well; we've only been friends for a couple weeks, and it's hard to believe he already talked about me to his mom.

I take off my sweater, fold it up neat and tidy, unbutton the top three buttons of my shirt. Luke watches me from under his long blond bangs and squints like he's thinking about something.

"I'm going to sit," I say. "Do you want to sit here?"

"On the sidewalk?" he says.

"Why not?" I say.

I sit on my sweater, back to the wall, face to the sun, eyes closed. Normal.

I don't hear him do anything, and I wonder if he's going to sit or what.

He lets out a deep breath, and then I feel him next to me. I open my eyes and smile at him. Luke arranges his long legs cross-legged and then takes off his letterman jacket, lays it over his lap.

"Don't you ever sit in the sun?" I say.

"Yeah," he says, one hand pushing his hair off his eyes, "but not at school on the sidewalk."

I lean my shoulder into his shoulder.

"When you live in a place that has almost no sunshine," I say, "you'd better do it when you can."

He smiles, but in that smile, I know he waits for an answer about dinner.

Up until right now, Luke and I have been having fun. We're friends, we flirt a little, make each other laugh about silly things. It's nice, it's easy, but what if it turns out like that first guy? What if I start to like him and then, boom, he's howling at me too?

On top of that, there are all these rules at my house, tough love, which mostly turns out to be a million rules: no talking on the telephone, no dating until I'm 16, a mountain of chores, and if I get out of line with a "bad attitude," I can be put on restriction or even spanked with this big wood paddle.

Luke sits with his face to the sun, eyes closed, head tipped back and the scars on his neck stand out even more.

I want to reach out and touch them.

"I have an idea," Luke says, opening his eyes. "I could call your mom and dad, you know, if you want me to."

I push my fingers into my palm and roll my hand closed. "No," I say.

"No?"

I clear my throat and rub the back of my neck. "They are very strict," I say.

Luke leans forward then, elbows on his knees, hands together. "They are probably just looking after you," Luke says. "That's normal."

"No," I say, "it's not that."

"What?"

I'm pulling what little normal I have apart, and I wish I could think of the right thing to say. "It's not a personal thing," I say. "They just aren't the easiest people to talk to."

"I can be pretty charming," he says. Luke nudges his shoulder against me, smiling all the way to his eyes, and it's true, he is very charming, but sometimes, it takes more than charm.

I put my head on my knees and Luke leans forward too, face close to my face, the smell of his spicy woody cologne mixed with something else, his own body maybe.

"So what are you going to do?" he says.

I look right at his mouth, and in my head is this idea that I could kiss him. I sit up, sit back.

There are kids all around, some walking past us, others in the hall slamming lockers, yelling out to each other, and I bite my lip hard.

Luke smiles, and I wonder if he knows what I was just thinking, wonder what he's thinking.

"I'll ask," I say.

Luke's smile goes up into his eyes, and he claps his hands together. "Great," he says.

"But don't count on it."

"Come on, now," he says. "Think positive."

Any other time, I could crack a joke and we'd be laughing at nothing, but now I can't. I'm different, he's different, and it's all because of dinner.

✦ ✦ ✦

Every girl has to take home economics at St. Helens High. You learn how to cook and sew and take care of medical emergencies in the home, as if all of us are getting married straight after high school.

The second bell rings, and I slide into my desk next to Megan.

"Tell me everything," she says. "Did he kiss you or what?"

"God, no," I say, tucking my hair behind my ears. "Of course not."

I roll my lips together, look left, look right, all the other girls settling in around us, jackets off, notebooks open.

"I almost kissed him," I whisper.

"When?"

"When we were outside."

Megan looks at me, mouth open. "I can't believe you," she says.

"It's not like I did it," I say.

"You are smitten," Megan says.

"Come on," I say. "It's not like I did it."

"You are love bitten and smitten," Megan teases, finger pushing into my side. "I knew it would come to this."

"Pay attention now, ladies," Mrs. Oelson says.

Home economics is the last thing on my mind, but I sit up, at least looking like a good student.

Part of me is still out in the sun with Luke, another part of me is trying to figure out how to ask Mom if I can have dinner at his house, and another part of me wants to just gossip with Moog.

Mrs. Oelson writes a recipe on the board, tells us to copy it down—strawberry crepes.

"I see absolutely no point in crepes," Megan whispers, taking a sheet of paper out from her desk, looking up at the chalkboard.

I laugh at her and doodle Luke's name on the side margin of my paper.

The bus drops me at the end of our road, and I walk home alone, book bag over my shoulder, the sound of a train far off. Luke is heavy on my mind, the open way he smiles and that serious way he watches me, the possibility of him around and around.

Nothing in me planned for someone like Luke. I never imagined it.

My plan is to get through the next three years of high school, just get through it and move out, move on. In three years, I'm going to college right out of high school. My sophomore year of college, I am going to spend three months in France, backpacking, and then I'll come back, finish school, have a great career doing—something—and then I'll get married, maybe have a couple kids.

My plan is so clear in my own head, neat and tidy, like boxes all lined up in a row.

Sure, I don't know what I will study in school, where I will even go, and I don't know what I want to be, but the rest is there, a plan I can see and count on.

Luke doesn't have a plan; as a matter of fact, no one I know has one. Megan doesn't; none of the other girls either. Everyone here just goes day to day. The biggest thing to plan for is homecoming week.

At the dead-end turnaround of our house, I go to the mailbox and gather up the papers inside. There's never anything for me except a birthday card every year from Aunt Georgia and Uncle Charles in Carson City and the two brown envelopes that come at the beginning of the month. Social Security and Veterans Administration. They say my name and Mom's name, but I'm not allowed to open them. Still, there's something nice about how those checks always come, and they make me think of my father, driving, smiling, and wearing a sweater.

I've already tossed out my big plan to my father, not in some haunted-house-talk-to-the-dead way, just like testing the idea against what I know about him.

I know he always wanted me to do my best and that he always wanted both Bryan and me to go to college, and knowing those things makes me sure he would like my plan a lot.

I balance the mail on my chest and go into the house.

RC runs to meet me, happy someone is home, happier to get outside since she has to pee. I pet her and then hold the door to let her out front.

I put all the mail on the buffet so Mom can look at it first thing, the way she likes.

I toss my book bag on the steps to the attic and look at the clock, three in the afternoon, two and half hours before they come home.

Part of me wants to call Luke right away, just to talk, but that's stupid, I just saw him at school.

Instead of embarrassing myself, I do the chores the way she likes too. I pick up the living room—Dad's balled-up yesterday socks, a bowl of dried-up ice cream someone ate last night, dirty ashtrays full of cigarette butts. I pick up Kimmy's toys, put them into her room, make her bed, fold her pajamas, put them under her pillow. I put a dark load into the washing machine, one cup of powder detergent, cold-water setting. I unload the dishwasher, put in the ice-cream dish, and then dump out the ashtrays and clean out the stuck-on ash before putting them back on the coffee table and end tables.

At three-thirty, the telephone rings, just like it always does, Mom checking in.

"Hi," Mom says.

Her work voice is happy today and she asks how school was, if I have much homework, and then she talks about how Kimmy was so cute when they dropped her off at day care.

This is the time to ask.

"Hey, Mom?" I say.

"What?" she says.

"I wanted to ask you a favor."

"What?" she says.

I put my finger into the telephone cord, wind it around and around.

"There's this boy at school."

Mom is quiet on the line.

"And, well, he asked if I could come to his house."

"His house?"

"For dinner."

I tell her how I've known him a couple of weeks, how he's Megan's cousin, how he's a good boy from a good family, and that it's really his mother who invited me to have dinner on Sunday afternoon, just dinner.

I talk too much, Mom always says that, and so I make myself stop.

Mom clears her throat. "You cannot date until you are sixteen," she says.

"I know," I say. "But this isn't really a date."

"It's like a date," she says.

"We're just friends," I say.

My finger is all wrapped in phone cord and it's blue. I unwind the cord, holding my breath.

"I think dinner would be fine," she says.

"Great," I say, letting out my breath and putting an arm up in silent victory.

"I have to ask your father first," she says.

"But you think it's okay," I say.

"I don't see why not," she says, "but we'll talk about it tonight."

"But you will tell him that you think it's okay?" I say.

"Jenny, don't push it."

"Okay," I say. "No problem. Thanks."

It's an absolute miracle, but Dad says yes and Mom says she will drive me up to the Lucas place after church on Sunday. Dad tells me again that I'm not allowed to go on dates until I am 16 years old and that I'd better watch myself with the boys since they are usually out for just one thing, even though he doesn't say what that one thing is. Mom tells Dad that all boys aren't that way, says it's fine to be friends, that she knew lots of boys who were just her pals in school. After that, Dad just laughs and shakes his head the way he does when he thinks someone is full of shit.

We go to Sacred Heart Catholic Church now, even Dad, who isn't Catholic. The church is stucco painted a lime green and there's a tall bell tower off to one side. Inside, the benches are wood and the windows are made from yellow-brown glass with smaller designs in the top sections. One of the windows has a cup with this red heart in it and a cross coming out one side.

The mass is an hour long, but it seems like a year, readings about something written in the Bible a million years ago that are impossible to understand.

The priest is Father Hubert and he wears socks with these leather sandals, even on Sundays. No one around here wears sandals except in the summer, but Father Hubert wears them all the time, and I like that about him.

After the readings from the prayer book, everyone in the

church sits, and Father Hubert tries to connect the readings to everyday life.

Mom listens, Dad sits on the other side of her, chin to his chest, nodding off, and Kimmy lies on Mom's lap, fingers fiddling with the hymn books.

I look up at the stained glass window, a warm light through the yellow-brown glass.

I have on jeans, a black button-up sweater, this white T-shirt with pretty lace around the neck and the arms, and white tennis shoes.

I hope I look okay, not too dressy, not too casual.

There is a nudge against my shoulder.

"Get up," Mom whispers. "What's the matter with you?"

Everyone reads out loud and I stand up fast, thumb through the prayer book to find my place. By the time I do, it's too late, and now everyone sits down so Father Hubert can mess around with his cups of wine and the tray of round wafer crackers.

Mom sits down, a stiffness to her shoulders and a set to her jaw that says she's mad now. It was just a matter of time.

She takes being Catholic very seriously and hates if I don't pay attention. I can't help it though, everything about the mass is so boring.

Being Catholic is okay, I guess, like being members in some exclusive club, but I just don't get it, and more than that, I don't feel it. It's not like I don't believe in God or even Jesus; I'm scared to death not to believe. Anyone who doesn't believe has a ticket straight to hell, but the rest is a mystery.

When church finally gets over, Dad and Kimmy go over to the Duemore place and Mom drives me up to Luke's house.

"Anything to avoid Grandma Duemore," Mom says, driving west past The Stump and out of town. Her car is a little red Volkswagen bug that has a high, whiny engine. She shifts through the gears as we go up a hill to the other side of town.

"I'm sorry I'm going to miss her today," I say, leaning against the door, arms crossed over myself.

"You can still come," she says, looking my way with the beginning of a smile.

"I could if I was crazy," I say, which makes her laugh like she used to.

"Where in the world do they live?" Mom says.

The directions are on a piece of a paper in Luke's handwriting and I read them out loud.

"The road dips, there's a big white house at the top of the hill, and then you make a left."

I point to the left where there is a white house and Mom makes a left on a narrow driveway that goes over a railroad-tie bridge. Their house is built at the top of a ridge that gives them a view of the land below and even the mountain off in the distance.

"Very swanky," Mom says, turning off the car.

Luke comes out the side door of the house, arm waving.

"That's him," I say.

Mom leans to the windshield, adjusting her glasses.

"He's a skinny kid," Mom says.

It's true, Luke is slim but I hope he didn't hear her.

I open the door of the car and get out quick.

"Hey," Luke says.

"Hey," I say.

Luke shakes Mom's hand before she is even out of the car. "Nice to meet you Mrs. Duemore. Thank you for letting Jenny come up. My mother can't wait to meet her."

Luke smiles his winning smile and escorts Mom to the

house with his hand on her elbow. Mom looks flustered, embarrassed, charmed.

Inside, Luke makes introductions.

"This is my mother, Shelly, and of course, this is Jenny's mother, Mrs. Duemore."

"Peggy," Mom says, shaking hands, all polite. "Please, just call me Peggy."

"Peggy, it's a pleasure to meet you," Mrs. Lucas says.

Shelly Lucas is smaller than Mom, a round woman with her blond hair twisted and put up on the back of her head.

Luke comes to where I am, shuts the door behind me. "See," he whispers, "it's going fine. Mom," he says, voice louder, hand on my elbow.

Mrs. Lucas turns from Mom, smile still on her face, Luke's smile.

"Of course this is Jenny," Mrs. Lucas says, hands clapped together.

She comes to where I am, shakes my hand with both of hers and they are so soft and warm. "Our boy can't say a sentence without your name in it. What a pleasure to meet you." She's such a mother, a real mother and all I can do is smile and nod.

"May I take your coat, Mrs. Duemore?" Luke says, same winning smile on his face.

"Yes, won't you have a cup of coffee?" Mrs. Lucas says. "I'm just cooling some rolls."

"Well," Mom says.

Luke is already helping her out of her coat, Mom shrugging it off, keeping ahold of her purse, first with one hand, then the other, and then Mrs. Lucas leads her away to the kitchen.

Mrs. Lucas says how sorry she is that her husband isn't here or her other boy Billy, but there was some work to do at their shop, and then asks questions about Dad's line of work and where we hail from.

Luke hangs up Mom's coat in the closet, rubs his hands, and walks to me, like business is all taken care of. He is dressed nice, a button-up shirt with jeans that are pressed perfect.

"Let's get out of here," he whispers. "I'll show you around." Luke pulls on a coat, adjusts his collar, zips up.

"I'm going to show Jenny around," Luke says.

"See you kids," Mrs. Lucas says, hand wave, not even looking our way. Mom turns to me then, mouth open like she might say something, but she just waves at me, all casual.

"I'll see you tonight," she says.

"Okay," I say, "see you."

An Indian summer sun is in the clear blue sky and it's a nice day.

Luke shows me everything; the swimming pool, the farm buildings out back, the land behind the house, the creek that runs through their property. He says his father owns a plumbing business and they are putting in a Christmas tree farm next summer.

He crosses over the narrow section of the creek he calls King Creek and then reaches back to help me cross.

"Step on the rock," he says.

I put my foot on the rock that lifts from the water.

"Thanks," I say.

Luke lets go of my hand, looks around and sits on the trunk of a fallen tree, long grass stomped down around his feet like he has been down here before.

"You wanna sit in the sun?" he says.

Luke unzips his jacket, takes it off, and folds it over the end of the tree. "I hear Nevada girls love to sit in the sunshine."

He leans behind the log, pulls a long piece of grass, chews on the end. I smile at his joke, but inside my stomach is a fly-away feeling, part nervous, part scared. I unzip my own jacket and then push my hands into my pockets.

It's beautiful here, the mountain with its white bowl top, the tall pine trees, the creek with sunlight shining on the surface of the water.

Far off is the sound of the Volkswagen and I look up to Luke's house.

"She's leaving," I say.

Luke twists around, looks up the hill too. "She's nice," he says.

The sound of the car is far off and the wind blows strong through the tops of the pine trees.

"Yeah, she's nice," I say.

"She's a lot younger than I thought; she must have had you really young."

I look down at his face, which is such a nice face, his eyes the color of honey. There's something about him, something special, and I take a deep breath.

"She's not my real mother," I say, voice low. "She's my aunt, not my mother."

Pieces of my hair blow into my mouth and eyes.

Luke sits with his knees wide, face without any kind of expression.

I push my hair off my face and sit on the ground, my back against the tree trunk, Luke's knee next to me. It's quiet for a minute, a strange, wide-open quiet.

Luke leans over, the shadow of him blocking out the sun.

"So," he says, "why do you say she's your mother?"

The water of King Creek moves slow and lazy.

"They adopted me," I say to the water.

I can feel his questions in the silence. He's going to ask, "Where are your real parents?"

And then: "They died? How did they die?"

And then: "You mean you were adopted another time too, and then your parents who adopted you died?"

He will ask about any brothers and sisters and I'll sketch the story of Bryan in Oklahoma and how I don't see him anymore.

Luke asks all those questions, and I answer them. I should cry when I talk about it since it's all so sad but I don't. I keep my own story away from myself, as if I talk about another girl, and as I tell it, I watch his face and worry about him. Will he still look at me that way he does? Will he be upset I didn't tell him sooner? Will he think I'm different, weird, wrong?

"Wow," Luke whispers, fingers twisting the strand of grass around and around.

"It sounds a lot worse than it is," I say, flicking nothing off my pants.

He rolls his lips together then and looks at me in a different way.

"It's not that big of a deal; it was a long time ago," I say, looking at the creek.

Luke moves from the log to sit on the ground next to me, and puts his arm around my shoulders.

"I'm really sorry, Jenny," he whispers.

I try to shrug my shoulders under the weight of his arm.

"Thanks, but I'm fine," I say, smiling and nodding.

"It's got to be hard," he says, his breath on my face, the smell of his cologne. "I mean, I wouldn't know what to do without my folks."

I push the tip of my tongue against my teeth and just nod my head since what else is there to say?

He reaches to me then, hand to my face, and even though I don't want him to, he moves my head so I'm looking right at his eyes.

I feel wide open with the wind rushing through the middle of my body, afraid and worried and nervous and a million other things, but at the same time, he's here, thumb moving so slowly along the line of my jaw and who knew this was the way it was going to be.

Luke kisses me one time, simple and careful, lips against my lips and then away. He looks at me, the question in his light brown eyes, and I stay so still, like *Yes*.

He licks his bottom lip, a deep breath in that lifts his chest and puts his other hand on the other side of my face like cupping water he's about to drink.

Luke kisses me back and back until I'm against the earth and the weight of him is along one side of my body. He kisses me like this is the only kiss there ever will be.

I hold on to his shoulders, the warmth of his body through his shirt, and Luke presses his lips against my closed eyes, my nose, my cheeks, my ears and then whispers into my ear.

"You smell nice."

I don't want to but I open my eyes, the blue sky so much more blue now.

"It's jasmine," I say.

He moves my hair a little, over my neck, picks out pieces of dead grass. I can taste him on my lips, and I roll my lips together, clear my throat.

"Moog loaned it to me," I say.

He nods, a shy smile all the way into his eyes. "So," he says, "that was okay?"

"Okay?" I say.

"You know," he says, pulling another piece of grass of out my hair.

I laugh and then stop laughing. "Sure, of course," I say.

He laughs then, warm and loud, happy to be alive laugh, and rolls over on his back, face to the sky. He puts his hands behind his head, not a care in the world, and then looks at me, one eye closed to the sun.

"I wanted to do that so many times," he says.

I move my fingers over my own mouth and turn my head to look at him. "I wanted you to do that so many times," I say.

"Really?" he says.

"Yes," I say, shifting over on my stomach, weight on my elbows.

Luke looks up at the sky again, closes his eyes on whatever he's thinking, and the scars of his neck are right there, close enough to touch.

When you've told someone all the worst things and they still want to kiss you, when you have been kissing that person for what seems like forever, well, it's probably okay to ask the question you don't know how to ask.

Careful, careful, I put my fingers out and touch the edge of his scar.

Luke opens his eyes then, the smile off his face.

I let my finger stay slow and careful to the next scar and down.

It's such a personal thing, touching another person where they've been hurt and I can almost feel pain from him through my hand. Luke looks at me for a long time, a quiet in him.

"Cancer," he says.

"Cancer?" I say.

Luke nods.

I look at his neck again, the side-by-side scars, the way the skin is white-pink and torn looking, only healed now.

"Just here?" I say.

"No," he says.

Luke shifts around a little, pulls his shirt up and up and left of his belly button, just below his ribs, is another scar, at least six inches long, and the skin is threaded and pink. Luke is so thin, you can see all of his bones and the lines of his muscles.

"It's like a snake," he says, laughing a little, and the scar shimmies on the surface of his skin.

I sit up and away, the scar so wrong against the rest of him, like a crack.

"Is it gone now?" I say. "The cancer?"

"Yep," he says. "They say it's all gone."

His voice is light and breezy.

"Is that why you don't gain weight?" I say.

"They think so," he says. "Something to do with my thyroid."

I look at his face, at his stomach, at his face again. I want to ask so many questions: When did it happen? How long did it last? Did he think he was going to die? I look away from his face to his flat stomach again, the turn-in of his belly button, the white of his skin.

I bite my lip and lay my hand over his stomach, over that terrible scar, and Luke sucks in his stomach so it's curved in, like a bowl. I move my thumb over the threads of skin, over the length of the scar, over the smooth of his white stomach, and somehow, it just doesn't seem fair that such a sweet guy would have cancer to begin with.

"Do you think it will come back?" I say.

"The cancer?" he says.

I nod, no words for how bad I would feel if he got sick again.

Luke sits up on his elbows then, takes my hand off his stomach, moves his fingers into my fingers, and brings my hand to his mouth. He presses his lips against my palm, where I was just touching his stomach.

"No," he says, "I don't think it's coming back."

It's Luke and me, all the time. At school, on the phone, on weekends.

I have a whole wall dedicated to him in my room; a cutout of his name, photographs, a few ribbons from these flowers he gave me.

We are one of those couples in the halls, his arm draped over my shoulder, my hand in his back pocket.

Everyone knows—I'm Luke's girl.

It's nice to be someone's girl.

It turns out he had Hodgkin's disease. The dictionary says only how it's a malignant disorder that enlarges the lymph nodes and the spleen.

In the corner of the history class, all the other kids already leaving, I pull out the *H* encyclopedia and sit down at a back desk.

I open to *Hodgkin's,* my finger back and forth over the three paragraphs written there. Signs of the disease are fevers, night sweats, weight loss. Hodgkin's shows in people as young as 15, is a cancer where the big immune cells take in outside bacteria; if you catch it early, there's a 90 percent chance of a full recovery.

I put my elbow on the table and face into my hand. On the chalkboard are words about the structure of representative government. The room is empty—even the teacher is gone—and I just look at the board for a long time.

Even though I don't ask Luke about it and it's really not my business, I couldn't help asking his mom when I was out there for dinner. Shelly was so nice, almost glad to talk, and told me about the six months of chemotherapy and surgeries and how he might never gain weight like other kids do. While she talked about him, her eyes, so much like his, filled with tears, and she told me how scared she was when he was sick, how she cried all the time, and now, almost to make up for it, she spoils him rotten.

✦ ✦ ✦

That winter, I go out for the basketball team. It's Luke's idea. He says it's good to be involved in extracurricular activities, says that's what high school is all about. He plays football and basketball. They don't let him play that much, and I wonder if it's because he was sick or that he is so thin.

It doesn't seem to bother Luke, though. He sits on the bench the entire game and claps, happy just to be on the team. It breaks my heart for him, since I could never sit on the sidelines the way he does—it's too humiliating. But at the same time, he's like an example of goodness to follow.

Every day after school, I'm with a bunch of other girls, freshmen to seniors. For two hours, we practice bouncing the ball, shooting the ball, and passing the ball. And we run.

When I was eight years old, I ran on a team where you put in eight miles a day. Compared with running on that team, this running is easy.

The day I find out I made the junior varsity basketball team, the coach says I should think about going out for the track team too.

"Thanks," I say, "but I really don't like running."

"Really?" she says.

"No," I say.

"There's a lot of running in basketball," she says.

"That's true," I say, "but it's not the same."

Our coach is a nice lady, thin face, round cheeks and glasses. She looks down at me the way grownups do, eyes like she has other ideas in her head only she won't say them.

"Well, congratulations anyway, Duemore," she says. "We're glad to have you on the team."

She gives me a bunch of forms for taking a physical, for getting my parents' permission to play and travel, for the kind of shoes I am supposed to buy, and then helps me pick the right size uniform. My number is 12.

Out the gymnasium door, I go into the main building where the juniors and seniors have their lockers. With school out for the day, it's empty in the hallway, almost too empty. I run past the closed doors of empty classrooms, past the trophy case in front of the main office, my book bag heavy over my shoulder.

Luke leans against his locker, looking in my direction.

I stop in front of him, my shoes squeaking on the floor. "I made it!"

"Congratulations," he says.

I drop my bag on the floor, and he pulls me so close, it makes me think of being swallowed whole. It's wonderful to be held that way but a little scary too.

I try to press back from him but Luke keeps me in the circle of his arms, hands around my waist.

"Now we both play basketball," he says.

"You have to help me with my free throws," I say.

"Maybe you can come up to the house and we'll shoot some baskets," he says.

"Maybe this weekend," I say.

"Cool," he says.

He lets me go and takes up my backpack, putting it over his shoulder. "I have an idea," he says, arm around my shoulder the way he always does, draped over and relaxed. "Let me take you home," he says.

"Oh sure—that's a great idea," I say, moving my fingers into his hand that's over my shoulder.

"I think so," he says.

"Hello?" I say, looking up at him. "You are kidding, aren't you?"

"Come on, Jenny," he says, "I mean it."

I stop then, my hand out of his, and I shift myself from under his arm and away. "You cannot be serious."

"I want to give you something," he says with a lift of his blond eyebrows. "A surprise."

"What is it?"

He puts his hands wide and shrugs. "It wouldn't be a surprise if I told you," he says.

"Luke," I say. "I don't know."

"Listen," he says, hand on my shoulder, "if you let me drive you home, I can give it to you in the car."

He moves his hand up to my neck then, thumb over the space of skin from neck to ear. I'm like one of those cats that goes around and around in circles when you pet it. When Luke touches me, I practically purr.

I hold my breath and shake my head. "Luke, if I get caught . . ." I say.

"You won't," he says. Luke moves closer, bends down so his face is to my face, and he presses his lips on my forehead. "Listen," he says, "I'll drop you at the Quik-Mart. That way, you won't get caught and I can be with you, alone."

Outside light comes through the windows of the double doors at the end of the hall and makes side-by-side rectangles on the floor. Soft lips on my face, hand on my neck, Luke is so close I can't think. I put my hand up then, hold on to his wrist, stop him from moving his hand on me, stop everything.

I stand extra still, not even a breath in my body, and it's very hard to say no to Luke.

"Okay," I say. "Let's go."

Outside, the air feels wet, clouds are low in the pine trees, and it's cold. Except for a couple of teachers' cars, the lot is empty, and Luke opens the passenger door, all polite.

"Thanks," I say.

His car is called a Savoy, this great big blue thing with wide seats, and it's already warm inside.

Luke comes around to his side, opens the door, tosses his book bag in the back, and then picks mine off the middle of the seat and tosses it in the back too.

"You don't have to sit all the way over there," he says. "Come closer."

"Your car is already warm," I say.

"I wanted it to be nice for you," he says.

"How did you know I'd say yes?" I say.

He shrugs just one shoulder the way he does and pats the middle of the wide seat.

I move over to him and he puts his arm around my shoulder, his other hand flat on my stomach.

"Alone at last," he whispers.

"Luke," I say against his mouth.

"Shhh," he whispers against my lips. He kisses the side of my mouth and then my neck to my ear.

Chills are all over my body, and I put my head back, talking up to the ceiling of his car.

"I have to go home."

Luke kisses the other direction, all the way to my mouth, and moves his hand around my waist, fingers under my shirt, against the skin of my back.

The word for him is *hypnotizing,* or maybe it's the way he touches me that's so hypnotic. I'm trying to figure out exactly what it is about Luke, but I haven't, not yet anyway.

His hand outlines the shape of each bone in my spine, fingers soft on my skin, lips moving full over mine.

A few minutes aren't going to hurt anything. I can do my chores in time. This is not a problem.

I move with him, to him, the taste of his mouth in my own, my hands inside his jacket, and I spread my fingers wide over the shape of his ribs.

Luke makes a sound deep in his throat, kissing down my neck and to my ear, his hand over my skin to the edge of my bra and he's never done that.

I open my eyes and press back from him.

"Luke."

"Relax," he says.

"No," I say, my hand over his hand on my chest, moving him off.

Not many people say no to Luke—you can tell in the way his eyes narrow a little and how he shifts away so quickly.

I adjust myself on the seat, the feel of him still on my skin, and there's such a lonely feeling through me.

"Luke," I say, "don't be mad at me."

He wipes the foggy window with the sleeve of his jacket and starts up the car.

"Come on," I say, my hand on his arm, "don't be mad."

Luke shifts his car and drives out of the school lot, and I feel terrible, worse than terrible.

It's quiet in the car and outside it starts to rain a fine mist.

The Quik-Mart is just a few minutes' drive, and when we get there, Luke pulls around the side and parks at the backside of the brick wall where you can't see anything but pasture land.

I hate how quiet he is, hate that he gets like this, and I wish I could do something.

He shifts the car into park, keeps it running, and turns himself on the wide seat so his back is pressed against the door.

"Do you have time for me to give you something?" he says, voice different.

I shift my knee up on the seat between us.

"Don't be like that," I say, reaching my hand to his, my fingers into his fingers.

He looks at our hands together and lets out a deep breath, looks at me with this sad expression.

"I just want to be with you."

"I know," I say, shifting closer to him, "and I want to be with you too."

I move my shoulder around like I don't fit in my own skin. "It's just, well, we shouldn't go too far," I say, "especially in a car, especially when I have to be home, and . . . nice girls aren't supposed to do things like that."

I talk too much, words around and around about something no one talks about in a serious way.

He smiles a crooked kind of smile and puts his hand to the side of my face, moves his thumb over my bottom lip.

"You're very cute," he says. "You know that?"

"I'm serious, Luke," I say, my hand on his wrist.

In his eyes is such a look of pure want, and that's normal, guys are like that. It's my job to say no. He knows it; everyone knows it.

He lets go then, smiling. "Close your eyes," he says.

I shift myself back, closing my eyes. He moves around on the seat, the sound of the zipper of his backpack, papers being moved around.

He takes my hand, then puts something square on my palm. "Open," he says.

In my hand is a small box of light gray velvet.

"Go ahead," he says, nodding his chin up.

I lift open the lid, the box making a cracking sound in the quiet of the car. Inside is a silver bracelet, JENNY engraved in cursive letters and then '82 next to my name for the year I am going to graduate from high school.

"Oh, Luke."

He lifts the bracelet with his fingers and turns it over. On the other side is his name, LUKE, in cursive letters.

"Do you like it?" he says.

"I do."

He opens the bracelet clasp and holds it wide for my arm. Luke has such a serious look on his face, his eyes staying on me.

I put my wrist up and he pushes the ends together with a snap.

"This way, my name is on you all the time," he whispers, "like a secret."

The metal of the bracelet is cool on my skin and I move my wrist around, front to back.

"Thank you," I say.

The windows are foggy again, streaks where he rubbed at the windshield with his sleeve earlier. The wiper blades move back and forth and the engine hums.

Luke licks his lips and takes a deep breath.

"I love you," he says, voice low and different.

Time stops, not even a breath in my body.

"I wanted to tell you so many times, but then," he says, "I wanted it to be special, something you could remember."

I watch him talk, his mouth moving, and I don't even remember the last time I heard a person say that to me. I can't even take the words into my body.

"Luke," I say, "that's so nice, this is so nice . . ."

I look around at everything, the rearview mirror and the glove compartment.

"But?"

"Well, it's so quick, and you don't know me that well."

He laughs a little and shakes his head. "I know you," he says.

"No, that's not what I mean," I say, looking right at him. "Things happen," I say. "You get to know people, and then things change."

He looks at me, blinking his eyes. "I'm not going to change."

He reaches to my hands, fingers into my fingers, and I look at our hands together, the silver bracelet on my wrist.

"I love you," he says, and lifts my hands up and down, like he's making his point. "I knew it right away; I know it now. I'm probably going to love you until the day I die."

He's so confident, it's in the sound of his voice, it's in his light brown eyes and I've never been that confident about anything.

Both hands on my face, he kisses me then, sweet and careful and so sure about this thing. I have to get home, I have a mountain of chores, but the bracelet, the "I love you," the confidence in him . . . and I can't say no to Luke again.

I don't get back to our house until four-thirty, which gives me less than an hour to do the chores and start dinner. I go through everything as fast as I can and then call Megan while I do the dishes.

"Did you tell him you love him back?" she says.

"No," I say.

"You have to, you know," she says. "A guy tells you that he loves you, well, you just have to say it back or it's hanging out there, like your underwear is showing or something."

"Jeez, Megan," I say, phone balanced between shoulder and ear. "How did this get so serious?"

"It's not serious," she says. "You just think too much."

I put clean dishes in the strainer and rinse gunk out of the sink. "I don't think too much," I say.

"You think too much," she says.

"Well, this is serious, Megan," I say. "You should think about serious things."

Megan is quiet on the line, and I can just see her, blue eyes up to the ceiling. "Love isn't something you think about; it just is. You love him. He loves you. Case closed."

I wipe the countertop off with the washrag. "But why?" I say. "Why me, why now? I just can't believe it."

"You just don't have enough confidence," she says. "That's your problem."

"I have confidence," I say. "I guess."

Megan laughs at that, and I don't know why, but it makes me mad at her, at myself.

"I have to go," I say. "I still have to start dinner."

"Call me later," she says.

"I will."

Mom and Dad say there is no way they are going to pay for a new pair of basketball shoes.

"Just wear the shoes you have," Dad says.

"My coach says I need this kind of shoe," I say, pointing at the papers I brought home.

"That's ridiculous," Mom says. "Those shoes cost at least twenty dollars."

"I bet the coach is getting some kind of kickback from the shoe company," Dad says.

"That's not true," I say. "Those are basketball shoes."

We are in the living room. Kimmy's in bed already, and the papers for basketball are on the coffee table between dirty ash-trays and half-full cups of coffee.

All they have to do is read and sign off their okay for me to have a physical, to be on a bus going to out-of-town games, and to practice between two-thirty and four-thirty. It should take only a little while, ten minutes, but they've been with these papers for an hour, questions about why I need a physical, warnings about how I will be punished if I let the chores slip, even a joke by Dad about how all girls who play sports are lesbians, ha, ha, ha.

I sit extra still, elbows on my knees, hands together like a prayer.

The silver bracelet is on my wrist, the secret of Luke's name on the inside and I can't believe he said he loved me. Me. The new feeling of being special to someone makes everything different tonight, especially Mom and Dad. I clean the house, cook the meals, do the laundry and the dishes and they never say 'thank you,' or even 'good work.' It usually doesn't bother me they are like that but tonight, it bothers me a lot. It bothers me that they are rude and unfriendly and now, giving me a hard time about a pair of shoes.

"When do you need these shoes?" Mom says.

"Next week," I say.

She sits next to Dad, legs crossed at the knee, papers in her lap.

Dad sits stretched out at the corner of the sofa, stomach pushed out from the bottom of his undershirt, cigarette in his hand.

RC sits on the sofa between them, her poodle body like an armrest for Dad.

"I'm not paying for 'em," he says, tapping the edge of his cigarette on his ashtray.

"I'll pay for the shoes," I say.

"How?" Mom says.

"I have a few dollars saved," I say.

"How much?" Dad says, looking my way.

"I don't know," I say. "Ten dollars, I think."

Mom puts the papers on her lap, crosses her arms.

"That's not enough," Mom says.

"I can baby-sit," I say. "Cathy Anderson says there's a lady who lives by the Quik-Mart and she's looking for a baby-sitter."

"Who said you could baby-sit?" Dad says.

I put my hands out then, palms up, the bracelet on my wrist, and Mom puts her hand on Dad's leg.

"She can baby-sit," Mom says, "but she needs these shoes now."

It's quiet in the living room, another commercial, and Dad watches it.

"Dick?" Mom says.

He looks at her then, the two of them doing that thing, talking without words, and finally she shrugs and looks at me.

"We'll get them this weekend," she says.

"She has to pay us back," he says, as if I'm not here.

"Fine," I say.

Mom looks at me like she has just done me a huge favor, like I should be grateful.

"Thank you," I say.

Star Trek is on again, and Dad adjusts himself on the sofa, shakes a fresh cigarette out of the pack sitting on the arm of the sofa.

I push myself up, hands on my knees and Dad looks my way, points to his coffee cup. "Get me another cup."

"Me too," Mom says, reaching to her cup and Dad's cup, handing them both to me.

I take the coffee cups from her, go through the dining room to the kitchen, and pour them fresh cups of coffee.

When spring comes, basketball season is over and the extracurricular activity isn't at school anymore.

Luke drives me home almost every day.

That's bad.

Worse is how he talks his way into the house, "just for a little while," he says.

Worse than that is what I'm learning in Sunday School. Father Hubert, socks and sandals, talks about staying pure for Jesus, avoiding temptation and sins of the flesh.

Personally, I don't believe God is going to punish me for Luke, especially if we just fool around. I mean, it's not like we're having sex or anything. Still, some things you can't know for sure.

I do know if Mom and Dad catch me, it's going to be worse than hell.

The funny thing is, Luke doesn't struggle at all.

When I say, "That's not a good idea," he says, "Close your eyes and just relax," unbuttoning my shirt, soft mouth on my bare skin.

When I say, "Wait a minute," he says, "You can trust me," and moves his hands down my stomach and over the bones of my hips.

When I say, "Luke, please," he says, "I love you," and persuades my body to lift into another place altogether. And I go It's just a matter of a few kisses, really, and I am out of myself and into a dream of visions and instead of the dark inside my own head, I see mountains and canyons and a horizon of light blue sky that meets the darker blue of the ocean.

"It's an orgasm, you big dope," Megan says.

"How do you know that?" I say.

"I know," she says.

"How?"

"Trust me," she says, laughing too loud. "I know."

I have the telephone balanced between my shoulder and ear,

hands free to peel potatoes, and Luke's bracelet lays at the bend of my left wrist, my name spelled out on top, his name a secret against my skin.

Megan clears her throat and in a low voice says how she was in the laundry room with Paul, messing around, and boom, it happened to her too.

"Oh my God," I say.

"I scared Paul to death."

"Why didn't you tell me?"

Megan laughs and makes her voice all normal. "Yeah, my mom is right here," she says, "Mom, Jenny says hi."

In the background I hear Megan's mom say hi.

"Oh that's great," I say. "Let's get your mom into the conversation." I rinse the potato off under the faucet, picking up another one to peel.

"You should have called earlier," Megan says.

"I would have but Mr. Lucas just left."

"You are kidding me?" she says. "This just happened?"

"Duh."

"Oh, my little girl is growing up," Megan says, voice all high.

It's quiet on the telephone, the feeling of Luke still on my skin, the taste of him on my mouth, and Megan tells me to hold on.

I want to ask if she had the same visions behind her eyes, mountains and canyons and the ocean, and then after, whether they fell away to a terrible darkness where in the end, she was alone and sad, ashamed and afraid.

What Luke has done shook out something old, like a memory I can't reach or maybe don't want to reach, and I wonder how something so wonderful could make you feel so bad when it is over.

When Megan comes back, her voice is normal again.

"She's gone," Megan says. "Now tell me exactly what happened."

I stop peeling and look out the window. Outside is Kimmy's swing set built from logs and under it the grass is so long, it reaches to the seat of the empty swing.

"I don't want to talk about it," I say.

"You have to tell me," she says.

"You didn't tell me about your deal."

"Okay, tell me this," she says. "Did you have your clothes on?"

Potato peelings are in the sink, a pile of them, dirty and brown.

"Um," I say, "yeah, a little bit."

"You were not naked?" she whispers.

"No," I say. "Not completely."

"And did he do this thing with his hand?"

"Megan . . ."

"Or his mouth?"

"Megan!" I say.

"Come on," she says.

I turn off the water and take a deep breath.

"Both," I say.

"Oh my God," she says.

I adjust the telephone on my shoulder, dry my hands off on a towel. "You cannot tell a soul," I say.

"I swear," she says.

I open one of the side drawers, take out the big knife.

"Did he know what happened?" she says.

"He knew," I say.

I cut a potato in half, the sound of the knife on the cutting board.

He knew what he was doing, but he had no idea I would cry after, a wave of shame and grief so deep, I couldn't talk at all.

Poor Luke was just confused.

I don't want him to see me like that; I don't want to be like that.

I cut the potatoes into smaller cubes, the chopping sound on the cutting board, faster and faster.

"It's too much," I say. "This is too much. I feel like this is getting out of hand."

"Don't worry so much," she says. "It's absolutely normal."

I put the knife down and hold the telephone with my hand.

"No, listen," I say. "It's going too far and I don't know how to make him slow down."

"Tell him that," she says.

"You can't say no to him."

"Yes," she says, "you can."

"He is very persuasive," I say.

"Luke is a spoiled-rotten little brat," she says. "Tell him no, and no is no."

I laugh at how simple it sounds but Luke is like a big bag of M&M's: Once you start, you can't help but eat the whole bag. Of course, after, you feel sick.

I take the cutting board to the stove and push the potatoes into the hot oil. Grease splatters and spits.

"So," I say, "was this a sin?"

"What do you think?" she says.

I move the potatoes around with a spatula.

"I don't know," I say. "It doesn't really matter, I guess. I'll just go to church and confess and it's three Hail Mary's, right?"

Megan's Catholic too, knows all about the stupid rules, and she laughs out loud.

We talk a little bit more, about nothing compared to this, and then I hang up the telephone, wind up the cord, put the phone where it belongs so they don't know I've been dragging it around and talking forever.

The rule is just 15 minutes per day, but I've figured out how to extend that by talking during the time they drive home. If I pick up at five o'clock, I can talk a whole half hour, no problem. Besides, I'm breaking so many other rules, what's one more?

I finish setting the table then, Dad and Mom's place on one side, Kimmy and me on the other. Against the back wall of the dining room is a mirror, and I put my hair behind my ears. There's no sign of what happened here today, nothing in my expression or in my eyes or the shape of my mouth. It's like Luke's bracelet on my arm, the secret of it is on the inside.

Easter is a week-long break, no school. Dad has this idea to put a new porch around the house, and Mom goes on a cleaning rampage.

I'm in trouble again—seems like that's been happening a lot lately. This time, for not cleaning the dishes well enough and letting chores get sloppy, and so over Easter break, I'm on restriction, which means no Luke, no Megan, no telephone, and being stuck at home.

On top of that, Mom is on another diet, only it's not working fast enough for her. I tell her she doesn't need to lose weight and it's true; she's not fat at all but there's no talking to her when she gets this way.

"I can't wait until you get fat," she yelled at me, "and it's going to happen one day, and on that day, I'm going to laugh my head off."

She always says things like that, as if her way is going to be my way.

Before I started my cycle, Mom warned about cramps and being sick once a month and how I might get all these breakouts on my face since it changes your whole chemistry.

"You will probably get bloated too," she said. "You can gain as much as ten pounds."

"You're kidding," I said. "That's disgusting."

"No, it's not," she said, all mad. "It's totally normal."

When it actually started, none of those things happened. It just came as quiet as a whisper, no cramps, no vomiting, no pimples, no bloating. Mom was furious.

On Saturday, I'm upstairs sorting Kimmy's clothes for Mom, as if this is what I really want to be doing with my time. There's a pile of things that are too small and another for what needs mending.

"Jenny!" Mom yells.

"What?" I yell.

"Get down here right this minute."

I fold a pair of Kimmy's pants, put them in the too-small pile, and go downstairs.

Mom waits for me in the dining room, hand fisted on her hip. She has on this striped shirt that makes her boobs look huge, and her jeans are tight and too short.

"When I call you," she says, adjusting her glasses, "you don't say 'What,' you come, immediately."

"Fine," I say. "I'm here."

I know I'm pushing it with her. I can see it, that hard expression on her face, but I'm worn out from this week.

She takes a deep breath then, the red stain of her anger rising up her neck, and she points at the wood box that holds the nice silverware.

"What the hell is this?" she says.

I look into the drawer and then at her again.

"Forks and spoons?" I say.

"Don't get smart with me," she says.

"I don't know what you are asking me," I say.

"These forks do not go in this slot," she says, picking up a fork and holding it close to my face.

"This is a salad fork and it goes in the salad fork slot," she says, moving the small fork down the line of silverware and putting it in the correct row. She picks up a bigger fork and holds it in my face.

"This is a dinner fork," she says. "It goes in the dinner fork slot."

She goes through the whole routine again, like I'm some kind of idiot.

"I know where the forks go," I say.

"Then put them where they belong, God damn it."

She slaps my face then, her whole hand wide open. I fall back a step from her and put my hand to my own face.

"If it wasn't for you, I could have had another baby," Mom yells.

For a moment, there is the sting of her hand on my skin, the sound of her voice in the room and those words that make no sense and all the sense in the world. It's not about forks or even babies, it's that she blames me for being here, as if I wanted to come here and ruin her life somehow. As if I had any choice.

I take my hand off my face and stand up to her.

"I never had a choice," I say, "and if I did, I wouldn't have come to live with you to begin with."

She inhales a quick breath, a look on her face like she might hit me again, and I just stand there like *Go ahead, hit me. I dare you to hit me.*

"Get the hell out my sight," she says.

Any other time, I would scurry to my room, but this time, I don't. Instead, I curl my hands into fists, my fingernails into my skin, *Come on, bring it on.*

"Go," she yells, arm up and pointing to the ceiling.

I step back from her, just in case she is going to hit me again, and then, extra slow, I back up, turn, and go up the steps to my room, my feet taking one step at a time.

I sit on my bed, head in my hands and what just happened between us is everywhere, going down into my heart like a rock sinking to the bottom of a deep pond.

My face and neck hurt from being hit so hard and I rub my hands up and down over my face.

On my wall are photos of Luke and me, goofing off at his house, a shot of us in the hall at school, always smiling, always happy. On my wrist is his bracelet with his name against my skin, a secret.

Just like with Mom, I've been kidding myself about Luke. He says he loves me but I know what he loves and it has more to do with my body than me. No one loves me, not really and I might as well face it.

Downstairs, I hear Mom move around in the kitchen only she is extra quiet, like she thinks I'm asleep. Outside, I hear the truck pull up and then Kimmy's voice yells something, the two of them back from the lumberyard.

Mom walks from the kitchen to the dining room and I hear her open the front door.

How do any of us go on now? How do I even face her again?

I put my head in my hands again, close my eyes and I don't know why, but I think about Bryan. I haven't talked to him in a long time but I heard he's graduating high school this year, that he's at the top of his class, that everything is just great for him. It figures.

✦ ✦ ✦

We do go on though, just like nothing ever happened, dinner, dishes, "get me a cup of coffee, Jenny," and a few days later, there's a letter on my bed with Mom's careful printing on the envelope. I hold the paper in my hand, the fold of pages on the inside, three pages written in perfect letters of wide circles and open spaces.

The words actually say, "I apologize for losing my temper" and "We say things in anger we don't actually mean," and at the end of the letter it says, "Love, Mom."

I look at the letter for a long time, the smallest flicker of hope in those two words, "Love, Mom." But I know they aren't true.

Outside, a car pulls into our driveway and I listen for it to back up and drive away like cars usually do but it doesn't.

I throw Mom's letter on the bed, go through the attic to Kimmy's room, and look out her little square window.

Luke's blue car is down in the driveway, and he gets out, looking around.

I can't see him right now, I can't keep up with us anymore. At school, I've been avoiding him and then riding the bus home before he talks me into riding home in his car.

There's a knock on the door and RC barks like she always does. Thank God she's not outside.

Luke knocks again, three times and the door of the screen squeaks on its hinges.

I wouldn't be surprised if he opened the door, walked in, and even came up the stairs.

I sit on Kimmy's bed, hiding in the box of her room.

Luke knocks a few more times, RC barking all over again, and then, finally, I hear his footsteps on the porch and the gravel driveway.

I sit alone for a long time, knees to my chest, flat feeling in me and I can't make Mom love me but I can stop this thing between Luke and me. I can.

Breaking up is a lot harder to do than I thought it would be. There was Luke's birthday and now prom is coming. Moog says I absolutely cannot ruin prom since we are double dating.

Knowing I want out and pretending I don't is terrible. Everything Luke does irritates me, how he hangs on me in the hall, how he kisses me in front of everyone, how he pulls me behind the school during lunch and, right in broad daylight, unbuttons my shirt.

"Stop it," I say.

"Come on," he says. "Just relax."

I put my hands on his wrists and squeeze. "God damn it, Luke," I say. "I want you to stop, right now."

For once, he stops moving his hands and I push back from him, buttoning back up again.

"What's wrong?" he says.

Even though summer break is a couple of weeks off, it's cold and wet out here, clouds low in the pine trees.

I look out at the roads that lead away from the school. Just down that road is Grandma Duemore's place, that one takes you to the freeway, and that road takes you to our house.

Luke snakes his arm around my waist, so familiar but I shake him off.

"What is wrong with you?" he says.

I rub my hands over my face, up and down, and I have to do it now.

"Jenny?" Luke says.

"Let's sit," I say, looking around for a place. "Over there," I say, pointing to the edge of the dry sidewalk.

I go past him and sit on the sidewalk, back to the brick wall of the school. Luke comes over then too, sitting down with his knees to his chest.

Pushing my hands through my hair, I look straight ahead at the roads that lead in so many directions away from here and it starts to rain this fine mist.

"I have to take a break," I say, "from us."

Luke holds extra still and I can feel his eyes on the side of my face.

The edge of the sidewalk meets the grass and I pull a piece of grass up, twist it in my finger.

"It's not you," I say. "It's me. I'm just—I don't know—overwhelmed by us, by this thing between us."

"I don't understand," he says, a raw edge in his voice.

Tossing the grass back to the ground, I push my hand over the side of my face and tuck some hair behind my ears.

"I just can't keep doing this," I say. "Every day at my house, at school, we're so physical, and we are going further and further. God, we're going to end up having sex, and I'm not ready for that, and then there are my parents. I feel like I am on the brink of getting caught by them, and if they catch me, they will go completely ballistic . . . and—I don't know—I just need a break."

It's too much talk for him and I make myself stop.

Luke stays extra still, swallowing hard, his Adam's apple up and down on his throat. He reaches for my hand and holds it in both of his. "But I love you," he says.

I look at his hand holding mine, that stomped flat feeling in me.

"Luke," I say, "come on, let's be honest here—don't you really love getting your hands all over me?"

"Of course," he says, thumb moving over the top of my hand, "but it's more than that."

"I don't think so," I say, taking my hand out of his.

He's quiet for a long time and his whole face shows the pain, from his eyes to his mouth.

"I don't want to lose you," he says, tears up into his eyes and then down his face. "Please, Jenny," he says, "don't leave me."

I've never made another person cry, never, and his tears break my heart, waking me up to some feeling for the first time since Mom hit me.

"Oh Luke," I say, "don't cry."

I sit up on my knees and gather him into me.

Luke holds around my waist like he's clinging for dear life, deep gulps of breath. I lay my face on top of his head, his blond hair so soft and I hold him tight.

Rain falls on the grass, makes it shine wet and I tell him I'm sorry, that I was wrong, that I'm just having a bad day. I talk it right again and rock him at the same time, back and forth, giving him what he wants, and making it better.

The bell rings, lunch over, but we don't get up to go to class, we just stay like that behind the school, making all sorts of promises. Luke says he won't press me to do what I don't want to do, that we can slow down, that he's sorry. I promise to be more open with him, tell him how I'm feeling, talk things through. We are desperate to make it right, and on the surface of things, we do.

When the tears are gone and our faces play at smiling again, he kisses me extra careful, and we walk back to class in a new silence. I hold his hand, act like I'm still his girl, but deep down, I know something has changed between us forever.

I'm going to Reno for two weeks, just like that.

Mom says a big reunion of cousins is coming together, that they are even going to buy me an airplane ticket so I can go, and Dad doesn't even say I have to pay them back.

The whole thing is centered around Bryan. I guess he

moved to Reno after graduating from high school, at the top of his class, thank you very much. He has a job in Reno, is living with some guys, and wouldn't it be just great to see him again?

It's almost funny, the way she acts like he's my brother again when I haven't seen him or heard from him in years, but I don't say anything, just smile like *Yeah, that would be great!*

"I can't believe I won't see you for two whole weeks," Luke says.

"It'll go by quick," I say.

Luke is quiet, the sound of other people in the background, and I know he's calling from his dad's office.

"I'll see you when you get back?" he says.

"Yeah," I say. "I'll call you."

We are still a couple, I love you's, double-date at the prom, making out in the afternoons at my house. Of course he doesn't slow down—that's an old idea that got lost after a couple weeks. We've actually started talking about birth control, Luke suggesting condoms, but I do not want to do that with him, no way.

"Jenny?" Luke says.

"Yeah?"

"I miss you," he says.

"I'll be back soon," I say.

"That's not what I mean."

"I know."

"I love you," he says.

Mom is in the kitchen, Dad in the living room. I clear my throat and look down at my feet. I cup my hand over the telephone and whisper. "Love you too."

Leaving St. Helens in an airplane is a taste of sweet, perfect freedom. You just get on an airplane and leave everything behind. You can be anyone, a brand-new person, and on the way to Reno, I actually make up a new me.

I'm Suzanna from Georgia.

I've never been to the South, not once in my life, but this sweet old lady who sits next to me on the airplane doesn't know that. I ya'all and ma'am her for the whole plane ride, eating peanuts and talking about my daddy's plantation where we grow cotton.

Who knew I could speak with a Southern accent? But I do, and it's the most fun I've ever had.

In Reno, I get off the airplane ahead of my new friend, just hoping she doesn't catch me talking normally to Grandpa Ed.

He waits for me in the terminal, big wave of his arm over his head.

I make my way to him quick, hugs and how-are-you's, and I rush him out of the airport before I get busted.

"You remember the old car?" Grandpa says, when we get to the parking lot.

"You bet," I say.

He unlocks the door of his green Toronado, only the metallic green paint is faded now, chipped here and there and inside, it smells wet.

Before, I was so short, I could barely see out the window but now, I can see everything.

Grandpa gets in with a grunt and groan, pulls his door shut, and even though I'm big now, I feel small like a little kid. I hold my hands in my lap and smile over at him.

"Good to be back?" he says.

"It is," I say.

"Better buckle up," he says.

I do like he tells me, seat belt over my chest, and we drive out of the lot.

Grandpa asks about Mom and Dad, how life is treating us in St. Helens, if I like my school.

I look at his profile, white bushy eyebrows, the same old wrap-around sunglasses on his face, the way he holds both hands on the steering wheel. Mom hates me and pretends she doesn't, Dad calls me a no-neck, good for nothing pain in the ass, there are the mountain of chores that I never seem to do exactly the way they want and every moment with them is a kind of hell where you feel like you are slowly being choked to death.

I clear my throat and look at the road again.

"Oh, everything is just dandy," I say.

"That's good," Grandpa says.

He takes the exit off the freeway, drives up the hill to their mobile home park, same old pool, same rows of trailers that shine in the sunlight.

"Everyone is here," he says.

"Everyone?" I say.

"Most everyone," he says. "Beth, Chris, the girls, Andy, Mark, and I think Carol will be up later with Faith and Tracy."

Grandpa navigates into the parking spot under the carport, just a few inches from his golf cart and trailer.

"Is Bryan here?" I say.

"You bet," he says.

Grandpa turns off the car, gets out, and holds the gate open while I go through, chitchatting about how all the kids are so big now, how Grandma is cooking up a big pot of spaghetti, and the weather is just perfect for a reunion.

I forgot how hot it gets here, dry hot, and I smooth myself down, tuck my hair behind my ears, and go into the front door that Grandpa holds for me.

"Welcome back," he says.

"Thanks," I say.

The air of the trailer is air-conditioned cold and they've changed things around. The green plaid sofa is still against the wall, the chairs are in their same place too, but the hide-a-bed sofa is out here now and the plastic fireplace is in the dining room.

The living room is filled up with Andy, Mark, a blond-haired girl, another girl who's chubby and has blond-brown hair, Aunt Mary Beth, her son Chris, who is the same age as Kimmy, and Grandma Maggie sitting with her legs curled under her, long brown cigarette between her fingers.

I smile, "Hi," "Nice to meet you" to the two girls who are supposed to be my cousins even though I've never met them and have already forgotten their names.

I look around for Bryan but he's not here.

Grandma crosses the living room and puts her arms out.

"My goodness, look at this tall drink of water," she says, and she's just the same, white hair cut short, bangs across her forehead. "Hi, Grandma," I say. She hugs me around my waist.

"I bet she's at least five foot eight," Grandpa says, shutting the front door.

Grandma keeps her hand on my waist and she's so tiny next to me now, as if she shrank or something.

"The boys love tall women," Grandma says. "You are the lucky one."

Everyone in the room laughs and I look around at these people, family but strangers.

Across the room, Bryan stands apart from everyone, his shoulder leaned into the wall between the dining room and living room.

Grandma follows the way I look and puts her arm out.

"Well," she says, "here's your sister."

Bryan nods his chin up, and he's just like I remember, black hair, black eyebrows, eyes so dark they look black and that mole just off the side of his lip. The difference is that he is a man, or on the edge of being a man, anyway. He's tall and muscular and very handsome.

I want to say to Grandma, "Look at how handsome he is," but I don't.

I take a deep breath and adjust my backpack over my shoulder.

"Hi, Bryan," I say.

Grandma laughs at that and takes ahold of my arm, pulling me into the dining room.

"Doesn't he look good?" she says. "All grown up and graduated from high school, top of his class."

"Yeah," I say. "I heard."

"Doesn't Jenny look good?" Grandma says to Bryan.

Bryan watches Grandma, one eyebrow up like he's bored or about to laugh, I'm not sure. Grandma lets go of my arm, looks back and forth between us and she wants something—I don't know what—probably a big sloppy hug and maybe a kiss on the cheek. If he started it, I would probably go along, just for the show, but he doesn't.

Bryan stands up taller then, reaches out and kind of nudges my shoulder.

"Good to see you, kid," he says. He goes past me then, his body shifted at this slip-past angle.

"Kid?" I say. "Good to see you, 'kid'? What's that?"

He ignores me, going into the living room and sitting between Andy and Mark, everyone around him like he's the center of the universe.

I look at Grandma then, a funny look on her face.

"Kid?" I say.

"He's glad to see you," she whispers. "He's just a little moody right now."

"Right now?" I say.

She puts her hand out, squeezes my wrist with her soft hands, and nods.

"It's so good to see you again," she says.

The trip is a joke. There's no reunion of the cousins. If I ever see Bryan, he ignores me and the rest of the time, he's off with Andy to play golf or go to the movies or just hang out with the older girls. There's some kind of serious boy-girl thing going there, Andy paired off with the chubby one and the blonde paired up with Bryan.

I would never admit it but it hurts my feelings I came all this way and he doesn't care at all.

I spend a little time with Tracy, Faith Ann, Auntie Carol, Aunt Mary Beth, and her little boy Chris, and the rest of the time, I hang out with Grandma at the trailer.

Over those two weeks, I pick up Grandma's habit of reading one paperback romance a day and they're really not that bad. Girl meets boy, girl hates boy yet is undeniably drawn to him, girl needs boy's help, they realize hate is love, and then there is a great make-out scene at the end.

I read one of those books down at the pool when Bryan shows up out of the blue and announces he's going to Carson City to see Aunt Georgia and Uncle Charles.

"You want to come?" he says.

"Me?" I say.

"Who else?" he says.

I sit on a lounge chair, shading my eyes to look up at him. I'm in the part of the book where the girl is in the "hate the guy" stage which makes it easy to hate Bryan in a polite but cool way.

"I'm sorry," I say. "I don't believe we've actually met."

He looks at me, no expression on his face at all, just blank. "What are you talking about?" he says.

"Hello," I say, putting my book down on the chair. "You've been ignoring me since I got here. What is the deal now?"

Bryan laughs a little, like he thinks I'm kidding, but I'm not and he stops. He has on a pair of faded jeans and a black cowboy hat. Who wears a cowboy hat in the desert? The hot wind blows hard, and he puts his hand up to keep it from blowing away.

"I'm talking to you now," he says.

"I can see that," I say.

"Do you want to go or what?"

I look up at him, close one eye like I can see him more clearly that way. "How are we getting there?" I say.

"Grandpa's car," he says.

"You are driving?" I say.

"No duh," he says.

"You think you can do it without killing us both?" I say.

"Ha, ha," he says.

I push off my chair and gather up my things. "Fine," I say, "I'll go."

In the car, Bryan has the radio tuned into something like hard rock, a guy screaming in a high voice.

Something is alive in the silence between us, you'd have to be a moron not to notice it but Bryan doesn't say a word. He just drives, head up and down to the music, fingers drumming on the steering wheel.

I've met guys like Bryan before, at least seen them at school. They are great-looking, smart, and completely stuck on themselves. They look down their noses at you, as if you are lucky to be in their presence.

I make a point to act extra bored, face in my hand, eyes out the window the whole time.

Outside is Paradise Valley, this windy no-man's-land of salt flats that reflect the light so it looks like they hold water.

There's a change in the car, the heavy frame of it shaking.

I look over at Bryan, casual, bored, and he has both hands on the steering wheel, chin tucked, eyes on the road.

His foot is pressed all the way to the floor and the speedometer needle moves past 70, 75, 80.

"What are you doing?"

Bryan looks at me then, big grin.

"Let's see if this baby can crack one hundred," he says.

The speedometer needle moves to 90 miles an hour and Bryan weaves between cars that don't go nearly as fast.

"Bryan!"

I try to reach to the dashboard, only the speed presses me back in the big leather seat. The needle rounds 95 and shakes around 100.

I don't even know I'm holding my breath until he eases off the pedal and my head is dizzy from no air.

The needle moves down, the car slowing, and what seemed like a reasonable speed before actually feels slow now. Bryan licks his lips then, high red color on his cheeks, and he looks at me quickly.

"I didn't scare you, did I?" he says.

My soft-cover romance heroine wouldn't take this crap from any guy. "Is that the plan?" I say.

Bryan looks over at me again, eyebrows up, Mr. Innocent. "I was just kidding around," he says.

I sit back and look out the window again.

It's funny how you can be away from a person for years, yet they don't change at all. He's as big a jerk as he always was, so full of himself, almost crazy sometimes and then pulled back into a shell where no one can touch him.

Bryan drives the big car through Carson, down the main street past the Golden Nugget and the silver dome of the capitol.

I act bored, face in my hand, but my eyes take it all in like I'm starving. I remember all this, I can feel it.

Bryan drives to the southern end of town, snow still on the tops of the Sierras, and he makes a left up the hill to Aunt Georgia and Uncle Charles's place.

They are just like always, tan and happy. Uncle Charles has on his mailman's uniform; Aunt Georgia wears white-and-blue shorts with a matching powder blue top. There are the kids—Carrie Sue, who's the same age as me, and Jeffrey, who is 10.

We haven't seen each other for years, but we act like it was just a few weeks ago—hugs all around; "Wow, you are getting so big," from Aunt Georgia; "Not too big for a tickle," from Uncle Charles, who needles my side and then hugs me with one arm. The two of them smoke cigarette after cigarette, offering sodas and chips, getting us into the house and into the living room.

"How're Dick and Peggy?" Aunt Georgia asks.

"Fine," I say.

"Kimmy?"

"Fine too," I say. "Everyone is fine."

"How do you like St. Helens?"

"It's great," I say.

It's strange having them ask so many questions, especially personal questions and I don't know if I can tell the truth here, so I just keep it nice and polite and normal, big happy smile on my face.

The living room has rusty orange carpet, black leather sofa, a gold swivel chair, a bureau with the television inside, and a dark wood coffee table. Aunt Georgia is right next to me on the sofa, Uncle Charles at the far end of the room in his chair.

I don't know why, but Mom and Dad do not like them at all, never have. It's that way with Grandma and Grandpa Lauck too. Mention Aunt Georgia and Uncle Charles and it's eye-rolling and head-shaking. I know the reason is mixed up in the past with how my mother was sick, whispers of "mental instability," and that everyone on her side of the family is "crazy." I know it's not true about my mother, but all that is like a million years ago, and besides, what does it matter now anyway?

Uncle Charles talks to Bryan, something about sports, and Carrie Sue stands with her back against the wall, one arm crossed over her stomach, and listens to them.

Aunt Georgia puts her hand out, finger into my leg.

"Did you get our Christmas packages?" she says.

I stop smiling, finally, the feel of it around the edge of my mouth.

"I did," I say, "I'm sorry; thank you."

She waves her hand in the air, *Forget it,* and I feel so stupid for not thanking her, not even calling, but I flat out forgot. Every year they send presents, records, jewelry, baubles for my hair, but Christmas is such a nightmare at our house, Mom going in and out of her moods, and I just forget.

"I tried calling," Aunt Georgia says. "Peggy said you were at a basketball game."

"You called?" I say.

She uncrosses her legs, crosses them the other way, and readjusts her ashtray on her lap.

"I'm really sorry," I say. "I didn't know."

"Don't worry," she says. "You've got enough on your plate. I just wanted to make sure you got the things, that you were doing okay."

I move the soda can in my hand, turn it this way and that, look at the label. I wonder what she means, enough on my plate. Bryan sits on the floor, with two pillows under his elbow, and he laughs at something Uncle Charles says.

"So you are playing basketball?" Aunt Georgia says.

"Yeah," I say.

"Do you like it?" she says.

"I do," I say.

"What position?" Bryan says, looking my way from where he is on the floor.

"What?" I say.

"What position do you play?" he says.

I clear my throat. "Center," I say.

Bryan nods like that makes sense. "How are your grades?" he says.

"What?"

"Your grades? Are you getting good grades?"

I laugh out loud, *Who the hell are you,* and I look at Aunt Georgia, *Can you believe this guy?* but she just puts her cigarette between her lips and squints as she inhales.

The whole room is quiet, watching, waiting, and I look over at Bryan.

"My grades are fine Bryan," I say. "Don't you worry yourself about me."

Bryan lifts his eyebrows up then, surprise in his dark eyes.

"Now, now," Aunt Georgia says, tapping my leg with her finger again, "he's just asking."

The room has a tense feeling now. I want to say, *Screw him.*

He doesn't call me for three years, ignores me the whole time I've been here, scared me to death on the drive over, and now, he wants to know about my grades.

I just shake my head and look at the top of my soda can.

Uncle Charles says something to Bryan about his job at the casino where he's parking cars, and I just look into the can of soda, moving it around like it's the most interesting thing in the world.

I can feel Aunt Georgia watch me, and I tilt my head to look at her. She has warm brown eyes and a nice face, high cheekbones, straight nose. More than that, she has a stillness to her that sees things that most other people don't. She watches you; she knows.

She smiles and nods her head up.

"So are you getting good grades?" she says.

"I am," I say, tilting my head in Bryan's direction. "Not like him, but good."

She nods.

"What about after high school?" she says. "Are you thinking about college yet?"

"Absolutely."

"I'm not surprised," she says.

Bryan and I spend the whole day with them, together but separate. He goes outside with Uncle Charles and the kids; I sit in the kitchen with Aunt Georgia and talk. She tells me all about Carrie Sue and Jeffrey, things they're doing at school, the boy Carrie Sue is dating. I tell her about Luke, that I think we are breaking up though, and how I like this other boy from my Sunday school class, but it's not serious. We talk a little bit about Bryan, why I was so rude, and then she tells me not to be too hard on him, how he has troubles of his own.

I sit on a stool at the end of the kitchen nook, my elbows on the counter, face in my hands, and from where I am I can see Bryan out back, throwing a football with Jeffrey.

"What could possibly be wrong with him?" I say. "The guy is brilliant and he graduated at the top of his class."

Aunt Georgia leans her hip into the counter, ashtray by her cup of coffee and she has her legs crossed at the ankle. She looks at her cigarette in her ashtray then, picking it up, studying the end that burns a line of smoke up.

"We wanted both of you kids to come live with us," she says, and it's such a surprise, so out of the blue really that I sit up in my seat.

"Did you know that?" she says, shifting her eyes to my face.

"No," I say, laughing a little, except it's not a joke.

"It's true," she says. "We had Bryan first, and we wanted you to come here too, but . . ." She moves her jaw side to side, holding something back.

"But what?" I say.

"Mom and Pop Lauck didn't want you kids with us."

"Why not?" I say.

She puts her cigarette between her lips and shrugs one shoulder, looking out at the yard.

Their back windows look over a wide stretch of grass that runs to a fence where she keeps two horses, and off in the distance, the Sierra Nevada Mountains lift up and are covered with snow.

"I don't know, Jenny," she says then, "maybe they thought we were after the money that came with you kids."

She looks at me, such a tired expression on her face.

"We never cared about that darn money," she says, "they could have had it for all we cared. Chuck and I just wanted you kids and we wanted you to stay together."

I look down at my hands in my lap and it's as if a door has

been opened inside of me, a door leading to a room I never knew about.

We talk then, really talk, and Aunt Georgia tells the story of how things were after they found us in L.A. with Deb. She says they wanted to take both of us kids right away, but legally, they couldn't. Instead, they came back to Carson and called a lawyer, and Deb agreed to give up Bryan first. After that, Bryan went to Grandpa Ivan, my mother's father in Boise, and then, he came here.

She says they were all set up to keep Bryan, had this lawyer draw up custody papers and were going to get a new house, but that Grandma Lauck wouldn't hear of it and sent Leonard over to change Bryan's mind.

"I thought he got to choose," I say.

"Sure," she says, snuffing out her cigarette in the ashtray and shaking a new one from the pack, "but you have no idea the pressure he was under. He was just fifteen years old and he wanted to make everyone happy."

Aunt Georgia bites her lip then, like she should stop telling me this stuff, only we've crossed a line and can never go back.

"We tried to get you too," she says, arms crossed over her stomach, "but Deb sent you off to Mom and Pop Lauck, and they wouldn't give you up."

"Mom and Dad said no one else wanted me," I say, the words stuck in my throat, almost hurting as I say them.

"Oh, honey," she says, coming to me, her hand on my shoulder like a mother would do. "That's just not true."

I want to believe her, I really do, but I don't know if I can or if I should.

When we leave, I'm not the same as when we came. I'm out of sorts, I'm angry and sad, and I just want to get the hell out of here.

"Write a note every now and then," Aunt Georgia says, hugging me good-bye. "Just let us know how you are."

"We worry about you," Uncle Charles says then, messing my hair and telling me to be good.

Aunt Georgia hugs me one more time, hands on my arms, like she doesn't want to let me go and I don't know how to be around people who are this nice, I don't know how to feel or trust their kindness.

"If you ever need anything, just call," she says, "Do you understand?"

I nod and look down at the ground since I can't look at her right now.

She hugs me one more time, and finally, we drive away.

The ride back is just like the ride there, except Bryan doesn't play the radio. Instead, he is quiet and I am too.

All this time, Mom, Dad, Kimmy, and me, our pretend game of being a family, how Mom slapped me and said it was my fault she couldn't have a baby.

I move my hand over my face, the sting of being hit just under the skin and my head hurts.

I can't believe Aunt Georgia and Uncle Charles wanted me. I can't believe they tried to fight for us and deep down, I wonder if Aunt Georgia is just being nice, but then there's how they were the only ones who ever came to L.A. to see how we were doing, and how they fought to get us away from Deb.

We drive past the capitol building, the Golden Nugget, and somewhere over there, the house on Mary Street. I look over at Bryan then.

He looks at me looking at him, just a quick glance. "What?" he says.

I move my tongue against my back tooth. "Nothing," I say,

looking away from him and out the window, chin in my hand, fingers over my mouth.

The sagebrush grows over the hillsides in tight little mounds of gray and green, and the sun moves its way down, turning the sky yellow and gray. Way up there, you can see the beginning of stars, tiny sparks, so far away. As we leave town, we pass a sign that says YOU ARE LEAVING CARSON CITY.

When I get back from Reno, I try to make myself forget what Aunt Georgia told me, even though it's always there now when I look at Mom and Dad—hope mixed with doubt.

I tell them what they want to know about the trip, how much fun I had, how Bryan is doing just great and has a job at a casino parking cars, and then, it's like I never left at all.

I have to play the game with Mom and Dad, but I can't keep it up with Luke.

He leaves messages but I don't call him back, and I keep myself busy with baby-sitting and this new waitress job at Spiffy's. My rationale isn't good but I figure if I dodge Luke long enough, he'll get it and go away.

I'm getting to be pretty good friends with a guy I know from church, this redhead named Randy who has the most beautiful blue eyes I've ever seen.

Randy is easy to be with even if he is painfully shy. We play tennis together sometimes, hang out after church, or just talk on the telephone. He's nice, he's sweet, he's safe.

Randy knows that technically I'm still Luke's girl but we don't talk about it, which is fine with me. It goes on like that until August when Luke shows up at Spiffy's, just after the lunch rush.

I work the counter, pour coffee for a couple guys who eat while they read the newspaper. At first, I look right past him, another guy in dirty coveralls with grease on his face and a hat on his head. Those guys come in all day long, timber workers mostly, and a few mechanics from the truck stop.

I put the coffeepot on the burner, go to the front counter to help him, and Luke takes off his hat, moves his hair with his hand.

"Hey," I say, laughing and forgetting myself for a minute. "I didn't even recognize you."

He smiles but it's not in his eyes. He puts his hands on the front counter where there are packs of gum and mints and odds and ends for sale. His fingernails have grease up them and I've never seen his hands like that.

"I've been trying to call you," he says.

I nod, *I know.*

"What's going on?"

He looks at me and I look at him and then I look away, down at the packs of gum; Juicy Fruit, wintergreen, peppermint.

Luke, we need to take a break.

It seemed so simple in my mind, but now he's here it's not simple at all.

A paperback romance heroine wouldn't be so weak; she'd be smart, cool, confident—or she would stall.

"I can't talk right now," I whisper. "I have to work."

He looks around the restaurant.

"Do you get to take a break?" he says.

"No break," I say.

"When are you off?" he says. "Can I give you a lift home?"

"My mom is coming to get me," I say.

A big man in a flannel work shirt comes to the counter then, bill in his hand, and he says hey to Luke, asks how his dad is. Luke smiles, all polite, says his dad is fine, the business fine, everyone is fine. I ring up the bill, give the man his change, and he leaves me a dollar tip.

"There you go, honey," he says.

I smile my waitress smile, fold the dollar up, and when he's gone, I roll my eyes. "I hate how they call me that."

"What?" Luke says.

"Honey," I say. "I'm not his honey."

Luke looks at me like he has no idea what I mean and what's the use.

"I have to get back to work," I say. "I'll call you."

"But you don't call," he says.

"I will," I say. "I promise."

Luke leans closer to me.

"Someone told me you are hanging around with Randy Harris now," he says.

"What?" I say, my best surprised expression, hand over my heart.

"Are you?" he says.

"Please," I say, waving off that idea, "he's in my church classes; he's a sophomore."

Luke leans back then, eyes on my face, and he moves his hand over his mouth.

"Where's your bracelet?" he says.

I look down at my own wrist but I already know his bracelet is in my jewelry box at home.

He leans closer to me, mouth set tight. "Did we break up?" he whispers, "because I don't remember us breaking up."

I look over my shoulder and the guy in charge of the restaurant looks my way, *What are you doing?* on his face.

"You are going to get me in trouble," I whisper.

Luke looks at me and I look at him, a terrible feeling between us.

"I can't believe you're doing this," he says.

"I'm not doing anything," I say. "I just have to work."

Luke knows I'm not telling the truth, in the same way he knows so many other secrets about me, and I wonder how that happened, how I let it happen. I clear my throat.

"Why can't we just take a break for a while and then—I don't know—we'll see."

"Why?" he says, "what's happened?"

"I can't explain it here," I say.

Luke looks at me for a long time and in that look I see how he wants to get me alone to show me how wrong I am—and he could do it too.

I step back from him, and Luke pushes his hand through his blond hair, puts his hat back on his head.

"Fine," he says. "When you're ready, call me."

"Fine," I say.

He leaves then, going out the door and not looking back.

I let myself fall into being Randy's girl even though the fire isn't there. He's so, I don't know, careful and innocent. The way he fumbles around is almost funny, not in a mean way, just in the way things are.

Part of me aches for Luke, for what he knew about me, for the way he kissed and touched and was. How many times I've almost called him, actually dialed his number and then put the phone down when it started ringing.

I got lost with Luke. With Randy, I know exactly where I am.

I wonder if I'll ever get Luke out of my system or worse, if I made a terrible mistake. I wonder if I was in love with him but didn't know it or didn't know how to feel it.

I think that's the truth, I probably made a terrible mistake and I will never find another person in the world who will make me feel the way Luke made me feel.

Sophomore year is just like freshman year but without Luke. I go out for basketball again, play on both the junior varsity and varsity teams.

Megan is a cheerleader now so I don't see her as much as I used to. Besides, things aren't the same since Luke and I broke it off. After all, she is his cousin.

Mom and Dad and Kimmy are about the same, same stupid jokes out of Dad, same rules, same mood swings, only now Mom says the reason is something new that her doctor calls PMS.

It turns out that Megan was right—I am blind—at least too blind to drive, so I miss driver's ed. I did get glasses, but Dad wouldn't teach me how to drive, so I taught myself when they were off at work, only Kimmy told on me and now I'm on a year's restriction. I can't get my license until I'm 17.

When I turn 16, I can go out on dates, finally, but it's just not that big of a deal. All this waiting to date, all the times Luke and I talked about what it would be like and now, I'm not even with him.

One month after my birthday, January 1980, Dad announces we are moving to Spokane.

No one moves their sophomore year of high school, no one has to start all over, but Mom and Dad say it will be good for all of us, that Dad will make more money, is on track for other promotions, and right away, a For Sale sign goes up in the front yard.

It's just a couple weeks before we are going to move when Mom, Dad, and Kimmy go to Spokane together so Mom can look at houses. I stay behind for school, and the first night I'm alone, I pick up the telephone, hold the heavy receiver in my hand, and look at the round part where you talk, the little holes in the plastic.

I take a deep breath and dial.

"Hello," he says, the familiar warmth of his voice.

"Luke?" I say.

"Jenny?" he says. "What are you doing?"

"I'm calling," I say.

"What?" he says.

I turn around and look at myself in the mirror over the dining-room table. I have on my shorts that I wear to bed, my big Mount St. Helens P.E. T-shirt, and my hair is back in a ponytail.

What are you doing?

What are you thinking?

"I'm moving," I say, looking away from my reflection. "To Spokane."

"Yeah," he says, "I heard."

I bite my lip then and take a deep breath. "Luke?" I say. "Can you come over?"

"Now?" he says.

I nod but he can't hear that.

"My parents are in Spokane right now," I say.

"Kimmy too?" he says.

"Yes," I say.

He's quiet for a long time. I wonder what he's doing, what he's thinking. It's eight at night, a school night, and I bite my fingernail.

"Please, Luke," I say, my voice not my voice at all.

"I'll be right there," he says.

It's no time at all, ten minutes maybe, and Luke pulls his big blue car into the driveway, turns off the engine, and gets out.

I already have the door open, the screen balanced against my hip, waiting.

He's just like always, but different too. His hair is shorter, he looks a little taller, and I think he put on some weight—not much, but it shows in his face. The scars are still on his neck, side by side, and most of all, his eyes still have that look in them, like he was searching and then found me.

He walks up on the porch, a smile on his face, a question in his eyes.

I put my hand out to him, reaching into the dark.

I know this is wrong, that I'm breaking all sorts of rules and it would kill Randy but I'm leaving St. Helens soon and may never be cared for the way Luke cares for me. I don't care if I can't feel it. I don't even care if it's not really love. I can't cheat myself of the one person who makes me feel wanted in a world where everyone else treats me like shit. I can't go one more day without feeling alive in a world where people are either dead or acting that way.

Luke doesn't wait, not even a moment. He puts his hand in mine, that old fire between us and I pull him into the house, closing the door behind us.

PART FOUR

SPOKANE

FOUR

SPOKANE, WASHINGTON ❧ 1980

It's a Sunday morning, one of those lazy days with nothing much going on. Mom and Dad are off on a road trip to Idaho; I'm baby-sitting.

Kimmy's tummy-down on the living-room carpet, with her face in her hands, Bugs Bunny on the television.

The front door is open, and I sit on the stoop reading a book—*The Thorn Birds,* which begins with this quote: "For the best is only bought at the cost of great pain."

Since moving, I read all the time, and not paperback romances either, those are so boring. Now I read John Irving, William Styron, and a bit of Danielle Steele. My favorites are the ones like *The Thorn Birds* though, the ones that haunt your memory long after you are done reading.

The sun cuts through the trees around our house in bright white slices. It's not suntan hot but it's warm with that kind of promise.

I put my book facedown on the stoop, take off my glasses,

and look at the sky. Far off are storm clouds and I wonder if they are coming our way.

We live in a suburb of Spokane called Twelve-Mile Falls, and our house is in a new housing development where most of the houses are still for sale.

It's nice here, very nice.

Our house is a big split level with a two-car garage, wall-to-wall carpet, brand-new appliances. Out front is a wide stretch of grass, out back is a big yard, and all around are tall pines that make everything smell like a forest.

The best thing about this house is my own room with four walls, a closet, and a door that locks.

My princess bed would fit perfectly here now, but that's kid stuff. Instead, I have a double bed with a new bedspread and curtains to match.

There are no mice or rats here.

It doesn't rain every single day.

Dad goes to work in a suit and a tie.

Mom has been in a good mood for weeks.

I'm even getting used to my school, this huge place with 600 kids in the sophomore class alone. That's how many kids went to the whole school at St. Helens.

At first, I'd get lost in the maze of halls, hundreds of kids who moved in a river of elbows and shoulders. I even drew out a cartoon for Moog where there were hundreds of circles jammed on a page and then on one circle, a face and an arrow. In a caption, I wrote, "This is me . . . drowning. Ha, ha, ha."

Since then, I drew myself a map of the school and I stopped getting lost.

The sun lifts higher in the morning sky and the storm clouds spread thick under the blue sky like an ink spill. They aren't normal clouds at all; they are more like one big cloud that covers everything. I've never seen a storm move like that.

Grabbing my book and glasses, I go into the house. Kimmy looks my way and then at the television again. She's still in her nightgown, bare feet, long blond hair messed up and tucked behind her ears.

I think about telling her that it's going to rain but she doesn't care about rain.

On the television is one of those Roadrunner cartoons and I toss my book on the sofa.

"They all end the same, you know," I say.

She moves her whole face at me, scrunched in at the nose first and then at her mouth and eyes. "Shhh," she says.

I put my glasses on my face again, go into the kitchen and lean on the counter to see out the window. The cloud is over the house now, over everything else too, day turned to night and a couple street lamps flicker on. I lean closer, as if looking closer will change what is happening but right away I know this is one of those emergency things.

I go into the living room again.

"Kimmy," I say, "let me change the channel for a sec."

"No," she yells.

I take up the TV remote and change the channel and Kimmy rolls on her back, hands over her face, letting out one of her loud screams like she's being stabbed.

"Don't be so dramatic," I say.

I change the channels past a cooking show, *Bonanza*, something about gardening, and cartoons again.

"Thank you," Kimmy says, rolling on her stomach again.

I look out the windows to the backyard and out there is dark too. "This is not right," I say.

I go into my room and get my transistor radio. I turn on a

high-pitch whine and move the dial around through music until I get a voice.

Kimmy stands at the doorway of my room, a funny look on her face.

"It is night?" she says.

I hold the radio up to my ear and shake my head at her to be quiet.

The announcer says it's not safe to be outside, to move all animals indoors and to take cars off the streets if possible.

"Mount Saint Helens erupted," he says.

Kimmy looks at me, a big blank in her eyes.

"Where's RC?" I say.

"I don't know," she says.

"Go find her," I say.

Kimmy likes to say she doesn't have to listen to me because I'm not her mother. Usually, I have to ask her to do something three or four times but this time Kimmy goes right away.

The cloud over Spokane is volcanic ash and the man on the radio says it's dangerous to breathe. I close the window in my room, then go into Kimmy's room and close her window too.

"RC?" Kimmy yells. "Here, RC."

On the radio, the man says the north side of the mountain is gone, Spirit Lake is gone too and there is a flood down the Toutle River.

St. Helens is no more than 50 miles from the bottom of the mountain.

Kimmy stands in the hall then, points at Mom and Dad's room.

"RC is up here," she says, "on their bed."

I turn off the radio then, toss it on my bed, and reach out for Kimmy's hand.

"Let's call St. Helens," I say.

Downstairs, Kimmy and me stand in the kitchen and I break

the long-distance rule. First, I call Grandma Duemore's place, but it just rings 20, 30 times, and finally, I hang up.

"That's fine," I say, "I don't want to talk to that sourpuss anyway."

Kimmy puts her thumb in her mouth and I reach over, pull her hand down.

"Don't do that," I say, "you're too big for that now."

I dial another number for one of Dad's brothers and she puts her thumb into her mouth again.

"No," I say, shaking my head.

She sticks her tongue out at me and puts her thumb in one more time.

The telephone line makes a bunch of strange clicks and I look at Kimmy.

"Jeez, Kimmy," I say, "you are six. You can't keep sucking that thing; it's ugly and it makes you look like a baby."

There is a funny disconnect sound on the line and I take a deep breath.

"Shit," I whisper, "shit, shit, shit."

"Don't swear," Kimmy says.

"Sometimes you can swear."

"When?"

"When it's an emergency."

"Well shit, then." She leans against the counter, wiping her thumb off on her nightgown. I try to act calm but my fingers shake as I dial a number I still know by heart.

It rings two, three times and then, "Hello?"

"Moog?"

"Jenny?" Megan says, her familiar laugh. "What are you doing?"

"Me?" I say, happy to hear her voice. "What are you doing? Did everyone get blown to smithereens over there?"

"God no," she says, laughing.

"No, seriously," I say. "Everyone is okay, everything is still standing?"

"Absolutely," she says.

I let out my breath, didn't even know I was holding it, and I put my thumb up to Kimmy, everything A-okay.

"So how have you been?" Megan says. "We got your last letter, that cartoon of you in the halls. It was so funny."

Kimmy grins at me and goes to the kitchen window, hanging over the sink to look out the window.

"Everything is fine," I say. "I think I'm over the shock of this place."

Telephone balanced between shoulder and ear, I whisper to Kimmy to close all the windows downstairs.

"Shit," Kimmy says.

"Please, Kimmy," I whisper.

She goes out of the kitchen then, dragging her feet.

There is the sound of the windows sliding shut but then I hear the TV click on.

Megan chats about this and that, small talk, but there's a change between us. It might be the distance and time, out of sight of out mind, but since I broke up with Luke last summer, things haven't been the same between us anyway.

I stopped telling my secrets; she stopped telling me hers.

She has no idea about that last night with Luke when everything was exactly where we left off, hypnotizing, visions of mountains and canyons.

We didn't do it, no way, but we did move together to the same edge where the possibility of doing it was right there, a red light blinking *Danger, stop, turn back*.

After, I cried, like I always did, and Luke tried to make it better.

Something about the two of us together was just too

much, like being in the deep end without knowing how to swim.

The window reflects me standing with the telephone at my ear.

"How's Luke?" I say.

"Oh, he's okay, I guess," Megan says. "I think he misses you."

"Did he say that?"

"No, but he's not the same, there's a kind of hangdoggy look to him now."

"He's not dating anyone yet?"

"No. Are you?"

"No, but I did get a letter from Randy."

"Jeez, woman, you've left a trail of broken hearts over here."

"Ha, ha," I say.

On the line is the sound of static and even though she's just on the other side of the state, it's like Moog is on the moon.

That's the way it is.

You leave a place and people and after a while, you change, they change and whatever it was that connected you to begin with is gone forever.

Megan and me say good-bye and I hang up.

Outside, the ash falls like snow and covers everything in gray.

I never spoke with Luke again after that night.

I couldn't be with him the way he wanted and even though he made me feel so wanted and alive, I didn't feel that kind of thing for him, I don't know why. It's not like I didn't care about him, I did. It just wasn't love like you read about in the books and I knew I had to love him that way.

After I finally stopped crying, I told Luke how sorry I was for everything, for breaking it off last summer the way I did, for avoiding him and taking up with Randy when technically we weren't even broken up.

"It doesn't matter," Luke said.

"How can you say that?" I said. "I didn't even give you a reason, and now, I call you two weeks before I'm going to leave. Come on, Luke—you should be furious with me."

Luke, sitting on my little bed in the nothing of a room, held my hand to his mouth, kissing against the inside of my palm.

"I love you," he said.

"Please don't say that, Luke," I said.

"It's true," he said.

I took my hand from him then.

"You're going to forget all about me," I told him. "If you don't, you should."

In the dark of my room, I could see the shine of his tears.

"You're not the kind of girl someone can forget," Luke said.

It's too dangerous to drive in the ash, so Mom and Dad are stuck over in Idaho.

Kimmy and I make a batch of homemade doughnuts for lunch and play Dad's stereo so loud, the house actually vibrates.

That night, we watch the news, and the only story now is Mount Saint Helens—the number of people dead and estimates of money lost in timber.

The pictures on the television show pines stripped clean and laid out like matchsticks, a river of mud and a hunk of the mountain just gone.

A few days before we moved, there was a going-away party at Megan's house. I took down everyone's address and Randy and me promised to write.

Mom, Dad, Kimmy, and me packed up the house, loaded the U-Haul, and left on a Saturday morning, a clear day where we actually saw Mount Saint Helens in the distance. It was always such a fixture out there on the horizon, solid and quiet with its rounded-off white top, that I barely noticed it.

Dad and Kimmy drove ahead in the U-Haul, and Mom and me rode in the Volkswagen, RC sitting her poodle self on my lap.

"Good-bye, St. Helens," Mom said.

"Good-bye, Stump," I said.

"Good-bye, Grandma Duemore," Mom said.

"Good-bye, rats and mice in the attic," I said.

"Good-bye, rain," Mom said.

"Good bye, home economics!" I said.

Mom looked over at me, eyebrows up in the question. "You didn't like home economics?"

"I hated that class," I said, rolling my eyes.

She laughed at that, surprised and I laughed too, for no real reason, just because it was nice.

As we drove over the freeway, past the sign that read YOU ARE LEAVING ST. HELENS, POP. 1,000. I moved my hands over the soft gray fur of RC's neck, looked past the mountain, and thought good-byes to Randy and Luke and the girl I was in that place, the idea of a fresh start in my head.

All the people who lived around Mount Saint Helens were warned by geologists to leave, and apparently, just about everyone was off the mountain when it blew except one old man who lived near Spirit Lake. Before the mountain blew and there were just warnings, a news crew went up to ask why he wouldn't leave and he told them he had lived on that mountain his whole life, that it was his home and he'd rather die than leave. After the mountain blew, all the stations play his interview over and over, and in his eyes is such a stubborn look, gray stubble jaw, a *Get the hell out of here and leave me alone* expression on his face.

Watching the interview with Kimmy, I wonder if he changed his mind at the last minute when he heard the first rumbles of that mountain or if he was glad to die in the place he called home.

After the eruption, ash covers trees, houses, and lawns and there is no sound from the things you take for granted, like birds and bugs and airplanes.

Mom says it's like living on the moon.

On the news are stories about people who box up ash and take it to California, selling it in little bags on street corners of L.A. and making a fortune.

Dad says he wishes he had thought of that.

After a couple of weeks, St. Helens' ash washes into the ground, the sounds come back, and a new family moves in across the street.

On a Monday morning, I wait for the bus out by the mailboxes, book bag over my shoulder and my face in a book.

It's one of those misty mornings with fog.

Mom and Kimmy are still asleep.

Dad already left for work.

I read with my finger on the page, follow the words in the bad light, and across the street I hear the sound of a door open and then close. When I look up, a guy walks down the driveway and he carries a black suitcase.

I hold my place with my finger and think about taking off my glasses but that's stupid.

The guy stops on his side of the road, black T-shirt, jeans, and a black zip sweatshirt.

"Hi," he says.

"Hey," I say.

"Is this where the bus stops?" he says.

"Yeah," I say.

He puts the suitcase down, a little puff of St. Helens ash lifting off the gravel.

I close my book and cross the street to where he is because that's the side to get on the bus anyway.

"Welcome to the neighborhood," I say.

He looks at me, not really a look, more like a once-over glance. "Thanks," he says. He turns and looks down the street again.

I cross my arms over myself, book under my arm and tilt my head to the side.

He's my age—a little taller than me, though.

"It's supposed to come at eight," I say, "but it's usually late."

My voice sounds different, confident, as if six weeks of living here makes me something of an expert. He looks at his wristwatch and down the road.

I adjust my glasses on my face, take them off, hold them in my hand because, that's cool, I'm not reading anymore.

I move my foot around on the gravel near the black suitcase.

"What's in there?" I say.

He looks at me for a second, then down. He has a quiet way about him. "Sax," he says.

"What?"

"Saxophone," he says, "a horn."

"You're in the band?" I say.

"I'm going to try out," he says.

I nod like *Oh yeah, I know all about the band,* which actually I know nothing about.

"I'm trying out for the drill team," I say. "They march with the band, I think."

The new boy moves his face in what might be a smile but it's hard to read. Maybe he doesn't like the drill team.

"I should say 'might' try out," I say. "I'm still thinking about it. I really play basketball, but I didn't make the team. I mean I made the team, but it was just B-squad, and there's no way I am going to play B-squad—that's for freshman players, not juniors, you know?"

He watches me, eyebrows up a little. I shift weight from one foot to the other.

"Anyway, I was just thinking something else would be good. Some kind of extracurricular activity."

I close my mouth then, my side of the conversation waiting in the cool morning air but he doesn't pick it up.

God, I'm so stupid.

I cross my arms tighter then, my book wedging up in my armpit, glasses in my hand. I'm right here, two feet away, but he looks in the opposite direction and I guess that's a hint.

I put my glasses back on my face and open my book. What's the use of being friendly if someone is going to ignore you?

By summer, Mom has a job in the city where she commutes to work with Dad, and it's my job to stay home and watch Kimmy. Mom gets me up at five to iron her clothes, help make their lunches, and take down a list of chores. When they leave, I go back to bed and sleep until Kimmy wakes me up, usually after ten because she's a late sleeper.

After that, I make breakfast, brush her hair, get her dressed, and make sure she doesn't watch too much TV and doesn't get run down by a car when she rides her bike up and down our street.

On Tuesdays and Thursdays, I take her down to the lake for

swim lessons and rub sunscreen on her because Mom says that's the new thing now, something to do with the ozone layer.

After Kimmy runs off to learn how to swim, I lie on a towel and read *Endless Love* in the sun, no sunscreen for me. I don't care a thing about the ozone.

I did make the drill team, big deal, a bunch of loser girls who couldn't be cheerleaders but at least I'm doing something, I'm involved and I get to dance.

I haven't made any friends yet; it's a lot harder here than it was in St. Helens. In St. Helens, you were part of a family, but Spokane's attitude is more like mind your own business.

I did meet one girl, Debbie, who lives a few blocks away, except she has a summer job in Spokane. I haven't actually met the boy across the street, not in a formal way. Since that first day when I made a complete idiot out of myself, I avoid him anyway.

It's a hot day, too hot, and after a while, I put on a baseball cap and an old T-shirt and go down to the docks with *Endless Love* under my arm.

Kimmy splashes around with the other kids and waves at me.

I wave back and sit with my feet in the water, cloudy with green algae. There's a flat feel to the air, little white puffs like dandelion seeds lifting over the water.

A ways off is a speedboat that makes a lazy turn toward the docks. I squint in that direction, curiosity more than anything, and I can make out two guys but not much else.

The boat comes closer and I take up my new Spokane attitude, open book, head down.

The boat comes even closer but I don't look up.

The boat bumps against one end of the dock and still I don't look up.

"Good book?" a voice says.

Not ten feet from me, the guy from across the street leans out of the boat and jumps to the dock as light as a cat. Inside the boat is this other kid, a John Denver look-alike, all the way to his round glasses.

The guy from across the street stands with his feet wide, Levi cutoffs, no shirt, and he makes a long shadow down the dock.

Quick, I clear my throat. "Yeah, it's a good book." I say. "Probably my favorite."

The two guys look at each other, smiles between them, and my face goes hot. These dopey guys don't care if this book is my favorite—shut up anyway.

I smile politely and go back to reading.

"Here, Dave," John Denver in the boat says and the dock bounces a little. He says, "Here," again, tosses a rope on the dock next to a water ski and then gets busy in the boat.

From the corner of my eye, I watch Dave, lean and long, flat belly, the curve of muscles moving. He buckles a life preserver belt around his waist, the tip of his tongue out of his mouth, and then he looks at me.

I look away quick, moving hair behind my ear that isn't there to be moved.

"Is that a joke?" he says.

He nods at my shirt and I look down at the words: MOUNT SAINT HELENS P.E.

"No joke," I say. "I went to school there."

"Is it still there?" he says, a laugh in his voice.

"Yes, it's still there," I say.

He watches me in his quiet way and tilts his head to the side.

"So you're new here too?" he says.

"Yeah," I say.

"Ready, Dave?" John Denver calls out and Dave looks in the

direction of the boat that's pulled out a few feet now, the rope unwinding in the water.

"Almost," he calls out, waving his hand.

I wonder if that's it, if we're done, and I guess so, because Dave takes the ski, puts it on his foot and slides his other foot into a slot in the back.

He looks over at me again, one eye squinted, that small smile like *Watch this*. "See ya," he says.

I nod like *Yeah, I guess I'll see you,* and Dave yells, "Hit it!"

John Denver in the boat pushes into high gear, rope unraveling and snaps Dave off the dock.

It's called slalom and I've seen it before, lots of times. Last summer, I learned how to water ski on a camping trip with Mom and Dad and Dad's brothers, but that was on two skis, which is easy compared to one.

Across the lake, Dave skis a lazy S-curve over the water's surface, jumps the wake, lands on the other side, tilts to make a rooster tail of water off the edge of his ski, and does it all again on the other side.

He's so easy about the whole thing, a knife through butter, and if he'd wanted to impress me, he did.

After that day on the dock, I'm curious about the boy across the street and I think he might be curious about me too.

Every day, we do this thing where I sit on the front porch with a book at the same time that he checks his mail. At two forty-five sharp, Dave comes out of his house, usually barefooted and in cutoffs, walks a funny crossover step from his driveway to the gravel and then a careful light step over the gravel to the road. At the road, he checks the street for cars, crosses to the row of mailboxes, ours not six inches from his, and he tugs open the door.

That's my cue to look up from my book, *Oh, hi* on my face, distraction in my eyes, *What's your name again?*

Dave shuts the door of the mailbox, lifts one hand, just one for a wave.

I nod and wave too—*Oh yeah, I do know you*—and that's it.

Dave puts his hand back into the pocket of his cutoffs, walks the light step over the road and gravel and then the crossover step back to his house, door closed, a mystery on the other side of the street.

I'm not sure what it is about him that has my attention. Is it his quiet way, that smile with the promise of something, or how I can't get the lean look of him without a shirt out of my head? Whatever it is, we are never going to meet the way things are going and that's when I decide to try something new.

Across the street is the sound of his door and I look at my watch: Two-forty-five.

I take a deep breath and count to myself, *One thousand one, one thousand two, one thousand three.* I've worked out how it takes 10 seconds for Dave to cross the street, and at 10, when he pulls the door of the mailbox, I look up.

He stands there in a pair of cutoffs, a navy blue T-shirt, eyes squinted, making him look just like a cat.

Cats are funny animals, nothing like a dog. Cats won't come to you unless they are good and ready but it helps to ease them your way with the promise of something, food, a good pet around the ears, something.

I don't pretend not to know him this time. I smile, take off my glasses and close my book.

Come on, Dave—come on over.

Dave lifts his hand for the wave and I do it too, *I know you* in my eyes; *Come on over here—I'm not going to bite you.*

Dave looks down like he wants to hide his smile, and then, like magic, he doesn't turn around and go away. Instead, he light-steps up our gravel drive and at the cement sidewalk, walks normal again, that slow crossover.

I want to laugh at this game between us, but I don't; that might scare him away. When he gets to me, he stops, a long shadow of him on the concrete porch.

"You know," he says, "I don't know your name."

Dave is for David. David Ashe.

His father is Abe and is in the military—air force. His mother is Bev. His sister is Dina. His dog is Buster. His cat is Cleo.

It's funny how they all have names that don't go past D on the alphabet. They are A's, B's, C's, and D's.

David didn't cross the street all this time because he thought I was a snob; "stuck up," he said.

"I wasn't stuck up the first day," I say. "You were the snob; you didn't even talk to me."

"I was nervous."

"Nervous?" I say.

"You made me nervous."

"How could I make you nervous?" I say, my hand over my heart, "I was nice. I was friendly."

David has this cute way of going from serious to not serious. He looks down, rearranges his face, and when he looks up, it's one thing or the other. Smile, no smile. Serious, not serious.

He looks down, rearranges to serious and when he looks at me again, there's even a little tick in his right eye.

"I was nervous," he says, very slowly, "because you're so good-looking."

I look at him, my mouth open. "Okay," I say, "I am in total shock right now, which is why I am sitting here with my mouth hanging open."

I put my hand on my chin, make my mouth shut and that makes David laugh. I lean to him, tapping my finger between his eyes, just two times, very carefully so I don't spook him. "You've got bad eyesight, my friend," I say.

I go on and on about how my nose is too long, my butt is too big and my hair is just wrong, straight and flat, and who gave me such terrible hair to begin with?

David laughs so hard, his neck goes red and it's nice. "Well, now you mention all those things," he says, "maybe I was wrong."

I lean back, hands up.

"No, no," I say, "you can't take it back. It's out there and that's fine with me. Anyone with bad eyesight is a friend of mine."

He looks down again, works on arranging his face to serious but he can't; he just cracks up and shakes his head like he gives up.

After that, David and me are front-porch buddies almost every day, cracking jokes and laughing at how funny we are.

At night, we have these signals: light on and then off from our rooms to say hello; three on-and-offs mean, "Meet me outside." During the last hot nights of summer, we hang out together all the time.

David is the kind of guy I could like a lot. He's funny, cute, and then shy in this sweet way that makes you want to know more.

When I left St. Helens, I made a vow I was going to be different here, that I would stay out of trouble, stay away from the boys and keep my eye on the big plan, and so I keep things easy with David.

It's three weeks into the new school year when Mom knocks one time and then opens the door.

"Busy?" she says.

I'm at my desk reading a paperback, and as quick as I can, I close my book and set it next to my geometry book. "I'm doing homework," I say, adjusting my glasses on my face, all casual.

Mom leans against the frame of the door the way she does when she wants to talk about something. Her dark hair is gone almost gray now. She says it's premature for a woman her age, just 31. Dad's hair is completely white, which is supposed to be very premature for his age.

"I hope you haven't forgotten your father's birthday," she says.

"It's not the nineteeth yet, is it?"

"No," she says. "I am reminding you so you don't wait until the last minute like you always do."

"I don't always wait until the last minute," I say. "That's not true."

She looks up at the ceiling, her way of reminding me that I did forget her birthday. We all did, actually, three years ago, and it's a grudge she won't let go.

"Okay," I say, "I won't forget Dad's birthday."

I shift around in the chair again, my back to her, like *Go away.*

"What about your brother?" she says.

Outside is dark and my window reflects her still standing there, arms crossed, waiting.

Bryan's birthday is on the same day as Dad's. September 19.

"I won't forget, Mom," I say to her reflection.

"Don't take that attitude with me," she says, pushing off the door frame and adjusting her top around her hips in a huff, "I'm doing you a favor."

I take off my glasses and turn in the chair to face her again.

"Mom," I say, "I won't forget Dad's birthday." I put my glasses on my face again. "I won't forget Bryan's birthday. Thank you for reminding me."

She stops adjusting herself, puts her chin up like *that's better,* and leans against the door frame again, a sign that she's still not done.

Mom wants to talk about what I'm getting for Bryan, how I intend to pay for it, and because I don't have much cash, why not make a nice batch of chocolate-chip cookies. "Nothing says home like cookies," she says, "and if you make them this weekend, I can box them up for you."

When she's like this, you just have to shut up and listen until she's done, and so she talks and I focus on that space right between her eyes.

Bryan is in seminary now; he went in this fall—voluntarily. And I'm in shock about the whole thing. Bryan a priest? Heaven help the people he preaches to. He'll scare the shit out of everybody.

No one here talks about why he's doing it but Dad was on hand to crack a redneck joke about how Bryan's probably a homo, ha, ha, ha.

"If you bake them on Friday," Mom says, "there will still be time to get them out on Saturday."

"Great," I say, smile on my face, focus shifted to her eyes again. "That sounds just great. Thanks. Thanks a lot."

Mom isn't the brightest bulb in the pack but she's no dummy either, and by the way she squints, I know I might be over the top with my enthusiasm. I keep smiling but tone it down and finally, she leans off my door frame and pulls the door closed.

"Well," she says, "I'll leave you to your studies."

"Thanks," I say.

"You bet," she says and closes the door with a click.

I let my smile go and blow out the air I was holding. It's so much work to be a fake.

I lean my elbow on my desk and reach for my book again, and across the street is a light on and then off.

That makes me smile and I reach up to my lamp on the desk and flip the switch so my room is dark too.

One after another, my thoughts are around David. What's his room look like over there, does he have a big bed or a little one, does he make it up every morning like I do or is he a slob, and at night, right before he falls asleep, does he think about me?

Jeez, what's the matter with me?

David flicks his light on again, bright now compared to the dark and he lifts his hand in a quick wave, a serious expression on his face.

I want to turn my light on too since that's what we do but I don't. Instead, I sit there in the dark and look at him in the light for a little while, as if I can hide from him and myself.

Dave comes to his window then, presses his forehead to it, his hands shading the sides of his eyes so he can see out. Finally, I turn my light on again and wave at him.

David says there's this new film he wants to see, asks if I want to go with him, very casual, not a big deal and so I say sure, why not, what's the film?

David says it's a surprise, which makes me wonder.

At the movie, I pay for myself even though David says he

should pay, and that's strange. More strange is the movie, *Endless Love.*

"It was your favorite book," he says.

"You remember that?" I say.

We go into the theater, Cokes and popcorn between us.

"How could I forget?" he says. David is going both ways on his face, a smile on his mouth but that right eye tick that means he's serious, and goose bumps run a race over my skin, up my arms, and meet between my shoulder blades.

We find seats off to the side, sit down, act normal but I chatter on and on about nothing and eat popcorn like I'm starving.

Thank God the theater gets dark and the previews start.

I sink down low, knees up on the seat in front of me and from the side of my eye, I watch David.

He's very cute, high cheekbones, straight nose, dark hair, and eyes this green color that changes based on what he wears.

He looks down like he knows I'm watching him and I shift my eyes to the screen.

Endless Love turns out to be a very bad film to see with a friend. During the opening scene, filmed in blue, the boy crawls into the bedroom window of his girl and in no time, the two are completely undressed, wrapped up in sheets, a shoulder here, a bare leg there, and they are doing it. I mean there is no doubt about it.

I can barely watch, squirming in my seat.

David looks down at me and I roll my eyes like *Can you believe this stupid stuff?*

He reaches over then, puts his hand over mine, fingers pressed between my fingers.

I look at his hand over my hand.

This is fine; this is just a couple of good friends holding hands.

I look up at him again, *Oh my goodness—what are you doing?* and in that quiet way of his, the reflection of the film in his eyes, David leans over and presses his lips to mine.

I haven't been kissed in a long time—seems like forever—and my vow to be a good girl disappears in the softness of his mouth that tastes like salt.

This is no first kiss, at least not for me, and the way he kisses back, I don't think it's his either. His mouth moves on mine, just right, and his hand moves flat over my stomach and around my waist.

Chills race around my body faster than cars on a Los Angeles freeway.

I lift my hand to David's face, tracing to the soft part of his cheek along the cheekbone to his ear.

If a kiss could be music, this one would be a symphony.

It a kiss could be a season, this one would be spring.

If a kiss could be one word, this one would be perfect.

David actually looks surprised when he stops and looks into my eyes. He rests his forehead against mine, moves his nose back and forth over my nose like *Hey, I know you,* and then he puts his hand on the side of my face, the same way I touch him. We don't laugh out loud but I swear I can hear the sound of laughter in the smile on his face.

Just after my seventeenth birthday, Dad and Mom say the no driver's license restriction is finally over. Dad picks me up after school one afternoon, takes me in for the written test, the driving test and then to get my photo taken. He even lets me drive his new van home from the Department of Motor Vehicles. It's all so nice of him, I'm in a state of shock.

"Thanks a lot," I say, driving extra careful.

"Maybe you won't screw it up this time," he says.

I look over at him.

"Pay attention to the road," he says, cigarette in his hand, pointing at the road.

I hold the steering wheel at 2 and 10, like the driver's manual says to do, and watch the road.

His new van is a stripped-down-to-the-metal kind, just two seats up front and the back as hollow as a soda can.

"The only reason I drove by myself before," I say, "is because you wouldn't teach me."

"You couldn't see," he says.

"I could after I got glasses," I say.

Dad pushes his cigarette out the side window, lights another one, and then hooks his head.

"Pull over," he says.

"Why?" I say.

"You're making me too damn nervous," he says.

"You said I could drive home," I say.

"Just pull over," he says. Dads sucks hard on the cigarette like it's pure oxygen.

I ease to the curb and shift to park.

"What did I do?"

He blows cigarette smoke out in a narrow stream at the windshield, little eyes squinted. "I don't need a reason," he says. "Just switch."

He opens his door and goes around the front of the van. I unbuckle my belt and cross over the wide, empty space from the driver's side to the passenger's side. Dad gets in on his side, shifts his butt back and forth in the seat like he's reclaiming his territory. I roll my eyes and look out the side window.

"Don't get all pissy," he says.

"You said I could drive home."

"Well, now you can't," he says. He moves the shifter into drive and looks into his side mirror.

"Don't forget your signal," I say.

"You'd better watch yourself," he says.

He pulls into the road and drives off faster than the speed limit.

I look over at his profile, white hair now, a nothing of a chin, little blue eyes set close together.

The great thing about Dad is how consistent he is. I can always rely on him to be a jerk.

How many times has he flat out told me I'm living with them on pure luck? That if it weren't for them, I'd be on the streets of L.A.?

Each year I get older, his story of what might have happened to me gets more extreme. A couple of years ago, I would still be on the streets begging for money. Last year, I'd still be on the streets and probably hooked on dope. Now I'm seventeen, I'd still be on the streets, hooked on dope *and* a prostitute.

I don't even listen when he says that anymore, ever since my talk with Aunt Georgia; I know it's a lie anyway, and besides, it doesn't matter. He's not my father; he never wanted to be and he never will be. At times like this, I go right to my own father in my mind; smiling, driving, wearing a sweater, and looking down to make sure I'm okay.

I may not be driving, but I do finally have a driver's license. I am going to get my own car and a job to pay for it, and in one more year, I am out of here.

I look out the windshield then and cross my arms over my stomach.

Yes, I would say that I'm doing okay.

✦ ✦ ✦

David's room has a twin bed with a navy blue bedspread. From what I can tell, he makes it every day. Under his window is a set of shelves that hold books about cars and airplanes, airplane models, and a piggybank that looks like a safe with its own combination.

In his room, we've listened to his favorite albums, Chicago, John Denver, James Taylor, and I think I've shocked him with how fearless I am about this whole thing. I've been here before; I'm not afraid at all.

"I Don't Want to Be Lonely Tonight" plays on his turntable, and of course you can touch me there, and you know what? I'll just lift your shirt right off your body and throw it over there in the corner.

David's body is wide shoulders, narrow hips, long legs and he moves like water, quiet and cautious. He has his own rhythm that runs deep and takes time.

Something about him has shifted me into that place I wanted to be with Luke but never was. I feel so much for David that I might burst from it. I know this is being in love and more than being in love, it's like being awake to the possibility that you never even considered before.

On the south side of our house is a cord of wood for the woodstove.

Black widow spiders live in that pile, red hourglass on the inside of their black hourglass bodies. They will run after you if you get too close.

It's my job to chop the wood and bring it into the house, and Dad says I shouldn't complain because this new axe he bought practically does all the work for me.

The new axe has this little gadget at the end that forces the wood apart once you lodge the main blade in but Dad's wrong;

it is hard work. I hate to cut wood. I'm scared to death I'm going to swing wrong and cut into my leg and I hate those spiders. I check each log over before I split it in half and then half again, and if there's a spider on it, I'll throw the whole thing five feet off and scream at the same time.

Dad calls me a pussy girl.

"Up yours," I say, not to Dad, never to Dad, but as I raise and then drop the axe into another log, I say those words to the wood, to the spiders, to myself.

It's one thing to be strong when you are awake, but at night, in my dreams, the spiders are always there now.

I can even feel them move between the sheets, can see them crawl right to me, spider legs on my hand, then my arm, and when I have that dream, I'm scared wide awake and out of my bed.

There's a free clinic near Mead where you can get birth control pills for eight dollars a pack. The pill is supposed to be 99.8 percent effective.

On my first visit, I talk with a doctor, explain how I'm not sexually active but there's a chance I will be, soon.

She gives me three months' worth of the purple packages and a prescription for another nine months. There are warnings about not missing a day and about if I do, what that means. She tells me to start taking them when my cycle ends, use the whole pack, stop for seven days and start up again.

It's amazingly easy, so matter of fact.

I leave the clinic, packets of pills in my purse, and in the car, I take them out and look. The package is purple and on the cover is a design of a butterfly and a flower, the butterfly just about to land.

I have a job now, part-time secretary for a real estate company that is part of a work–study program at school and I'm buying the Volkswagen from Mom and Dad on this payment plan they set up. They practically take every dime I make for the payments and the insurance but I have enough money for my prescription and even to save for the day I move out.

One more year.

I put the three packages of pills back into my purse and start up the car.

One more year and I'll be free.

That spring, Grandma and Grandpa Lauck move from Reno and into the lower floors of our house.

Mom is all excited about the move, says Grandpa can golf at the course nearby and Grandma can get all the paperback romances she wants at the library at Seven Mile.

Dad renovates the house to fit them in, makes a bedroom and bathroom by the laundry and finishes the basement with sheetrock and carpet.

All their things are moved in by May: green Barcaloungers, the shiny green globe lamp, the big table that sits between their chairs, green plaid sofa. Right away, they are into their old routine; mornings with sourdough toast and Mr. Coffee coffee, afternoons with cocktail hour and Merv Griffin, and then, plug in the fake fireplace at dinnertime, all six of us together in the dining room.

Whenever we can, Kimmy and I go down to their basement living room.

Kimmy sits curled up on Grandpa's lap, Grandpa's big arm around her shoulders. He tickles and teases and she soaks up all the attention.

I sit on the green plaid sofa, close to Grandma and catch her up on everything: David, drill team, my job, and my grades, which hold steady at a B average.

"You can do better than a B," Grandpa says.

Grandpa's glasses take in the shine of the light from the green globe lamp and he's just the same: bald on top, wide around his middle, and the color of his eyes that remind me so much of my father.

"Math is killing my average," I say, "and I bombed in chemistry."

Grandma sits with her legs curled under her tropical print dress, white hair cut short like a man's. "Bryan was an honor student," she says.

"And he's keeping a 4.0 in college," Grandpa says.

"Seminary college, no less," Grandma says.

"Much harder than secular schools," Grandpa says.

"What's an honor student?" Kimmy says.

"Straight A's," Grandpa says, a tickle into her stomach, and Kimmy giggles and squirms around.

On top of their television is a high school graduation photo of Bryan and he has that smug straight-A look on his face.

"Bryan is brilliant," I say, "I'm a mere mortal."

Grandma laughs and shakes her head, reaching over to pat my arm.

"Don't sell yourself short," she says. "You are very clever."

"Are you kidding me?" David says. "You are joking, right?"

"I am not kidding," I say. "I wouldn't joke about this."

"Jeez, Jenny," David says, face gone more serious than I've ever seen, a tick in both the right and the left eye.

We are in my car, driving to school through the winding roads of Bigelow Gulch and this might have been the wrong time to bring it up.

David actually looks scared over there in the passenger seat, all the color drained from his face.

"I'm sorry, David," I say, trying to take his hand.

He moves away fast, turning in his seat, his back against the door.

"And you went to get these pills?" he says.

"The pill," I say. "I heard about it from Rondi—you know, Rondi from drill team?"

"God," he says, shaking his head like a cat does when it gets wet. "You didn't tell her about this, did you?"

"Of course not," I say.

I put both hands on the steering wheel then, cold from the way he didn't take my hand, mad at the way he acts.

It's quiet in the car except for the music playing low on the radio.

David clears his throat and shifts around in his seat, the cold shoulder.

There's been a change in him—not a big one, because he's not like that—but a change of sorts I can feel more than see.

It started just after I told him I loved him, the words out loud between us in his little bedroom, a shock on David's face that hurt my heart. I backpedalled, tried to make a joke, but then David took my hand, kissed the lines of my palm, and looked at me, dead serious, tick in his right eye.

"I love you too," he said.

Since then, Grandma and Grandpa moved in, I've been working all the time, but when I try to see him, there's no more time to be alone because he's flanked by his two buddies, Mike and Tim, the three of them rebuilding the engine of David's Nova.

I've been scrambling to get him back—thought this would get his attention but apparently not and it stings like a million pins being pushed into the back of my neck.

"You know what?" I say. "Forget it. Forget the whole thing,

forget I brought it up, and you know what, forget us—just forget it."

I shut my mouth before I say *Forget it* one more time and hold my hands so tight on the steering wheel, my knuckles hurt.

I feel him watch me but don't look his way, make a big show of ignoring him, turning up the radio as if I want to hear a commercial for Zip's Hamburgers; "Tuesday is Belly Busters for a buck."

We go the rest of the way in silence and at the school, I pull up to the drop off curb, wait for him to get out.

"We should talk about this," he says.

"No," I say, finally looking over at him. "We should not talk about it. Get out."

He moves his jaw a little, side to side, that tick in his right eye. I look away from him, *Get out of my car* still on my face and when he gets out, I grind the gears and drive away.

The far off ring of the telephone wakes me out of a deep sleep where I was dreaming of being under warm water with my eyes open.

I blink in the dark of my own room like I don't know where I am or what day it is. Around the edges of the shade I pulled down over my window is bright sunlight that reminds me of everything. David, this morning, me coming home and crawling into bed.

The telephone stops ringing and then it's the sound of Grandma's ring against the metal handrail as she comes up the steps.

"Jenny?" she calls in a rough voice, "are you up there?"

Even though I don't want to get up, I do, smoothing my shirt and jeans.

"Yeah," I say, opening the door of my room, "I'm here."

Grandma leans over the railing of the steps and looks up at me, bright blue eyes behind her glasses, white hair cut short like a man's, tropical print dress.

"I didn't know you were home," she says.

I go down to where she is and comb my fingers through my hair. "I wasn't feeling good, so I came back from school."

She stands so small compared to me—smaller, because she's down a couple of steps.

"Your young man is on the phone," she says.

"He is?"

"I guess he's calling from school," she says.

I take a deep breath and wouldn't it be nice if she knew what was going on, got on the telephone to David and said, "Jenny does not want to speak with you, so kindly stop calling her anymore. Good-bye."

Grandma Lauck, such a good Catholic, so thrilled that Bryan is in seminary, would die if she knew what I proposed to that young man today, would send me straight to church for confession if she had any idea of what I've been doing with him across the street. If Grandma knew anything about the real me, I'm sure I'd be packed up and sent to the nearest convent. No questions asked.

I put my hand on top of her hand, the feel of her skin so delicate and dry. "Thanks," I say. "I'll pick up the phone in the kitchen."

Grandma puts her other hand on top of mine then, holding on.

"It's hard to be young sometimes, isn't it?" she says.

I just nod my head, her words so true they actually hurt.

The same way I drove this morning, I go back to school to pick up David. On the phone, he was irritated I left to begin with, says I'm acting too emotional, that running away is not the way to work out a problem. He was all stern and serious, part father, part big brother.

I wanted to say *Up yours, David* and hang up the telephone, but then he said, "I love you Jenny," and what could I do?

I drive the back route to the school, radio on loud and in the rearview mirror, I see my own face is messed up and wrong. My hair is wild, mascara is under my eyes and it's so clear I've been crying.

I look at the road, then look in the mirror again and wipe the mascara from under my eyes. I look at the road again, look in the mirror, and comb my hair down with my fingers again.

When I look at the road again, it's one of those tight corners and I'm going too fast. I take my foot off the gas, brake a little, and coming my way is a truck, a big black truck. We pass each other, close, way too close. I come around the corner too tight, slide a little on the slick road and try to steer out, only it's too late.

"What the hell happened?" Dad says.

"I don't know," I say. "It happened so fast. The road was slick, the pine needles were wet; I just skidded off."

"What were you doing on that road that time of day?" Mom says.

I sit in the middle of the sofa in the living room, hands on my knees, and I've told them the whole story over and over. I got sick, I came home and then went back to school when I felt better.

"Let me get this straight," Dad says. "In the middle of broad daylight, a truck runs you off the road and into the boulders."

"Not exactly," I say, looking at my hands for the right words. "I thought he was close to me and I just steered too far to the right."

Dad paces around the living room in his suit pants that are wrinkled and low around his hips and a button-up shirt that is wrinkled too and untucked from the front of his pants.

Mom has her work clothes on too and she sits in a dining-room chair, legs crossed, ashtray balanced on her lap.

"But the guy in the truck didn't stop?" Dad says, "and you didn't get his license?"

"That's right," I say.

"Bullshit," Dad says. "That is the biggest bullshit story I have ever heard." He turns his back on me, hands into his pockets.

I look at Mom, and she takes a deep breath. "Dick," Mom says, "accidents happen."

"Bullshit," Dad says. He paces the living room and stops at the sliding glass door that faces the backyard.

After the accident, I wasn't hurt, just scared. I got a ride to a telephone booth and called Dad. He didn't ask if I was okay, just yelled about the cost of a tow truck and how stupid I was. It took the rest of the day to get me and the car back to the house.

I haven't talked to David yet. What happened between us this morning seems like a million years ago.

"You are off our policy as of now," Dad says to the sliding glass door, "and you are paying every damn dime to fix that car."

"Isn't that what my insurance is for?" I say, hands out wide.

Dad turns around then, dark circles under his small eyes. "Not in this house," he says. "You are on my insurance and if this accident is reported, my rates go up." He lifts his thumb up to the ceiling to emphasize his point.

Mom holds very still, eyes from me to Dad.

I close my own hands into fists. "I paid for that insurance," I say.

"This is my house," he says. "I pay the bills; these are my rules."

"Dick," Mom says.

He points at her then and that's different. Dad isn't much of a pointer. "It's about time she learned a thing or two about the real world," he says. "Goddamn ingrate doesn't know how good she has it here."

Here it comes: *If it weren't for us, you'd be on the streets in L.A., hooked on dope, a prostitute.*

"Hell, you'd probably be dead by now," he adds on to the story, "you're so damn stupid."

"Dick!" Mom says.

I push my tongue against the inside of a back tooth and hold myself so still, eyes on his face.

"You'd better wipe that look off your face," he says. "Your ass is grass right now." He always says that right before he punishes me: *Your ass is grass and I'm the lawn mower.*

"You are going to quit your job," he says. "No car, no job."

"What?" I say.

"That's right," he says. "You can just park your butt here until you get enough money to fix that car."

"If I can't work, how do I make money?"

He rubs his hand over his own face and looks over at Mom.

Forever, there's been this thing between them, a kind of communication without words that you can pick up on by the way they hold on to each other's eyes, a series of nods between them. They do that now and it's Mom who nods the last time, like *Fine—you tell her.*

Dad tells about this elaborate plan where I am going to baby-sit Kimmy for the summer and take on another kid, whom I will get by placing an ad in the Spokane paper.

"You pay for the ad," Dad says.

Once my mini-day-care operation is underway, they will take out the cost of food, the rental of the house for the hours I watch the kids, and in the end, after three months, I should earn just enough to pay for the damage to the car. I will have learned my lesson and will be a better person for the whole experience.

I listen and even though I'm here, I have such a strange feeling at the back of my head, as if I'm going to explode out of myself through some trapdoor back there.

With the plan all laid out, they are both quiet, watching me, waiting. Past how incredibly unfair it is, I'm struck by the complexity of the whole thing. It's like they had this all worked out way before I crashed the car into a rock and were just waiting for the chance to get a summer of free child care that also turns out to be a moneymaking venture. What a deal. I watch their child and pay them at the same time.

Mom's cigarette smoke lifts in a cloud around her face and to the ceiling. Dad bums a cigarette off her, lighting up in the silence of the living room.

I wouldn't expect more from Dad—he's always been like this, tight with money and mean-hearted—and so I look past Dad at Mom, who sits so prim and professional, legs crossed, pantyhose, blue polka-dot polyester blouse with the bow tied at her neck.

She knows this is wrong, I can see it in her eyes and I can't believe she would let him use me like this. I look at her like *Do the right thing here; prove you are better than he is; stand up for what is right,* but she just puts her cigarette between her lips, takes a deep inhale, and in her eyes is a look like I deserve whatever happens.

When the summer gets too hot, David likes to sleep in his basement. On the nights I baby-sit for other people, I call from the phone where I work, and he says, "I'll leave the door open."

The whole time I'm gone from the house, Mom and Dad

think I'm baby-sitting for this family or that family, and technically it's not a lie. I do baby-sit but I know they don't care when I come home. It's not like they ever wait up for me. All they care about is that I have a twenty-dollar bill for them come morning.

It's always late when I leave my baby-sitting jobs, midnight or later, but instead of going home, I go around the back of David's house. Like he promised, the door is open.

His dad isn't here anymore; he was stationed somewhere in Asia—Okinawa, I think. It's supposed to be this one-year mission and then he's going to retire early.

David's mom and sister are upstairs, two levels above the basement. David says they sleep like logs.

It's been a very strange summer. When you are on every possible kind of restriction and watching a little kid who will tell on you for just about anything, things have a way of cooling off.

Then David's dad left and David pulled me back into his world with these deep felt letters that said he missed me and that he was sorry and wrong and he mixed up his words with lyrics to his favorite songs.

In the basement, the only light comes from his black and white television, flicker shadows that move on the basement walls and around the shape of him in a sleeping bag.

Curled on his side, hand under his face, dark lashes against his skin, David looks like a little boy.

There's a cracking sound in the joints of my knees as I squat down to watch him in a way I can't when he's awake. I look at all of him, the width of his forehead, the line from his jaw to his chin, the shape of his nose. I memorize his features and the fine quality to the shape of his face, the length of his eyelashes, the softness of his lips.

As far as I can fall into another person, I'm into David. He's probably my best friend—at least I think of him that way. I've told him every secret I have and I have a lot of secrets. David has told me his too. I know how he can't talk about things the way he wants to, that he gets these deep nervous feelings inside his stomach that sometimes feels like acid eating away at him, that he feels responsible for taking care of his mother and sister, and that right now he misses his father so much it aches in his body.

As if he knows I'm there watching him, David opens his eyes fast and looks up at me, a slow smile moving over his face.

"There you are," he whispers.

He unzips his sleeping bag and I shrug out of my sweater and kick off my sandals.

David pulls me into his warm, sleepy body, and I go there as easy as going under water. He presses his face against that space between my neck and shoulder, breathes deep, and moves his hands up the back of my shirt, fingers spread wide and pressed down. Under his hands, I can feel every bone of my ribs, my spine, my shoulders.

The first time hurt, a lot. No one tells you about that kind of pain. They certainly don't write about it in any of those stupid romance books.

David says it was his fault, too rushed, too nervous, and ever since, he says he's on a mission to redeem himself.

That makes me laugh. I don't know why; probably because he's so sincere.

Now there's no pain at all, none, and there's a dreamlike quality to the slow way his hands outline my body. I trust him and follow his lead, my hands up his back, out to his shoulders, around his neck, down his chest, stomach, and hips.

There is no sound at all except my breathing mixed with

his, the kicking in of the heater that makes David stop like a cat to listen and then relax back to me.

Sometimes it makes me cry, not the pain, just the wave of love for another person, I guess. David kisses my face when that happens, like he understands, and I wish I could just crawl inside the person he is and leave myself behind.

When summer ends, I do not see a dime of the money I worked for. Big surprise. Instead, Dad goes through a series of car exchanges.

He switches my Volkswagen with another red one, a little older one with an electrical problem. Then he trades that car for an old Audi that doesn't run right, and after that, he says he's got a line on a great deal from a guy he works with.

I get a new job with another real estate company, better pay, and every time I get a few dollars into my checking account, Dad wants me to write him another check for the car of the week.

One day, out of the blue, this guy named Red shows up with a green dog of a car. AMC Hornet. 1973. It is the most unattractive car I have ever seen, this big hulk of metal with no shape, no personality, no style.

Red is this stubble-faced guy in a baseball cap, folds of skin under his eyes and around his jaw.

"She's going to love this car, Red," Dad says. "Aren't you, Jenny?"

I lean my shoulder into the door frame of the big garage door and cross my arms.

Red grins and rubs his hand over the green hood.

"I hope you'll be half as happy as I have been with her," he says.

"I'm sure she will," Dad says in his best good-ole-boy voice.

He talks to Red about car things, maintenance, rotation of the tires and then Dad directs his talk at me, says I have to write a check for the great new tires Red put on.

My eyes shift from the ugly car to Dad and I hold myself extra still. "Excuse me?" I say.

"I already told you," he says, good-ole-boy smile fading. "Write Red a check for these great tires."

I shake my head then. "You never said anything about tires."

Dad shifts his eyes to Red, who isn't grinning anymore and Dad shakes his head like *She's confused* and laughs a little.

"Go in the house, get your checkbook and write a check for Red."

I stand off the door frame then and I don't want to be rude, so I smile as I speak."I don't think so."

"Dick," Red said, "if this is a problem . . ."

"There's no problem," Dad says. "Jenny, get in there and write a goddamned check."

Red looks nervous and his eyes shift back and forth between Dad and me.

There's no use in being polite anymore so I stop smiling. "You're the one who wants this car," I say. "You pay him."

I can feel their eyes on me as I go through the garage and back into the house.

In the kitchen, Mom stands in front of the refrigerator, looking at everything in there, a pad of paper in her hand.

"I do not want that car," I say.

She closes the refrigerator door. "Now, Jenny," she says. "Dick has gone to a lot of trouble to get a car for you."

"I never asked for his help," I say.

The door from the garage opens then, Dad big in the open

rectangle of space and he slams the door behind him so hard it shakes the microwave oven that sits on the counter.

He comes at me then, as big as a bear. I back up against the counter until I can't move any further.

Dad gets into my face, small eyes squinted in his small head, jaw set tight and in a deep kind of growl, he says I've embarrassed him in front of his friend and that I'd better write him a check.

Hands on the counter behind me, I hold on.

"I'm not giving you another dime," I say, my words slow, one after the other and before they are even out of me, he grabs the front of my shirt and yanks me up to him, my feet almost off the floor.

I know I should be scared right now, but I'm not. I'm just fed up with him and this game we've been playing. I'm sick of it.

"Hit me!" I yell. "Go ahead, hit me!"

"No!" Mom yells. "Stop it, both of you! Stop now!"

Dad breathes bitter coffee and cigarette on my face.

He opens his hand then and drops me to the floor, my butt hitting hard. He yells that I have to pay him back and this is going to be my car.

He slams the back door again, the sound of it in the walls of the kitchen and the space where he was is empty but still filled with all that anger, as clear as heat rising from a hot pan.

I sit on the floor, hands flat on the indoor-outdoor carpet and everything is very quiet. Part of me wants to scream after him, call him a fucking coward but there's no use in pushing it.

Mom is quiet, eyes wide, mouth open too. She looks down at me then, blinks back to normal. "He could have killed you," she says, no air in her voice.

My palms are skinned and I blow on them, rub them together, blow again. "He doesn't have the guts," I say.

"Jenny!" she says. "What's gotten into you? What are you thinking?"

I stand up, pulling wrinkles out of my shirt, rubbing at the back of my neck that is stiff all the way down to my shoulders.

This is way more honesty and reality than she can take but for me, it's like a sweet breath of fresh air. At least we are being honest, finally, and if she can't figure it out, I'm not going to waste my time trying to explain.

I turn away from her then, go out of the kitchen and up the steps to my room.

Dad lost his job at Sears.

Mom says he was screwed by the corporate system.

Dad says it was a layoff.

Grandma and Grandpa say he was fired only they whisper it so the sound is like the hiss of snakes.

We sit in their basement and since the big fight, that's the way it is now. I'm either down here, in my room, or at my new job. I stay away from Mom and Dad, and they stay away from me.

I could care less about Dad losing his job, fired, laid off, whatever. I'm trying to figure out where to apply to school and what my major should be. My aptitude tests from school have my talent boiled down to two categories: art—dance, painting, drawing; and writing: creative, nonfiction, journalism.

I thought I could make a good interior decorator but there's nothing about that on the test. There's no way I'm going to be a dancer—too late for that now—so I guess I could think about writing. I love to read. Why not?

For about a year now, Dad and Mom have been saying I

should go into the military. Mom says I could see the world. Dad says that after four years, I get my college for free.

"Well, you are going to college," Grandma says, "of course."

"Absolutely," I say, "but where? Washington or California? And then, what should I study?"

They are set up with vodka martinis and a plate of crackers and cheese. I am on the green plaid sofa, closest to Grandma and I sit forward, elbows on my knees. On the television is *Wheel of Fortune* and some guy just won a boat. On top of the television is a new photo of Bryan in a black turtleneck sweater and a tan blazer. He's majoring in philosophy now, but from that photo, he looks like he's always looked, smug and smart and perfect.

"In state will be cheaper," Grandma says.

"And closer," Grandpa says, "so we can see you."

"You could even live at home," Grandma says.

I look at them. How do I say, *There is no way I'm living here any longer than I have to?* It's already too long to stay until next June, when I graduate.

"Money shouldn't be a problem," I say. "Mom has been saving money for school for years but maybe I should apply to just Washington schools, like WSU and UW."

Grandpa sips his drink and listens to me talk, eyes over his glasses and on my face. "Are you sure about that?" he says.

"About what?" I say.

"About the money for school," he says. "Are you sure you're all taken care of?"

There's such a strange feeling to the room as if he knows something that I do not want to even think about.

"Mom promised to save money for my school," I say.

Grandma picks up her cigarette that is almost burned to the end and takes a deep inhale, looking across the table at Grandpa. "Ed?" Grandma says then.

I roll my lips together and sit back in the sofa.

Grandpa puts his martini on the table, turning the glass around and around, eyes down at the ice cubes there. When he looks up, he makes himself smile over at me.

"I'm sure she did, then," Grandpa says.

Grandma nods quick, like she agrees.

David and his mom and sister have been gone for a whole month. They went to Okinawa to see his dad and when he comes back, I have so much to tell him I feel like I might explode. The thing is, he doesn't call me, he doesn't cross the street, and if I see him at school, he's flanked by Mike and Tim again. "Oh yeah, hi. I'm kind of busy; I'll call you later," he says, rushing past me.

There's such a bad feeling inside of me, since I remember avoiding Luke the same way and I remember why I did it but then I tell myself this can't be the same. David and me are in love with each other, we've been together in ways Luke and I never were and so, instead of making a big deal out of it, I just wait.

It's almost two weeks before he does get around to me. I'm downstairs with Grandma and Grandpa, filling out applications for Washington State University, Eastern, and the University of Washington.

"Jenny," Kimmy yells down the stairs, "David is here."

Grandma is curled in her chair and she eats her olive off her toothpick. "Is that your young man?" she says.

"Yeah," I say.

Grandpa is just back from golf and he's all relaxed in his lounger chair, the footrest up, his drink empty.

"Want me to fix you guys another drink?" I say.

"That would be lovely," Grandma says, "but what about your friend?"

"It'll just take a second," I say, getting up and taking their glasses.

I need something to do with my hands anyway, a way to look calm and cool. I go up the steps to the front door and David is out on the stoop with his hands in the pockets of his jeans.

I'm happy to see him, really happy, only I try not to look that way. "Hey," I say, "what are you doing out there? You can come in."

Kimmy, watching TV in the family room, yells up at us. "He didn't want to come in."

"You don't want to come in?" I say.

He shakes his head, "I thought we could talk," he says. "Maybe we can take a walk."

I stand in the entryway, two glasses in my hand, and I look down like I don't know what they are for. "I have to get them a couple of drinks," I say, clearing my throat.

"I'll wait," he says.

He met another girl—I bet that's it.

No, that's not it.

He's moving to Okinawa.

Maybe that's it and he just doesn't know how to say it.

My hands shake making the drinks, one shot of vodka, ice, water and toothpicks with olives.

Quick, quick, I take the drinks down to their living room, and they both smile at me, say "thank you," and I say I'll see them later.

David sits on the porch and when I come out he stands up quick.

"Okay," I say, "what's up?"

David looks right, left, and clears his throat. "Let's walk," he says.

"Okay," I say.

It's one of those days where you can still feel summer even though it's fall. We go over the lawn to the main road and walk around the corner. While we walk, we talk about his trip, his dad, but David is different. Polite.

We go down the hill below David's house and he says, "Let's go up there," pointing to this tree that grows sideways from the hill. It seems stupid to climb up the soft sand of the hill but David wants to, so we go. He climbs up on the tree trunk, swings his legs over, sits like it's a bench, and I do too, like this is totally normal.

"I like to come here sometimes," he says, "you know, to think."

I look out from where we sit and the sun is out on the horizon, blue sky, tall pine trees.

"It's pretty," I say.

He looks down, arranging his face and when he looks up at me, there's that little tick in his right eye.

I've never been dumped before but that's what this is. David has a speech all prepared about how we are too serious, that we need to date other people and have fun. They are words out of his mouth but they don't seem like his. David says that when he was in Okinawa, his dad gave him this "you're young, you should be having the time of your life, there's plenty of time later to be serious with one girl" pep talk. David almost apologizes for his dad, but then he says, "I think he's right."

A rush of wind blows up the hill and birds call to each other.

When they say your heart gets broken, it's kind of true, but it's worse. If your heart just broke, there would at least be tiny pieces you could sweep up somehow. My heart curls on itself like a dead leaf in the autumn sunlight and then breaks up into impossibly small pieces before blowing away.

I don't even know I cry but the tears are there, down my face and on my hands. I remember when I tried to end it with Luke and how he cried like this. I remember feeling so sorry for him and there's no way I want David to feel sorry for me. I push off the log then and go down the hill as fast as I can, feet sliding on the sand, some of it getting into my shoes.

When I get to the road, I walk as fast as I can, head down, David back there, who cares where.

In our house, afternoon sun comes through the windows and dust floats in the beams of light. The television is still on in the family room but Kimmy isn't there now. I can hear her down in the basement with Grandma and Grandpa, that sound of her laughter.

Dad's out working at some temp job today.

Mom will be home in an hour.

In 30 minutes, I'm supposed to start dinner.

Whatever was supposed to be is gone though, and it's an effort just to stand up, my hands on the edge of the counter, an empty ache in my whole body.

This is the kind of thing you need a really good friend for, a best friend but David was my best friend.

Tears fall on the countertop like raindrops. How could I make such a mistake? How could I have been so stupid? How could I fall so far into another person that way, trusting him? When will I ever learn. He didn't love me, he probably just said it to be nice and now I'm so embarrassed I want to die.

I put my hands over my whole face, shoulders shaking with a fresh run of tears and I'm on the wrong edge of myself where if I let it happen, I could cry and cry and maybe never stop.

As hard as I can, I push against my own face—stop it right now.

Taking in a deep breath that hurts, I yank a paper towel off the roll, blowing my nose loud in the kitchen.

The afternoon sun is just at the top of David's house now, a bright light that makes me squint. This doesn't matter. I don't need him, I don't.

On the counter is the big gallon of vodka I left out after making their drinks and the sun shining through the kitchen window reflects through the bottle that's smudged with fingerprints.

Looking across the street again, I throw the balled-up paper towel on the counter and open the cabinet to get a glass.

It's not good to drink three glasses of the vodka without so much as an olive in your stomach and after I finally wake up facedown on my bed, my stomach tells me this truth. I throw up until there's nothing more to throw up, and even so, I keep right on going.

Mom thinks it's the flu. Who am I to say she's wrong? I can't talk anyway.

I'm hunched over the toilet spitting out dry heaves of bitter yellow bile.

When I was really small, three, four years old, my father let me have a sip of his beer, Coors. It was a little ritual on the weekends: He'd sit in his big chair watching something on the television, drinking a cold beer and eating macadamia nuts. I fit on his lap just perfect and the smell of that chair was a cool, musty leather mixed with the smell of him. He'd let me have one sip of salty beer and a nut, the two tastes together like nothing I've ever had before.

I've never had anything else to drink.

Past those sips of beer, I've never been drunk and I certainly have never had hard liquor.

In the thick of being so sick, I see my father in my mind,

driving, smiling, and wearing a sweater. He would say this is my own fault, tell me to tough it out, pay the price, and more than that, learn a lesson.

I stay sick for two whole days and instead of feeling sorry for myself about it, I make myself go to school and to work. I drag myself through the day, throw up if I have to, and then go back to whatever I was doing.

After a couple of weeks, I'm better in my body, my head stops hurting, and David starts to call again, sending little notes across the street.

I have no desire to talk to him at all.

Just thinking about David makes me taste bile again—I guess the vodka taught me my lesson.

Grandpa turns out to be right about Mom.

They didn't save a dime for school.

All this time, more lies. Why am I surprised?

They give me the news in November and the only reason they tell me at all is because of new legislation that cuts off all Social Security benefits for kids who are not in college by March of 1982.

I'm not supposed to graduate from high school until June.

There's no money for school, my Social Security benefits that would have been available for four years of college will be gone, and guess what, I can't qualify for financial aid. Mom and Dad are my legal parents, they make too much money for me to qualify and besides, the deadline for that and scholarships is way past.

Mom is incredibly thorough when it comes to all the research to support her bad news. Too bad she wasn't that careful when she promised to save money for college, but now, she says she never made that promise, and Dad backs her up.

"We don't know what you're talking about."

Past the shock of bad news and the lie about the money, Mom has done a little more homework on my options.

She says to save my benefits, I can graduate from high school early, register at the nearby community college, and live at home to save expenses.

"You don't even have to pay rent," Dad says. "At least not until you can afford it."

When my early graduation day actually comes in January, there's no cap and gown, no ceremony, no speech from the class valedictorian. There is a dinner out at a nice restaurant, a small gathering in the basement with the six of us, and everyone gives me cards that say silly things about how real life now begins. It seems like my real life has been going for quite a while now.

When my graduation day is over, Mom and Dad and Kimmy go upstairs, Grandpa goes to bed, and I stay in the basement with Grandma. She reads a book, and when she's not looking, I turn around the photo of Bryan's face so I can watch the late movie in peace.

Grandma's cigarette burns down in her ashtray, and at the last page, she closes the book the way she always does, hand on the cover, a wet look to her eyes.

I have no idea why they make her cry—they are just so predictable—but that's it—she reads, she cries.

"Good one?" I say.

She nods, eyes watching the television. "What's this you're watching?" she says.

"That lady there has amnesia," I say, pointing at the TV,

"and that guy is her husband but she doesn't remember him."

Grandma still looks nice from the day, light pink lipstick a little worn off her lips, a pair of pearl earrings, her hair combed neat and tidy and she wears the long tropical dress I got her for Christmas last year.

She shakes off the funk of ending her book and tosses it down into the brown grocery bag where all the other finished books pile up for another run to the library.

"I have a little surprise for you," she says, hand digging along the hip of her deep pocket. She pulls out a white box and hands it my way.

Shifting up on the sofa, I look at her, at the box, and she lifts her hand a little, like *Take it.*

"You didn't have to do that," I say, taking the box and holding it with both hands.

She dusts nothing off herself. "It's not what you think," she says.

I look at the box again and then at her, the lines like a map around her face. "Thank you," I say.

"Don't thank me until you see what it is," she says, smiling even though she tries not to.

I open the box then and inside is a small pendant I've seen her wear before.

The gold is curved in the S shape of something you'd see on a musical scale, and two diamonds are set in the curves, one small, one big.

"There's a story behind that," she says, the far-off sound in her voice that she gets when she goes into the past.

"Your father gave it to me," she says, "when he started his own accounting business in Carson."

I lower the pendant into my palm and watch her talk.

"All the other young men went to work at big accounting firms," she says, "but Bud wasn't like other boys, he was a go-getter."

Grandma has told me so many stories in this basement, all of them when Grandpa is gone, all of them late at night.

She told me how my father was brilliant, always at the head of his classes, and when he was in college, he didn't even go to his classes, just showed up on the day of the test, took it, and got an A for the whole term.

She told me how he once lied about his age to get into the navy and Grandpa had to get him out before they shipped him off to the Korean War. He was drafted the next year anyway and ended up in the army, which he hated.

She told me how he married my mother, even though he knew there was something wrong with her, and how he went so deep in debt with her medical bills that according to Grandma ruined his heart and probably killed him.

In all the stories about my father, I've learned a deep truth about Grandma. He was her favorite son and his death killed her in a way. Even now, she blames herself, saying she was the one who encouraged him to marry my mother and that she could have changed his destiny by telling him not to marry her.

"He gave that pendant to me on the anniversary of his first year in business," she says.

Her lips quiver and her eyes are full of real tears that move down the lines of her face.

The diamonds sparkle up to me with the shine of his success and even though it's a nice story, part of me just feels tired. What would he think of me? Before I even leave high school, I'm a failure. I get marginal grades and now, I'm going to a community college, no money to even cover the cost of books.

Even though I love him more than I can say, sometimes it's hard to live up to his memory.

Grandma, curled up with her legs under her body, reaches for a tissue and dabs at her eyes under her glasses. "Let me put it on for you," she says, sniffing.

I let her have it then and kneel down in front of her chair as she opens the clasp and puts it around my neck.

Grandma smells like medicine and wine and cigarettes. Her hand presses over the pendant on my chest, her fingers adjusting it just right.

She smiles then, nodding like *That's right,* and I sit back on my heels, touching the pendant with my fingers. "I know he would be proud of you today," she says.

The light from their green globe lamp reflects in her glasses and it's the best thing she could ever say to me, even though I know it's not true.

As careful as I can, I hug her small, soft body and press my lips to the lines of her face. "I love you," I whisper.

PART FIVE

COLLEGE

FIVE

FALL 1982

There's only one good thing about Economics 101 and it's this blue-eyed guy with the best butt I've ever seen in a pair of 501's.

I know who he is—at least I've seen him around. He plays football, and his name is something like Larry or Lance.

Even though we don't have assigned seats, he sits next to me in class every Tuesday and Thursday. Sometimes he sits behind or in front, but never more than one seat away. He takes notes like everyone else does but every now and then, I catch him looking in my direction, lips in the beginning of a smile and a light in his blue eyes.

David is a ghost now, shadows of what could have been lost on the day he dumped me.

I've got two jobs now, one checking groceries at Yokes, the other at the real estate agency, and I'm trying to save which is not easy to do. College is expensive, books are expensive, gas and everything else, all expensive.

It's a Thursday, three weeks into class, when the blue-eyed

guy leans over at the beginning of class and whispers, "I hate this class."

I look at him, really look, and I wonder, Do I talk to him or just smile and nod?

I'm in my third trimester at Spokane Falls Community College. Everyone calls this place The Falls. I went spring and summer, and I figure I can get through in less than two years and then transfer all my credits to a university. No one will ever know I went to a junior college and if the math is right in my head, I can be out of here by fall of '83.

I sit back in my desk, take my glasses off my face, and he's pretty cute. Why not?

"I hate it too," I say, only loud, because I don't give a shit who hears me.

He smiles completely then, and his whole face changes with that smile. He has this big grin like sunshine through rain clouds.

Our economics teacher comes in the room, and he's young with blond hair that's thinning at the top. He drops his books on his desk and says, "Let's open to chapter three in your main text."

I put on my glasses again, open my book, and take out my pen.

The teacher writes something on the board, and I can feel that guy watch me.

I don't want to, but I smile at being watched, and the guy leans over again, reaches out his hand into the space between us.

"I'm Lance, by the way," he whispers.

I look at his hand between us, very professional and very direct.

I put my hand into his and he shakes it with a confidence you don't see in a lot of boys.

"Nice to meet you," I say.

I try to take my hand, but Lance holds on, like he's waiting for more. I laugh a quiet laugh and tell him my name, just my first name, and then he lets me go.

"Nice to meet you, Jennifer," he says.

Lance is from Montana, and he's the youngest of four boys. His dad is a salesman, his mom is a secretary, and his brothers are all grown and off doing their own things.

He's at The Falls on a football scholarship and he hopes to get another scholarship to a university, maybe Washington State or Eastern. After football, he wants to run his own business, be rich or at least wealthy.

Lance is nice enough, he likes to joke around and I respect that he has a plan. Not a lot of people I know have one.

We've been dating for a while now, a couple of months, but it's just casual, and tonight, we went to a university football game he wanted to see.

I drive because he doesn't have his car here, and we leave the stadium parking lot in bumper-to-bumper traffic.

Lance is different tonight, more serious than I've seen him before. For the whole game, he just watched the guys play, elbows on his knees, and on his face was such a strange expression, like the game was so important. I don't know him well enough to know what's going on, and he is pretty serious about sports, one of those intense jock types, so I just stayed quiet.

Lance sits sideways on the seat and watches me, his fingers touching the side of my neck.

I look over at him and smile. He smiles too, but it's not in his eyes.

"I don't think I'm going to get a scholarship out of here," he finally says.

"Why not?" I say.

He moves his arm off the back of the seat and into his lap.

"In case you haven't noticed," he says, "I'm pretty small."

Lance looks out the windshield and then down at his lap.

"I'm fast but short," he says.

"The season isn't even over," I say, "and you guys are doing great. You'll probably win the championship this year."

The brake lights of the car ahead go on and I stop again.

"No," Lance says, "the coaches have already been here to see us play. I didn't make the cut."

He looks straight ahead, the red of brake lights shining on his face.

Since I've known him, football has been about all Lance has talked about. He played all four years of high school, even some junior high, and a few months ago, when the year started, he said it wasn't unheard of for a guy his size to make the NFL. I don't know a thing about football and I don't care either, but I can tell this is bad for him.

I touch his arm, just this quick squeeze.

"I'm sorry, Lance," I say.

He shifts in the seat, leaning his elbow on the side of the door, face in his hand. "Ah," he says, "forget it. Who needs it anyway?"

"No," I say, "I mean it. I know it was important to you."

"Yeah," he says into his hand, "well, it was more important for my old man."

I look over at him again, but he's off somewhere else, eyes out the window.

It's finally my turn to get out of the parking lot and I make a right, driving down the curving road that gets us back to the college.

Up until now, I've been careful with Lance. We've kissed a little, just in the car, and he is a great kisser, the kind of person

I could kiss myself into big trouble with. He's asked me up to his room at the dorm, says he can have company until ten on school nights, midnight on weekends, but I laughed him off and said, "What kind of girl do you think I am?"

Lance doesn't know anything about me at all, and that's fine; I like it that way, less explaining to do, less heartache later. I like being with him, but I like keeping myself from him too—it's safe—but here in the car, there's a shift in me, a softening maybe, like I want to do something, anything to put him right and turn him back into Mr. Confident Jock.

His dorm is in this historic part of the school where the trees are planted in tight rows that make a canopy over the road and I pull in front of his building.

The leaves are almost gone now, but a few still hang on up there, spinning in the wind. Through their bare branches there are stars in the black sky, and the moon is almost full, an edge of it shaved away to the dark.

Right about now, Lance usually puts his arm out and I scoot over. We'll kiss until my body gets that warm liquid feel and he starts to move his hand up the back of my shirt. Then it's, "Now, now, we'd better get ahold of ourselves," a few embarrassed coughs, and the adjustment of clothing.

Lance says good night, I say good night, and that's it.

Tonight, though, I turn off my car, take my keys out of the ignition, and hold them in my hand.

"So you can have company until ten?" I say.

For a second, Lance looks surprised, but he smiles it away with one of his big grins. "Midnight," he says.

I nod and he nods.

"Midnight is good," I say.

"Yeah," he says, "midnight is very good."

He nods and I nod, and I bet he's been with other girls before. Of course he has, maybe Montana girls who are wild and open and free like the big sky he's always talking about.

There's a little warning bell that goes off inside me, *Caution, warning! What about your promise to be good?*

I look at my hands, at my keys, and toss them back and forth.

Lance reaches across to me then, catches my keys midtoss, and holds them still in his own hand.

"Come on up," he says.

At first Lance is all embarrassed that his room is a mess. "I didn't expect company," he says. He picks up dirty clothes, straightens his bed, and fluffs his pillow.

I take off my jacket, toss it over the back of a chair. "Don't worry about it," I say.

His room has a narrow bed pushed in the corner where there are two big rectangle windows without curtains or shades. There are high ceilings, walls painted white, and an old fireplace. Lance has a football helmet in the space where logs would go.

I push my hands into the pockets of my jeans.

He clicks on a lamp by his bed, turns on his clock radio, switching around for music and then stops at what sounds like rock.

At his dresser, I touch over his things, a red toothbrush with white crusty toothpaste around the head, a black comb, a flat bottle of something called Skin Bracer. I open the bottle and that's what makes him smell so nice. Who would have known? Skin Bracer.

There's a circle of warm light by his bed that's made all neat and tidy now. The rest of the room is white with moonlight, a few shadows from the trees over the hardwood floor and across the bed.

Lance stands a few feet from me, and his body has this wound-tight quality, like he might just burst into a fast run or drop to do a few push ups. He stands there, so still, but wound tight at the same time, not sure what to do next.

That's okay, I'm not sure either.

Over his dresser, photos are pushed in around the edges of his mirror. I look closer at one in the corner.

"Your folks?" I say.

Lance comes to the mirror.

"Yeah," he says, "that was a ski trip, at Bozeman."

He's so close I can smell his Skin Bracer, clean and sharp. I look at him and he looks at me, moving his hand over his mouth.

I hold my arms tighter around myself and look at the photo again.

The man in the picture looks exactly like Lance only he's a bear of a man, he's huge—or maybe it's just how his mom is so small. I'm not sure. They both have big, outdoor smiles on their faces, and behind them is a mountain covered with snow.

"Did you tell your dad yet?" I say. "About football?"

Lance reaches to me then, barely touching the lower part of my back. "No," he says. "They are coming next week though, I'll tell him then." He moves his other hand around my waist, eyes on my mouth. "Maybe you can meet them," he says.

He shifts me so we are hip to hip, chest to chest, face to face.

"You might not want me to meet your parents, Lance," I say.

"Why not?" he says, stepping in a little closer to me.

I lick my lips. Where do I start?

"Well," I say, "here I am in your room, at all hours. I'm sure this isn't what they intended for your education."

He laughs a little.

"Oh, I want them to meet you," he says, voice very low, breath on my face.

Lance moves one hand behind my neck, the way he likes to do, and pulls me the rest of the way.

We kiss in front of his parents' smiling faces. No one has made me feel like this since David, only this time, I'm not in love.

I move my hands down his chest, under his shirt, and then flat all the way up, my fingers on his warm skin.

Who says you have to be in love anyway?

I lift his shirt with my arms, breaking off the kiss to take it the rest of the way over his head.

"What would your parents think of this?" I say, smiling and dropping his shirt on the floor.

He clears his throat and tries to be serious even though he's smiling. "Well, my father would be very proud," he says, kissing me at the same time.

"Really?" I say. I unbutton my sweater, shrugging it off my shoulders, and Lance helps me pull it off. "And your mom?" I say.

"Well," he says, dropping my sweater on the floor, hands on my shoulders again.

I lift my T-shirt off, nothing under it but my bare skin, and he rolls his lips together.

"You think she'd like me?" I say.

Lance breathes in deep, his chest filling with air, and he touches his palms to the shape of me.

I move my arms over his shoulders and close my eyes.

"Yes, Jennifer," he says, pressing his mouth to my chest, "I think she'd like you a lot."

He moves his hands all the way around my back, and it's like I'm starved for being close to someone, for being touched, and Lance is the same, almost urgent in the way his mouth holds on to mine.

I push him back to the bed.

He goes, kicking his shoes off.

I'm not supposed to do this. He is.

Girls are supposed to be innocent and pure. Boys are supposed to get laid.

Girls hold out for "the one." Boys go out and sow wild oats. Who made those rules anyway?

I sit on the edge of his bed, kick out of my own shoes, pull him down and he snaps off the light next to his bed and lays his weight over me.

Lance and I are legs and arms, around and around, and in this space before, the possibility is as perfect as a new day. David is still on the edges, the way he moved and talked and smiled, the green color of his eyes and the slow touch of his hand, but as Lance moves, more confident, more aggressive, it's a new rhythm, not better, not worse, just different.

I move the way I've always moved, matching my rhythm to the person I'm with, but this time, I'm different too.

Pushing him onto his back, I move over him.

I'm still on the pill. I told myself it was easier to stay on than go off, but maybe this is the reason. Maybe I stayed on so I can finally find my own rhythm.

On my elbows, I look down at Lance's face, the shadows of tree branches over the top of his head. Under me, he is wound tight and so strong.

"I'm on the pill," I whisper.

"You are?" he says. The look on his face is pure surprise and then, something else, maybe gratitude or thankfulness or just pure joy. I almost laugh at his expression, and I want to ask what his parents would think of that, but we're past jokes now.

For just a second, my own father is in my mind, smiling, driving, and wearing a sweater. All this talk about Lance's parents and he never asked about mine.

Lance gathers me closer to him and rolls me over on my back.

I close my eyes on my father, smiling and driving, and right now, I don't even care what he would think.

Lance pulls his blankets over us and lies close to me, his arm over my stomach.

Regret is all over my skin, in the cooling of our bodies, and maybe disappointment too. I figured he'd know more about this whole physical thing than me, but when it's all said and done, I guess he doesn't.

It was too fast, too new, and maybe it wasn't such a great idea after all.

I ease myself away, only his arm holds on.

"Hey," he says. He closes the distance, kissing my shoulder, chest, and neck until he is over me again. "Are you okay?" he says.

"Sure," I say. "I thought you were asleep."

"No," he says, "I'm not asleep."

Lance looks over my whole face and rolls his lips together. He moves his finger over my collarbone, touches the chain around my neck, and moves my father's pendant around.

"That's pretty," he says. "Are those diamonds?"

I nod my head. Where are my underwear?

He shifts around on the bed so we are side by side, his hand on my stomach. "You know," he says, "I don't know anything about you."

I move my feet between the sheets, searching, and then find

them wadded up. "Yes, you do," I say. Wiggling my toes, I snag my underwear.

"I don't," he says. He moves his hand up my stomach and over my chest. "Like where were you born?" he says.

"Reno," I say.

"Nevada?" he says.

"You're good."

"Ha, ha," he says. "See, I did not know that." He moves his leg over my leg, and my toes lose hold of my underwear. "So how did you end up in Spokane?" he says.

I look at him and he looks at me. "It's a long story," I say, "and you know what? I should go."

Moving my leg from his, I find my underwear again and sit up to pull them on.

"I don't want you to go," he says, reaching to my hips, but I shift off the bed and pick up pieces of my clothes. Jeans, socks, my T-shirt by the mirror. I turn my shirt the right way, pull it on, and in the mirror my hair is wild around my head. My face is heated up and pink.

"Hey," Lance says. "What's the hurry here?" He's still wound up in the sheets with a confused expression on his face. Without clothes, he looks younger, like he could still be in high school.

I come back to him, sit on the edge of the bed, close but out of reach. "I have a long drive home," I say, pulling on my jeans. "I have to work tomorrow. You know, I just should go."

Lance leans back then, hands behind his head. "That bad, huh?" he says.

"No," I say, touching his leg that is still under the sheet, "no, it's not that. I really do have to go."

He shakes his head and frowns. "No, it was too fast. I got too worked up," he says. "I was just . . . surprised. I mean—I didn't expect that at all."

"I know," I say, pulling on my socks. "It was fine. You are wonderful. Forget it."

Lance sits up, the sheet around his hips, the rest of him bare in the white light of the moon. "Let me have another chance," he says, hand moving up my arm and over my shoulder. "I don't want you to leave and think, *That guy—what an amateur.*"

I put my hand on his wrist and move his hand off me. "I don't think that," I say.

"Then why are you leaving so fast?" he says. "You are practically running out of here."

Lance isn't mad but there is the beginning of that in his eyes and in the tone of his voice.

The shadows of branches move over the sheets, the trees blown by the wind, and I move my hand over my own face.

Lance is right.

If he didn't stop me, I would leave, never talk to him again, and maybe even drop economics just so I wouldn't have to see him, but it's not Lance, it's me. This seemed like a good idea, but now, I feel stupid and embarrassed and bad.

"I'm sorry," I say.

"What's the matter?" he says.

"I'm just not myself right now," I say. "I'm not usually like this."

"What is it?" he says, hand to my arm again.

I shake my head and look up at the high ceiling. I wish I knew what it was, wish I could tell him and get it out of me, but I don't think it's one thing—it's more like hundreds of things tangled together.

I look around his room then, at the bed, at him, and it wasn't that long ago we were over by that mirror, dressed and practically strangers.

I put my face in my hands and laugh even though I really feel like crying. "God, what you must think of me," I say.

He scoots closer then, bare legs around my hips and hands around my waist.

"I'm the luckiest guy in these dorms tonight, probably in all of Spokane."

I push my hair back from my face, my hands in fists. "But I'm on the pill, you barely know me—"

"And I've been going out with you for two months now," he says. "It's not like we just met tonight, and it's great you're on the pill, it's amazing."

I'm all dressed and he's naked, just a white sheet that barely covers him.

"You're amazing," he says, so serious.

I roll my eyes and shake my head.

He moves his hands up my arms to my shoulders. "I mean it," he says. "I've never met anyone quite like you. You're funny and smart and I like you. Very much."

I bite my lip and look at him again, blue eyes so blue.

"I mean it," he says.

Music plays low on the radio and his clock says 11:00 P.M.

"Stay with me," he whispers. He presses his lips to my forehead and then my nose. "Please stay," he whispers again, his hand around the back of my neck. He kisses my mouth then, soft and careful, the taste of us on his lips and in me is a spark of something old that wants to believe.

I open my hand and press my palm in the center of his chest, the beating of his heart under my fingers and then, I close my eyes.

Kari is my best friend and has been since David dumped me. She has dark brown eyes, dark brown hair, and a pretty face that turns the heads of most boys.

We used to share a locker in high school, and on weekends,

we would hang out with her family. She has four little sisters, a nice mom, a nice father. The perfect family. Kari insists they aren't perfect, but she's wrong. They are.

Over the summer, we went to a Catholic youth retreat together, and her priest, this very cool guy who cracks jokes all the time, had us write our worst sin out and then burn it in a big forgiveness ceremony. Even though everyone was laughing and making jokes, I wrote out my worst sin and then watched it burn with everyone else's worst sins, and finally felt better about what I lost to David.

"What was yours?" Kari asked.

"David," I whisper, "the sex thing. You?"

"Swearing," she says.

When I started early in college, I took Kari to all the parties around town, these stupid keggers where you stand around looking bored. We had fun, though, laughing at all the idiot guys and their come-on lines, and then after, we'd go cruising Riverside Drive.

I've eaten a mountain of french fries with Kari, laughed so hard I thought I would pee my pants, and she's with me the day I find my apartment.

It was out of the blue really. We were driving around this older neighborhood that I thought was a back route to The Falls. Instead of making a left, I made a right, and we got stuck in Browne's Addition.

"This is wrong," I say.

"You need to go back to the freeway," Kari says.

I turn and drive to the dead end of a street called Pacific and there is an old brownstone building with a FOR RENT sign in the window.

"That's a cute building," I say.

Kari looks that way too. "That is a great building," she says.

I pull to the curb and there are six apartments, pretty plants around the windows, and a row of trees.

"It looks expensive," I say.

Kari opens the door then. "Let's go see," she says. Kari crosses the lawn and squats down to read the sign in the window.

I turn off the car, go to where she is, and she has a big smile on her face.

"One seventy-five," she says.

"That's cheap," I say.

Kari looks at me and I look at her.

Since I started school, Mom gives me the Social Security and VA checks, which aren't much, about $200 a month, plus I make about $500 checking groceries.

"Hold on," I say, my hand to her. "What about a deposit? Don't places like this need a deposit?"

"How much do you have saved?" she says.

"Eight hundred," I say, "but that's supposed to be for next term."

"You could defer your tuition," she says, "and maybe get a loan."

"That's true," I say.

Kari has a good head for things like that, always thinking about options. I stand up, look around the neighborhood, and it's perfect. Quiet, beautiful, safe.

"I love it here," I say.

She stands up too, looks up at the building, and nods like she approves.

Kari knows all about Mom and Dad and the bullshit of living at home. She's even seen them in action but since she was raised to only say nice things or nothing at all, she doesn't say much except how they don't seem to be very nice people.

I rub my hands together, push them into my hair, then

rub them together again. “Oh my goodness,” I say, “I can’t think.”

Kari laughs at me and goes back to the car. She gets her purse, takes a pen out, and writes the telephone number on the inside of a matchbook.

“We can go to my house,” she says. “You can call right now.”

“Or a phone booth,” I say, “I could call from a phone booth.”

She nods like *Yes, you could do that too.*

I push my hands in my hair again, push on the sides of my face like I might explode.

I love that she’s my friend, that she is here right now with the phone number already written down, and that there isn’t one bit of doubt in her eyes.

“God,” I say, “can you imagine?”

“Yes,” she says, “it’s time.”

It’s late at night and the house is quiet. Mom is upstairs watching a movie, Dad already went to bed, and Kimmy is asleep too. Grandma, Grandpa, and me are in their basement living room, the television tuned to news, and Bryan is there in his photo, like always, smug in the seminary.

I tell them how I found an apartment and that I am moving out as soon as the holiday is over.

“Sure you can afford that?” Grandpa says, so practical.

“Yeah,” I say, “just barely.”

“But you’re going to stay in school?” Grandma says.

“Absolutely,” I say.

“Good girl,” Grandpa says, and Grandma smiles.

I trace my fingernail over the pattern of a square on the armrest, so much to say but no way to say it.

“You didn’t tell your folks yet, did you?” Grandma says.

I shake my head, eyes down.

"I don't know if I will tell them."

I look over at him again.

"After this bit with the money," I say, "I don't think they deserve it."

Grandpa leans his weight forward in his chair and looks directly at me over the tops of his glasses. "Peg says she didn't make any promises to you," he says.

"She's lying," I say.

I look at him and then at Grandma.

"Think about it," I say. "I have no reason to lie and she has every reason to."

It's so quiet between us, the kind of wide-open truth that never gets spoken in this house, and Grandpa puts his fist to his mouth, coughing.

"They've done the best they can," Grandpa says.

Grandma nods and looks over at me. "They're so young," Grandma says.

"You should always remember that," Grandpa says. "They aren't much older than you."

Grandma nods again.

The space between us is how they can accept the lies and I can't. I don't know if that makes me a bad person or makes them good people or what. Mom and Dad didn't do their best, they used me and lied to me, hell, they were shoving the military at me as an option for college because they knew they hadn't saved a dime and now, they just keep on lying, innocent until proven guilty, with me as the one who gets screwed, over and over again.

I'm even getting screwed right now by the doubt that's in Grandma and Grandpa's eyes, doubt that's mixed in with loyalty to their daughter. Laucks always stay loyal to Laucks.

I look at both of them and bite back what I want to say, how every day since I came to live with Mom and Dad has been hard, too hard, that they never wanted me, probably wouldn't have taken me had it not been for the money and my housekeeping and childcare services, that things could have been different for me if Aunt Georgia and Uncle Charles had me instead.

I've wanted to say it for so long but didn't know how and even though it's so clear in my head, I don't know how to make the words come out right.

"Considering the way things worked out," I say, "do you think it was a good decision to send me here after all?"

It's so quiet in the room, too quiet, and Grandma looks like I hit her. Grandpa looks surprised too, a slackness to his mouth.

"What are you saying?" Grandma says, hand over her heart.

Looking down at my hands, there's a terrible feeling in my stomach, and I shake my head.

"I'm sorry," I say. "I'm not saying anything; I'm just tired."

Grandpa lets out a deep sigh then, his air filling the room, and he sits back in his big chair. "We understand," he says, "it's a difficult time." He looks over at Grandma again, but she's off somewhere else now, a look on her face like we've crossed a line and there is no going back.

On New Year's Eve, I was supposed to go out with Kari, but Mom changed her mind at the last minute, said I couldn't go out after all.

"I cannot believe this," Kari says. "What's the matter with her?"

"She has this bizarre fear of New Year's," I say, "she thinks that the moment the sun goes down, drunk drivers magically appear, and if I get hit, their insurance rates go up."

"My mom will come get you, then," Kari say. "She has to trust my mother."

"Nope," I say. "I'm screwed."

Kari makes a bunch of sounds on the line, disgusted with the whole thing. We were going to meet up with Lance and his friends at her house. We were going to have a good time and stay in—we've been planning it for three months.

"I already told Lance, and he's going to just hang out with some of his friends."

"Oh, I'm so irritated with your mother," Kari says.

"Kari," I say, "you will never be as irritated as I am."

We talk a little more, wish each other a happy new year, and hang up.

Mom and Dad did go out, just to play cards down the street. Kimmy is at a friend's house and so it's just me in the house tonight, Grandma and Grandpa downstairs.

Instead of just being angry, I use New Year's Eve to pack. It turns out that my big piece-of-junk car is good for something. My bookcases fit in the trunk, my pink trunk fits in the backseat along with most of my clothes, and the front seat is big enough for a chair, a lamp, and my stereo.

Through the snow, I stomp back and forth, carrying my things out of the house, and then I park my car off on the side so they won't notice it's all packed when they walk home.

New Year's Day, I get up before anyone else, leave a note that says I have to work, and drive to my new apartment.

Inside is cold, the heat off, and it smells like dust.

The apartment runs the length of the building and is painted a creamy white. The windows and doors are framed in dark wood; there are hardwood floors and arched doorways.

My shoes make the only sound in the empty space and I go

through the whole apartment, taking it all in. This is my space. Mine.

I turn on all the lights, turn up the heat, unload my things from the car. Each time I go out and then come back in, more of the space is filled with me. My clothes are in the closet, my bookcases are in the back bedroom, my pink trunk is in the living room.

It's not a lot but it's mine and I can already see a new bed in the bedroom, a dresser, a big rug for the living room, a sofa there, a TV over there, and maybe a coffee table with a glass top.

Crossing my arms over myself, I stand in the empty living room and over by the coat closet is my pink trunk.

The light in the living room comes from the wall fixtures, which make big circles of light on the ceiling and shadows of light on the walls and floor and trunk.

Crossing the room, I kneel down and push open the lid. Inside is a time capsule of pink bed linens that went to the princess bedroom, stuffed animals, and *Grimm's Fairy Tales*.

All this seems so silly now, pink and prissy and so little-girl.

I can't imagine showing Lance any of these things. What would I say? "This is my lamby"? He'd laugh his ass off.

One by one, I take all the things out of the trunk and make piles on the hardwood floor because I can still use the trunk for storage or something. Dust bunnies swirl around as I make a pile of the old princess bedding, of books, of stuffed animals, and there, under everything is the old Our Wedding Book and the black velvet bag.

I shift myself to sitting cross-legged on the floor and look around as if someone is going to barge in on me. Reaching down, I take the velvet bag, open the string, and tip it into my hand. A strand of pearls snakes out and then my mother's wedding ring falls out too, tipping out of my hand and rolling across the hardwood floor.

Dropping the velvet bag, I slap my hand over the ring, the sound of metal against the wood floor, and then move it over my first finger, lifting it up into the light.

It used to seem so big, but now, it's so small, a line of tiny diamonds on the outside, the date they were married engraved on the inside. I lift it off my finger and try to push it on my left hand, fourth finger, but it's way too small. Trying the pearls around my neck is the same, too small.

Overhead is the deep thump of someone walking and I look up. The sound stops, muffled voices talking or maybe a television turned on, and I look down again at the pearls and the ring. I never thought about her being so small; in fact, I haven't let myself think about her. So much has happened since becoming a Duemore, pushing the possibility of her as far away as the moon. Sitting here in my own living room, I have all the time in the world for her now but I can't feel her at all.

I put the pearls and the ring back into the bag and lift out the book that says Our Wedding on the cover. The cardboard is warped from time and it's dirty around the spine but the words are still there in big, curvy gold letters. The binding of the book creaks as I open it, and the black-and-white photos look so old now, dated, him with a crew cut, her with that dress that flares out like a big bell.

I used to look at these pictures all the time but then had to put them away. "If I see that thing again," Mom had yelled, "I'll throw it in the goddamned trash."

The memory of that terrible day is still alive in my body as if it was just yesterday. It didn't make any sense to me then and it makes no sense to me now. Why? Why wouldn't she want a photo of her own brother out? Why couldn't I have my memory and my mother? It's like Mom hated all those good things that came before her and wanted me to be like her, miserable and angry.

I take a deep breath that hurts my chest, as if there isn't enough air to breathe.

In her way, she won too. I can't feel my mother like I used to, I can't even feel what it was to be loved or to love. There's just anger, bitterness and how I can't trust anyone.

I move my hand over the photos of my parents, trying to get back what I lost but how can I change the past?

I stand up, the sound of me in my empty apartment, and I dust my butt off. Over the fireplace, I balance the book on its edges so two photos show, one where they are posed between two baskets of flowers, the other where they are feeding each other cake.

I step back then, arms crossed, and there's a strange shift that makes me feel restless and a little nervous.

Looking at my watch, it says five o'clock. I have to go—I'm actually late.

Quickly, I go through the apartment, turn off all the lights, and then lock the door without looking at the fireplace or my parents again.

Lance has moved out of the dorms too and shares a place with another guy that's not too far from my place. He's not going back to college for the winter term. He has a line on a job with this company that sells electronics. His oldest brother works for the same company, like a regional manager or something. Lance says he's going to work his way up to having his own store just like his brother did, maybe be a regional manager too.

Lance is full of plans and confidence, says the time to strike is now, college can come later.

I don't see anyone but Lance, even though I'm not sure what is going to happen with us. He says he's in love with me, but I can't let myself think about all that right now.

Lance and I are friends, that's the important thing, and tonight, I need a friend. He's helping move the rest of my things out. Of course, he has no idea of the real story until I pick him up and head out to Twelve Mile.

"You haven't told your parents that you're leaving yet?" he says.

"Nope," I say.

"Shit," Lance says, hand through his hair, voice with an edge to it. "They are your parents. You have to talk to them. I mean you have to tell them what's going on."

Lance is all big brother about this, outraged, a little mad, and I can't help but laugh.

"It's not funny," he says. "What is so funny?"

It's gray the way it gets around here in the winter, dirty snow piled along the sides of the bare roads.

"Let me tell you a few things about my parents," I say.

It takes all of the drive to give him the smallest idea and when I pull into the driveway, he looks like I hit him between the eyes. I shift the car to park but keep it running, shifting myself to look over at him.

"You look a little dazed," I say. "Are you okay?"

He shakes his head, mouth open a little. I pat his arm and laugh.

"That's okay," I say, "I'm a little dazed too, and it's my life."

Lance looks at me then. "I don't know how you can make jokes," he says. "That is serious."

Outside it starts to snow, big fat flakes that land on the windshield and melt right away.

I shrug him off, looking out the window at the house. No

one is in the kitchen. I would see them but there is a light from the back, probably the living room.

"God," Lance says, "your parents are dead?"

"Yep," I say.

Lance puts his hand on my hand then, holding it between both of his. "Why didn't you tell me any of this?"

"It's old news," I say, waving my other hand around, like *Big deal.* "It happened like ten years ago, longer than that for my mother, and besides, it's not the kind of thing that makes for good conversation, you know?"

Lance watches me talk, so many expressions moving through his eyes, shock, sadness, surprise. This is why I don't tell people about myself—this is what happens every time. People act all sorry for you, they look at you like you're different or cursed or something, and I hate it.

"We're having fun," I say, trying to take my hand away from him. "This isn't the fun part, but these people are very strange, and to understand what's about to happen, I thought you should know a little history."

Lance won't let my hand go, moving his fingers around mine to hold on.

"We are more than just fun, Jenny," he says.

"Yeah, well," I say, flipping my hair over my shoulder, "we were until now, but I wouldn't blame you for taking cover."

He looks down at my hand in his and for once, that wound-tight quality has shifted in him and he's more still than I've ever seen.

"This doesn't change anything," he says. "I mean, it would have been nice to know, but, God, what kind of guy do you think I am?"

"I don't know," I say. "What kind of guy are you, Lance?"

"I'm the one who loves you, Jennifer," he says. He lets my

hand go then, shaking his head and pushing his hand through his hair like he's the one under a lot of pressure. "You tell people you love about things like this."

"Look," I say, "I didn't tell you because most people don't understand."

"I'm not most people," he says.

"You're not like me, Lance," I say, my hand on my chest. "You have no idea what it's like."

"How would I if you don't tell me?"

I look at him and he looks at me and any other time, I could work this out, we could talk and make sense of it but right now, I'm going into battle in that house and I can't let myself argue with Lance when I know the biggest argument of my life is coming up.

Adjusting myself behind the steering wheel, I shift my car into reverse.

"This was a bad idea," I say. "Let me take you back, and I'll do it myself."

"No," he says, hand up to my wrist.

"Forget it," I say, shaking him off and looking out the back window for any cars. "I don't need your help. Let's just forget it."

Lance moves closer to me then, making me stop everything, arm around my shoulders, his hand over mine on the shifter. "Slow down," he says.

"Don't tell me what to do, goddamn it."

"Just stop for a second," he says. "Will you just stop?"

All I want to do is get out of here, get away from him and this house, and just go where I can regroup, think about a new plan, start over, but Lance holds me from going and it's all I can do not to hit him away from me.

I shift the car into park again with a hard thump, a tightness in my neck and jaw, holding myself together by holding my breath.

"This doesn't change anything," he says, holding on, his mouth close to my ear, his voice low and steady. "I want to help you. I'm glad to help. I'm just a little caught off guard, that's all."

Lance moves even closer to me, his hand up to the side of my face, making me look at him. "You have to trust people," he says. "You have to trust me."

He has eyes so blue you can practically see down into him, and what's there is as clear and wide open as the sky. He's one of those people who is young in his soul, and why wouldn't it be that way? His world is safe and sound, Mom and Dad in Montana and three big brothers. Lance can turn around, look back, and see how he went to the same school his whole life, had all the same friends, and can count the one disappointment in his life as not being big enough to play professional football.

Trust is natural for him, but it's a luxury I can't afford.

We look at each other, such a space between us, the kind of space that likely will never be filled. Even though we're the same age, he's so young and I'm so old.

Lance tries to cross that space in the only way he knows how to reach me, his hand around the back of my neck and his mouth pressed to mine, kissing me with all his strength and confidence. He moves himself so close that spark between us that takes away thoughts and words almost makes up for the differences between us.

"Of all the ungrateful things to do," Mom yells.

"You're not leaving this house," Dad yells.

Lance is in the entryway, hands deep in his jeans pockets, and he is actually white, in-shock white.

They were watching television when we came in, just the

two of them here in the living room, but now, Mom is pacing around and Dad is at the edge of his big chair.

The house smells like bacon grease and mashed potatoes, and the light in here seems extra bright, extra white. Up the steps, the hall is dark, and I know Kimmy is already in bed. Down the steps, it's quiet, and I wonder if Grandma and Grandpa are still awake or if they are in bed too.

"You think you can just spring this on us," Mom yells, "no warning at all?"

"I just found out about this place," I say. "It was pretty sudden."

"Oh, bullshit," Dad says.

"You are not moving out of this house," Mom says.

"I can leave and I am leaving."

Dad looks up at Mom, she looks down at him and then she throws her hands up, all dramatic.

"No warning, absolutely no warning at all," Mom yells. "Why would you do this to us?"

"I don't know why you are getting so pissed off," I say. "It's not like I'm asking you to help me. It's not like I want money. It's not like I've even been here for the last six months anyway."

"God damn it," Mom says. "That's not the point."

"You can't just move out and not talk about it with us," Dad says, trying to act like he's reasonable. "That's not the way you do things. Old Lance there, he wouldn't just move out of his folks' house without talking about it first, now would you, Lance?"

Lance looks at Dad, at me, and he shrugs his shoulders.

"Don't pull that with him," I say. "He's here to help me move, not take sides."

"You'd better watch yourself," Dad says, shaking his finger at me.

"Or what?" I say, my hands out wide. "What are you going to do?"

Dad looks at me and I look at him. He moves his mouth around like he's thinking about things. He reaches over the coffee table, takes out a cigarette, and flips his lighter open. RC comes over to him, pushing her face into his hand.

"You won't make it," he says, petting the side of the dog's neck, "not one month." He lights his cigarette, flips the lighter closed, and holds his hand up in a kind of peace sign.

"Two weeks," he says. "I give you two weeks and you will beg to come back."

Kimmy comes out of the shadows of the upstairs hall and leans against the wall at the top of the steps, a sleepy expression on her round face.

"You'll be back in a week," Dad says. "You have no idea how hard it is out there."

Mom stands with her arms crossed over herself like she agrees with him and Dad smokes with that smug look on his face like he knows all about me.

How did that happen? How did the two of them ever think they knew a thing about me? Have they ever asked what I was feeling or thinking or even about my life before I came to live with them? Back when I was ten years old, I knew exactly how hard it was out there, I knew it the day my mother died and the day my father died, the day Deb dumped me in that house in L.A. I've lived a hundred lifetimes "out there," but they just have no idea and the fresh anger of what he says about me is all I can feel, a shake of anger that goes all the way down my legs.

I go to end of the sofa and put my fists on the arm of it, bending down a little so Dad and me are eye-to-eye level.

"If I have to eat macaroni and cheese for the rest of my life,"

I say, my voice so slow and careful, "I will never come back to this house."

Dad looks at me and I look at him, and he looks away from me first.

Mom uncrosses her arms, puts her hands on her hips and then crosses her arms again.

"Well, you can't leave without proper linens," Mom says, her voice high-pitched, like a hostess's. "Just wait right here," she says. "I'll get you some sheets."

Mom turns, goes through the dining room to the garage, says something about how she has these extra towels and sheets and a few blankets.

This is an act I've seen before, all polite and nice in front of my friends and then completely crazy when it's just me. The only reason she is doing this now is to look good in front of Lance and I want to yell at her to stop it but I can't.

I look at Lance and shake my head like *Can you believe this* but he just looks at the floor and scratches his ear.

Mom comes back with a cardboard box already packed up with old saucepans, wooden spoons, and plates.

"Come on, Mom, I don't need that stuff," I say.

"No, no," Mom says. "It's the least we can do." She talks about how she wishes there was more to give, how a new home needs so many things, and then she goes up the steps, past Kimmy.

"Your sister is leaving," Mom says.

"I heard," Kimmy says.

I go up the steps to where she sits and kneel in front of her.

Mom is in the linen closet, bent over and talking to herself about old sheets.

"You're never coming back?" Kimmy whispers.

Mom closes the closet door, a pile of sheets and towels in her arms.

"Of course she's coming back," Mom says. "There are birthdays and holidays—we'll see Jenny all the time. What about a blanket? I know you'll need a blanket."

Mom goes down the steps and into the kitchen again.

"Dick," Mom yells, "don't we have an extra blanket in the camper?"

"I don't need a blanket," I say over my shoulder.

"She doesn't need a blanket," Dad says.

"Of course she needs a blanket," Mom says.

The door to the garage opens and closes again and Mom's voice is gone.

I put my hands on Kimmy's knees.

"I'm not going because of you, okay?" I say. "We are fine—I love you."

Mom comes back from the garage, slams the door. "Found it," she says.

"I wish you didn't have to go," Kimmy says.

She's grown so much from that first day I came to their house. She didn't even have hair.

I move my hand over her long hair, a mix of blond and brown. "I'll get you my phone number," I whisper. "Maybe you can stay the night sometime."

"Really?" she says.

"Absolutely," I say. "A sleepover. It'll be fun."

"Okay," she says, nodding.

Mom comes out of the kitchen, a second box packed up, and pushes it at Lance, who takes it in his arms.

After that, Lance and I fuss around getting the snow off my car, hauling out my desk, putting it into the back of the Hornet, tying the dresser to the roof with the length of rope. There are boxes and odds and ends and we make arrangements for when I can get my mother's dining-room set.

Dad watches from the kitchen window; Mom watches from the front stoop, hugging herself against the cold.

When we're done, Lance gets into the car and I go to the front stoop where Mom stands. I put my arms around myself but I'm not cold.

She's back to her old angry self, red stain up her neck, that look in her eyes like I'm so ungrateful for all they've done for me.

Snow falls on my face and I look away from her.

I am grateful, but I'm also tired of the weight of them, the anger, the lies, and this game of being a family. I want out.

"When I get a telephone, I'll call," I say.

"That would be good," she says.

"And I'll get you my address," I say.

"Good," she says. "We'll need that for your mail."

"Right," I say.

Dad is still at the kitchen window and I look at Mom again. I wonder why she is like this, so unhappy and so hard to me. All these years with her, the years of wanting her to be my mother but she's still a mystery.

I wipe snow off my cheeks. "See you later," I say.

"Okay," she says, arms tighter around her body.

I watch my feet on the snow and go around the front of the car and open the door. Lance has already started it up, and it's warm inside.

I sit behind the steering wheel, looking at the snow that falls on the windshield and melts as soon as it hits the glass.

"That went well," I say, "don't you think?"

Lance lets out a deep breath, a laugh mixed with a cough.

I look past Lance at the house and she's gone back in.

Part of me wants to cry, this feeling that it's my fault somehow, that I could have done that better or even be a better daughter from the very beginning but it doesn't matter now, I did what I had to do and thank God, I'm finally free.

I sit up in my seat and shift the car into reverse.

My own place is like paradise . . . better than paradise. I leave dishes in the sink all day, talk on the telephone for an hour, two, three, eat what I want, sleep when I want. If I don't feel like it, I don't even make my bed or pick up my clothes.

That first night, Lance and I picked up a pizza, built a fire in my fireplace and sat on the floor making all sorts of jokes about what happened at Mom and Dad's house.

"I told you they were strange," I said.

"Strange?" he said. "They are beyond strange." He sat away from me, tucking in his chin. " 'You won't make it a month,' " he said, all stern and fatherly.

" 'Two weeks,' " I said, fingers up in a peace sign.

" 'One week,' " Lance said. " 'You'll be begging us to take you back.' "

We sat on this makeshift bed of a sleeping bag and a bunch of blankets and I laughed out loud at his imitation of Dad, almost dead on even though he saw him only a couple of times. Lying back, I kept laughing, the shadows of the fire up on the ceiling. And then I stopped laughing.

"I'll be begging, all right," I said, looking over at Lance, fingers moving over the waistband of his jeans. "You can count on that."

Lance shifted around on our strange little bed, leaning down to me, his breath warm on my face.

"Oh, yeah," he whispered, "you will beg."

He laughed low and in the back of his throat, hands moving

up under my shirt. After that, we didn't talk about Mom and Dad anymore.

Lance is with me almost every night and we've taken a couple trips to Montana to meet his mother and father. After a while, it makes sense to split the expenses and have him give up his place—he's at mine all the time anyway.

I'm in school and working at just one job now.

Lance works full time at Radio Shack, was promoted to manager, and he's easy to live with. I even like taking care of him. I cook for us and he does the dishes, and we make love in every single room of my apartment.

It's nice, it's safe and past that, I feel lighter, as if a heavy load has been lifted off my shoulders just by being out of the house at Twelve Mile and away from Mom and Dad.

It wasn't my plan to have things go this way; it just happened. You fall in with someone, spend a lot of time together, meet each other's parents, have a couple fights, make up, make love—a lot, and it just happens.

People think we are too young to get married and it's probably true.

The thing is, I don't feel young, and frankly, I don't give a shit what anyone thinks. Getting married to Lance is a good thing. I'm still going to get my degree, I'm still going to travel, and I'm still going to have a career. Lance knows all about my plan; he's fine with it. He knows everything now about my real parents, my brother in the seminary, my completely insane family, and he still wants to be with me. It was his idea to get married. I just said yes.

The wedding is set for August twentieth. People come from all over. There are Lance's parents, his three older brothers, his best friend from high school, not to mention a bunch of his other friends from Montana. Lance is a very popular boy.

To keep up, I invited all my family too, even though I didn't expect many to come, especially the ones from out of town. Auntie Carol, Aunt Mary Beth, and Uncle Leonard aren't coming—no big surprise. I haven't seen any of them in years, but it turns out Aunt Georgia and Uncle Charles are coming from Carson City and Bryan is coming all the way from Oklahoma.

That's the biggest shock of all. I haven't heard a thing from him in three years. Through Grandma and Grandpa, I do know he left the seminary and that he's going to the University of Oklahoma in the fall.

Two days before the wedding, I leave our apartment so Lance can have a bunch of his friends stay over, and, without having to beg, I stay in my old room at the house in Twelve Mile.

The great thing about my family is you give things a little time and it's as if nothing ever happened. We've never talked about the day I left or any of the other things. All the lies and the meanness sit like broken glass under our feet, but everyone just looks up and keeps going. Now I'm getting married, they are the parents of the bride, and we are one big, happy family.

It's the same with Grandma and Grandpa. They're happy I'm getting married, relieved it's going to be a Catholic ceremony, and overjoyed that Bryan's coming.

The day before the wedding, I visit with Aunt Georgia in the living room of Mom and Dad's house. Uncle Charles is asleep in their trailer that's parked out front.

They got in late last night and it turns out they brought Bryan with them. Aunt Georgia says he took a bus from Oklahoma to Nevada and then came with them the rest of the way.

"Why didn't he fly?"

"Too expensive," she says, "and besides, we were glad to spend some real time with him."

"You must be gluttons for punishment," I say.

Aunt Georgia smiles with her mouth but it's not in her eyes.

"I'm sorry," I say. "I didn't mean that."

"He was very good company," she says.

Aunt Georgia is just the same, shorts and top that match, tan arms and legs, brown haircut neat around her head.

She smokes a cigarette, drinks a cup of coffee, and chats like this is the most normal thing in the world even though it's a little odd to have her here. Grandma, Grandpa, Mom, and Dad don't like them—everyone knows it—and I wonder why they came at all.

To ask now would be rude, and besides, I'm glad they came. I invited them here. It seemed important to have someone from my mother's side of the family.

We sit in the quiet, this feeling between us that there is so much to say and no way to say it.

I look down at the engagement ring on my finger, the circle of gold and diamonds. I turn it around with my other hand.

"Let me see," Aunt Georgia says.

I hold my hand up and she puts her cigarette in the ashtray, scoots to the edge of the sofa and holds my fingers.

Her hand is warm, and this close, she smells nice, like almond lotion.

"I had my mother's ring fitted," I say, pointing at the lower side of the ring. "It's going to be the wedding band that attaches to this."

She looks directly at me, her eyes to my eyes.

"Where did you get her ring?" she says.

"I've always had it," I say. "Ever since she died."

Aunt Georgia smiles, a small tilt of her head. "Since you were seven?" she says.

"Absolutely," I say.

I explain about Auntie Carol and how she told me to keep my mother's things forever, about the pink trunk with the lock, how I had the key tied into my shoe and hid everything from Deb. I tell her I brought that trunk with me on the bus when Deb sent me off, that I've had it ever since, and I still have it at my apartment right now.

Aunt Georgia listens in a way Mom never did and then shakes her head like she can't quite believe it. It's funny, I don't even believe it myself anymore.

She lets my hand go and pulls out a new cigarette from her pack. "I've never worried about you," she says. "I mean, I have worried, a lot, but more about the way you were being taken care of, not about you as a person." She puts her cigarette between her lips then and lights it with a match. "Do you know why?" She inhales and shakes her match out, dropping it in the ashtray.

"Why?" I say.

She blows smoke off to the side then. "You're a survivor," she says. "You always were."

I shift in the chair, my hand on my own lap again, the feel of her fingers still on my skin.

"I saw it in you when you were a little girl," she says. "I saw it when you were up in Carson a few years ago, and I see it now."

The way she talks makes me embarrassed, self-conscious, but there's something to her words that move through me, like potential in myself I don't even know about yet.

Up the stairs is the sound of someone walking around.

We both look toward the steps and Bryan stands there, tall

and dark, the same as before, but thinner, almost lanky, like he's in the process of becoming a different person.

I push myself to standing, feeling more nervous than I thought I would.

"Hi," I say.

Bryan doesn't say anything. Instead, he takes these long strides down the steps and covers the space between us, pulling me into one of those long-lost hugs that is so tight and such a surprise, I don't even try to respond. I'm more like a doll pulled in and then let go just as fast.

Bryan is all choked up, without words at all, looking at me for a second and then leaving the room out of the sliding glass door that leads to the backyard.

I watch him go, my whole body shifted by that hug and I can't help but laugh—not really a laugh—more like a cough.

Aunt Georgia sits forward, wrist balanced on her knee and cigarette smoke curving a line up in front of her face.

"Was that weird or is it just me?" I say.

She shakes her head and tips it toward the window that looks over the backyard. "He's just nervous," she whispers.

"That's nervous?" I say.

"He told us he was very nervous to see you again," she says.

"Me?"

"Just go talk to him," she says, waving her hand to the back window.

The backyard is all grass except this island where Dad and Mom planted a tree and a few bushes. Every year, she tries to grow roses, but they never seem to take, and so it's mostly grass and beauty bark and those tall pines that make everything smell that way.

Bryan sits on the edge of the patio with his feet on the grass, elbows on his knees, and even though he looks casual, I know he's waiting.

I smooth my shorts and go to where he sits, lowering myself about a foot away from him. Bryan holds a polite smile on his face and I smile that way too, as if it's the most normal thing to sit down with a brother you haven't spoken to in at least three years.

I can still feel his hug, if that's what you would call it, and I shift my head to the side, shoulders tilted, trying to get myself into myself again.

Small white butterflies move over the grass, lifting and then falling, and in my head are all the possible opening lines: *You look good; Nice to see you; Did you have a nice trip?*

Bryan clears his throat then. "I've always hated you," he says to the yard.

Or, we could go that way too.

He drops his head and starts to laugh, looking up at me fast with a grin on his face. "Sorry," he says, "I have so much to say." He shakes his head and laughs a little more.

"I was going to say that it's good to see you," I say, "but you know, that hating thing, I guess that's a good start."

He laughs harder then, as if what I said was just hilarious.

I push my hands through my hair and tuck it behind my ears. He looks at me again, this over-the-shoulder kind of glance, and lets out a deep breath with his cheeks puffed, like he's under a lot of pressure.

"What's the matter with you?" I say.

"What do you mean?" he says, that quick shake of his head so his bangs angle over his forehead. "You're acting—I don't know—weird."

He looks down at me, so much behind his eyes, things I don't know, things I couldn't even guess.

"I just have so much to tell you," he says. "I guess I thought about it a lot, but now I'm here, it's like you said, weird."

"Well," I say, "just take it easy and tell me."

He squints like he's trying to get me in focus. "You've really changed," he says. "I mean in a good way. You're all grown now and really pretty."

"Gee," I say, "thanks."

He puts his hand on my arm, this familiar touch that's so strange, I can only watch his hand.

"I'm serious," he says.

Far off is the sound of a lawn mower engine kicking in and then cutting out, the pull of the string, and the sputter of the engine again.

Bryan has changed in ways I can't even put together yet. He's just as serious but it's like he's found a way to be in himself, and maybe that's what happened in the seminary.

Bryan sits with his knees up, arms around them and hands together, all casual. He starts at the very beginning, with the story I already heard from Aunt Georgia, from when he was sent from L.A. by Deb on what she called a vacation but turned out to be a short stay with Grandpa Ivan in Boise and then a longer stay with Aunt Georgia and Uncle Charles. He says it was great to be back in Carson, to go to his old school with his old friends—how he was learning how to snow-ski and everything—but then it came down to a choice and he chose Leonard and Sylvia, which turned out to be the worst decision of his life.

"Why?" I say.

Bryan looks over the backyard and I see the line of his jaw to ear to cheeks, tanned skin, straight nose.

"Oh, it's complicated," he says, with a push of air, looking my way over his shoulder. "We all didn't get along that well."

He presses his mouth together on what else he might say and looks down. "It's not that big of a deal. I just screwed up."

He rolls his lips together. "I didn't know we weren't going to be together," he says, "not until Leonard came to get me and took me out to your place in Black Sparks. Remember that?"

"The golf-ball incident," I say. "How could I forget?"

He laughs but it's not a laugh at all. "Yeah, well, that wasn't a good time for me," he says. "I was upset we weren't going to be together."

"You're kidding, right?" I say.

"No," he says, shaking his head to the side again. "Georgia and Chuck were trying to get us together, but Leonard said it was out of the question."

The sound of the lawn mower goes from high to low, as if it's running out of gas and then it dies completely.

"You wanted us to stay together?" I say.

"Of course," he says, as if it should be obvious. "You're my sister."

"Bryan, come on—I'm your adopted sister," I say.

He frowns at that, dark eyebrows pulled together over his eyes, this little crease in the middle. "But still my sister," he says.

I rub my hand over my face, too much of a change to take in, he's not even the same guy. That seminary must be an amazing place. Bryan keeps talking, says he's sorry he wasn't a better big brother to me, that he hopes things have been good to make up for it. Then, he looks around the backyard.

"I can see you had things pretty good here," he says.

I watch him, my mouth open, not sure what to think or say.

"What?" he says.

I look at my feet, the grass coming up through my toes. Compared to his calm, I feel jagged and nervous and even angry, this feeling like I have to set him straight.

I tell a little about my life as a Duemore and Bryan listens, my words going into his impossibly dark eyes and not coming out again.

It turns out we had almost the same experiences growing up; no affection, tough love, chores and chores and more chores except Bryan also had to deal with some extreme poverty.

We go back and forth, telling our stories and all this time I thought he had it better than I did but it turns out, it wasn't true. Bryan had it worse.

Bryan gets quiet, lost in his own thoughts and I bite the edge of my nail, lost too.

The backyard, the sound of birds and sprinklers kicking into action around the neighborhood, the smell of pine needles burned by the sun and this feels like the most important conversation we will ever have, even though I can't say why.

"So why are you getting married?" Bryan says after a while, breaking the silence. "Do you love this guy?"

It's like Bryan just hit the nail on the head, asking the question I ask myself all the time. Do I really love Lance? Can I love anyone? Do I even know how to love or what it is to feel loved?

I straighten my legs out then, smooth my shorts, and put a smile on my face. "Sure," I say. "Of course I do."

"It's not just to get away from this?" he says, tilting his head at the house. "From them?"

"Of course not," I say. "I already live alone, and besides, I don't need some guy to take care of me."

I can tell he doesn't buy what I say; it's right there in his dark eyes and that pull at the side of his mouth. I look over the yard, at the grass, the trees.

"What about you?" I say, all casual. "Why did you leave the seminary?"

He stays still for a long time, just watching me in that same way of his, and finally, he breaks away and looks over the yard too.

"I was there for the wrong reasons," he says, "and I couldn't imagine a life without women." He tries not to smile, but then he does, embarrassed.

It turns out there is a woman in his life now, someone named Val who is small and blond, and he says she's just wonderful, the kind of woman who could restore his faith in womankind.

The way he talks, low and a little self-conscious, it sounds like this is a new relationship and I bet it's such a relief to be with someone, just to touch another person after three years of being in a seminary.

Of course, I can't ask him that stuff, there's no way, but I understand.

"You know," he says, "the reason I went to the seminary is because of women. I mean I didn't feel like there were any good ones; I didn't think I could trust them." A fly buzzes close to his face, and he shoos it away. "It might be hard for you to understand," he says, "but I feel like women have let me down my whole life, first Mom, by dying; then Deb, for just being Deb; Aunt Sylvia, who was so cold to me. You know, I don't think she ever told me she loved me."

His words hold a wisdom that touch me but it's a language I can't understand yet and I feel overwhelmed.

"And you," he says, "I've been really angry with you too."

I freeze then, not even a breath in my body.

"Why?" I say.

Bryan looks at his own hands, held together in front of him like a prayer and then he looks over at me again.

"I hated you for what you said about us," he says.

"What are you talking about?"

"You know," he says, "the reason we were separated."

He looks at me and I look at him but I really don't know.

"You told Deb we had sex together," he says.

I open my mouth and close it again, swallowing. "I don't think I understand," I say.

"Well," he says, voice matter-of-fact, "that's what you said."

I let go of my knees and shift on the patio, moving myself from him. "When did I say this?" I say, my hand over my chest. "Did you actually hear me say these words?"

Bryan turns too, just a little, one hand flat on the cement patio, his arm up on his other knee. "Well, no," he says.

Familiar anger moves through me, the language I do know.

"So what the hell are you talking about?"

He scratches his head then, frowning. "Deb said . . ." he says. "Well, I mean Leonard told me, which I guess he heard from Deb, or maybe it was Grandma and Grandpa."

He shakes his head a little then, like he's confused and moves his hand over his mouth. "You never said that?" he says, shifting his eyes on me again.

I put my hands up and let them fall again. I just can't believe this. "Why would I say something like that?"

There are a million thoughts in my head, none of them making their way out of my mouth. This lie is the true reason we were separated and how do I prove I didn't make this accusation. Why would he believe me anyway? Our past together is filled with terrible things. He used to terrorize me and I used to scream foul words at him; he used to hit me and I used to scratch at him to fight him off. We have a history of shadows and secrets and our own version of who's to blame. How do you reach through all that to prove anything?

Bryan just watches me, as if he can't figure things out, and I don't know what to do or say.

I put my head in my hands and rub them over my face, over and over again, to feel something past this terrible trapped feeling. "I would never say a thing like that," I say, "never in a million years." My own words sound so weak. All the bullshit lies in this family, all the sick, terrible things people say for no reason, and it's like being caught in the sewer. I feel dirty and ugly and wrong. I want to get away from him and this house and this family. I want to go home to my apartment, take a shower that lasts ten years, and get drunk.

Bryan reaches over to me then, puts his hand out, palm up. "Jenny, I believe you," he says.

I look at his hand, the lines over his wide palm.

There's no comfort in his belief, none at all. In fact, I don't believe him.

Squeezing my own hand into a fist, I look up at him, but he nods like it's true.

"I believe you," he says again, his dark eyes on mine.

I feel so awful, so small, and even scared, but he lifts his hand one more time, *Come on, take it,* and I open my fist and so slowly, lay my hand over his, palm to palm, sister to brother, stranger to stranger.

He closes our hands together with his fingers and holds on like he did when he first hugged me, like he found a long-lost friend, like a lifeline, but I don't feel it at all.

Trust is a luxury I can't afford, and this is why. The price is always too high.

Being married isn't much different than living together and if anyone asked, I'd say we were very happy.

We've filled our little apartment with new things: a sofa, a television, a little table in the kitchen, and pretty things in the bedroom. Mom and Dad let me have the dining-room set that belonged to my mother and with all the stuff we have, it's like a home.

I'm at Eastern Washington University now, majoring in journalism and I'm up for an internship at the city paper next summer. Lance works 10 hours a day, most weekends too and he's already one of the best managers around, breaking sales records and making big profits.

We've talked about kids, in a very casual way. Lance says he'd like to have four boys and maybe start in four years. I say, *Sure, why not;* four years is forever away from today.

I didn't see Bryan in a real way after that day, after he told me that terrible lie, just looking his way filled me with shame and embarrassment and so, I avoided him which turned out to be easy. The wedding took over. There was the rehearsal, the rehearsal dinner and then the wedding ceremony. Bryan just became another smiling face in the crowd of smiling faces.

He tried to give me a little brotherly advice about birth control and family planning, but I blew him off.

Bryan posed for photos and then left for Oklahoma right after the ceremony.

Lance and I go through the holidays together: Halloween, Thanksgiving, my twentieth birthday, and then Christmas. I got one letter from Bryan. He wrote that he was enjoying school and thinking about going into the military, but he didn't write anything about his girlfriend Val. He enclosed a couple of photos of himself and wrote out the lyrics for a song he liked off the new Yes album.

He was always like that, so into music. The song was called "Leave It," sort of about breaking down dreams to what is real, but it didn't make much sense to me.

At the end of the letter, Bryan wrote how nice he thought

the wedding was, that he hoped I was happy. He even wrote that he loved me.

Still queasy from what he told me at the wedding, I couldn't bring myself to write back.

I'm studying for midterms in late March when I get a long-distance call.

"Who is this?" I say.

"Leonard," he says.

"Who?"

"Your uncle?" he says.

"Leonard?" I say. "Uncle Leonard?"

"That's right," he says.

When Bryan was here for the wedding, he told me a bit of trivia I didn't know. Uncle Leonard is actually my godfather, his wife Sylvia is my godmother. I doubted it was true, because it's a big responsibility that Catholics take very seriously. Godparents are invested in your well being and are supposed to help guide you spiritually. I haven't heard from Leonard or Sylvia ever until today.

"Have you seen Bryan?" he says.

"What do you mean, seen him?" I say.

"Has he been to Spokane?" he says. "Recently?"

"No," I say. "What's going on?"

My books are spread over the dining-room table, a notepad full of lecture notes and a couple of pens on top of the papers.

I look at the mess on the table and listen to his voice through long-distance static. Leonard says Bryan is missing from school, that he's been gone at least a week, that his bike is gone too. "And he might have a gun."

"A gun?" I say. "Bryan owns a gun?"

"It's not his," Leonard says. "It's his roommate's gun."

Leonard won't tell me much more but what he did say is enough. I don't know why, but in that moment, I know Bryan is dead.

Lance says I shouldn't jump to any conclusions, that I don't really know what might have happened and that I should just wait.

What Lance says makes sense but I can't feel Bryan in the world anymore. I know in my bones, in my blood; I can almost taste his death in my mouth.

My head keeps things under control. My head tells me to finish midterms, to pick up milk and a loaf of bread at the grocery store and to have dinner ready by six. I even invite Kimmy to stay the night with me so Mom and Dad can go out for their wedding anniversary. April second.

On the third morning of April, Kimmy and I are in the kitchen where it smells like hot oil, nutmeg, and cinnamon as I make French toast for breakfast.

Kimmy sits at the round kitchen table and drinks a glass of milk.

Lance already left for work.

"You know, Lance eats his French toast with peanut butter," I say.

"Gross," she says.

"It's true," I say. "It's pretty good. You want to try it?"

She scrunches her face from the middle the way she does, nose all wrinkled.

I take the peanut butter out of the cabinet and put it on the table. "Just try a little bite," I say, "and then decide."

She's still not convinced when I put a slice of crispy toast on her plate.

Kimmy turned 10 last month and even though she's in a

chubby phase, I know she's going to be tall, and she has the prettiest blue eyes.

I put a slice of French toast on a plate and sit across from her. "I'll put some on mine and you can try that," I say.

"Okay," she says.

We eat and it turns out Kimmy likes peanut butter on her French toast after all.

"See?" I say. "Maybe you'll listen to your big sister every now and then."

The telephone rings and I wipe my mouth off with a paper towel, crossing the kitchen to answer it.

The line is static, the voice far away, saying Bryan's body was found, that he's been dead for at least a week and that it was suicide.

"Jenny?" Kimmy says.

That voice keeps on with all these specifics, how he was found on the outskirts of the University of Oklahoma in some forest, how he did take that roommate's gun, but details don't matter now. When you find out the thing you knew was true, when you don't have your head in the way to keep everything in control, what else is there but a kind of free fall where you can't even stand up anymore?

"Jenny?" Kimmy says again. "Are you okay?"

I lean back against the wall of the kitchen and slide down to the floor, my face in my hands. There are no thoughts at all, just a black hole feeling pulling me down and down, away from Kimmy and normal and this life I've barely started. There's no kitchen, no apartment, no Lance, no college. There's nothing but a terrible emptiness that owns me. All I can think is how everyone is dead now and I'm the only one left in this terrible life that feels worse than hell.

✦ ✦ ✦

The funeral is in a tiny Catholic church called Immaculate Conception, in a town called Seminole, on the edge of Oklahoma.

Outside, a storm rains and rages.

Inside, the church is filled with people and yet there is a strange stillness that makes me restless. I have on a black sweater and a black skirt made from black crepe with small leaves in the design of the material. I pick at nothing on my skirt and shift around in the pew, uncomfortable in my pantyhose and heels. I never dress like this.

A few aisles up are Aunt Sylvia, Uncle Leonard, their kids Erin and Ricky. I didn't know them before I got off the airplane, I don't know them now, and I know I won't know them when I leave.

I've been studying Aunt Sylvia though, this person who never told Bryan that she loved him and Bryan is right about her. She looks cold, an endless expression of failure etched into every line of her face.

Leonard isn't much better.

Bryan told me he was a career military man but then was something called RIF'd from his job, which meant a reduction in forces, early retirement, and then he lost his severance in a bad investment in a woman's clothing store. From where I sit, Leonard has that same look of disappointment and failure.

Someone coughs and another person blows his nose.

The casket is up front, too big for this church, and on top is a photo of Bryan that's at least two years old. It figures they couldn't even get a recent photo.

On my lap is this program someone dreamed up, a bunch of stuff about the service on the one side, and on the other side, the poem called "Treasured Seasons."

"For everything there is an appointed season, a time for everything under heaven."

How can there be a season for shooting yourself in the head? Don't these people have any common sense?

There's a shift in the room, a hush, and a priest comes in, this little guy with pale skin. On the program it says "Father Patrick Gaalaas."

That's really good to know. I'm so glad to have a program to get me through this bullshit. I toss my program on the floor.

"In the name of the Father, the Son, and the Holy Spirit," Father Patrick Gaalaas says, a little too loud.

I sit lower in the pew and cross my arms.

"Let us pray," Father Gaalaas says, and bows his head.

Everyone bows, but I hold myself tighter. I'm not going to pray.

Since the call came telling me Bryan was found, he's been everywhere, on the surface of my skin, a whisper in my ears, the beat inside my own heart. I don't have one thought that isn't about Bryan.

There's been all that so-called normal stuff, long telephone conversations with cousins I haven't spoken to in years, the retelling of the specifics of what happened, going over all of it again and again with Mom and Dad, Grandma and Grandpa, even Kimmy but I pulled myself away from all that and went into a kind of grief that seems to have no end.

I bought the album Bryan wrote about over Christmas and lying on the floor in the living room, I listened to "Leave It" so many times, the words burned into my memory.

It was right there, "good-bye, bad, hello, heaven." It was right there and I can't believe I didn't see it. I didn't even try. I didn't even write a fucking letter.

Lance can't reach me at all. He's tried, the way he always does, by trying to have sex, but I told him to get the hell away from me. He had the nerve to fight with me about this, as if he has a clue how I should feel. He can't know how I feel, how I can't eat and can't sleep and how the nights are the worst. In the dark I lay next to Lance, who actually sleeps, like a total jerk. Instead of sleeping, I close my eyes to see Bryan's last moments as if they were my own.

I see a forest and fog that hovers a foot over the earth and weaves around the trees and bushes.

I see us walk between a tangle of branches, and in our hand, the gun is heavy and cold.

I hear the snap of a twig that breaks underfoot and then the thump of one knee, as we go to the earth.

We kneel, as if asking forgiveness for a sin that supposedly cannot be forgiven but, how can that be true when the pain of this life is like hell?

Lance snores next to me, his back turned away and this thick pain lifts up in my throat like a stone.

I don't stop though; I can't. I stay in that moment where Bryan lifts that gun to his head and holds it there, looking at what?

Are our parents there? Can we see them? Are they reaching for us and are they saying, *Come on, enough already; just come.*

Can he see them? because I can't see them. Are they there?

They have to be there.

I freeze right then, on the possibility, and then, it's just me alone in bed with a man who can sleep with his back to me while I cry silent tears that make the pillow wet around my head.

Rain hits the roof and fills the church with that sound.

Father Gaalaas lifts his head, takes out a sheet of paper, and clears his throat.

"Life is a mystery," he says, looking around at all of us in the church. "Sometimes things happen that don't make sense."

He tells a story about how his own father was a helicopter pilot and how one day, some other helicopter pilot crashed. It's one of those stories inside a story, and just like that, he's talking about freak accidents. It's his own abstract, three-times-removed "brush with death" story that has absolutely nothing to do with Bryan or suicide.

I look around at the faces of the people here, at how they buy this crap, how they don't even blink at it.

"When we are presented with mysteries like Bryan's death," Father Gaalass says, "we must put our faith in God, we must trust the higher mystery of His love."

Is that the way it is when a beautiful, intelligent, and gifted 23-year-old man kills himself? It's just a fucking mystery and isn't that convenient for everyone? Why take any responsibility when we can leave it all to God?

Sylvia and Leonard up there, they don't have to take responsibility this way. They can just pull on those bland expressions they wear like a habit and raise their shoulders. "Gosh, it's just baffling to us."

I look up at a window where the rain makes thin rivers down the glass.

My father used to say, "You can't stay angry forever," but right here, right now, I know he's wrong. I will be angry forever at this death, at these people, and most of all, I will be angry with myself.

I rub my hand over the side of my face and close my eyes.

Father Gaalaas says, "Amen," everyone else in the church says, "Amen" back to him, and then, the rain stops.

As we go from church to cemetery, the clouds part, and the sun comes out, so bright, it hurts the eyes.

There's a caravan of cars and pickups and the hearse, all

winding over these narrow country roads for what seems like a hundred miles to a cemetery in the middle of nowhere called the Old Bokoshe Memorial Gardens.

Someone thought it would be dandy for Bryan to be buried next to a bunch of Aunt Sylvia's relatives, Rafertys and Tanners.

Cars park single file up the hill of the cemetery; some have to park along the road. Everyone walks head down to the tent where eight men take Bryan's casket.

Out of the car, the colors of this place shock my eyes. The grass is vivid green, the earth is a rich dark red, and the tent that covers the hole in the ground where the casket will go is a bright white.

I pull on my sunglasses and follow the crowd.

Someone rolled out an AstroTurf carpet around the hole in the ground and set up a few chairs where Leonard, Sylvia, Erin, and Ricky sit. Front-row seats.

I stand off, arms crossed, sunglasses on my face, and I look around at the strange names on the other headstones, not one Lauck in the place.

Of course, this is all wrong.

My mother was cremated, and her ashes are in Reno. My father was cremated, and his ashes were sent flying over the waves of the ocean. Bryan should have been cremated, his ashes placed in a vase next to our mother or scattered to ocean winds.

Instead, they're going to leave what's left of him here, for eternity, surrounded by strangers related to a woman who never even loved him.

Father Gaalaas is at it again, ashes to ashes, dust to dust, and I can't stand to listen. Instead, I turn my face to that sun that burns so bright in the blue sky. I let it fall over my face, the warmth on my skin, and I close my eyes.

✦ ✦ ✦

By the time we are all gathered at Leonard and Sylvia's place, the rain is back and it hits the house in waves. The wind shakes the frames of the storm windows, and on one, the plastic pulls away and slaps back at the window like a child's hand.

Post-service is a potluck with people who come and go but I don't know any of them. They are Sylvia's people, some friends, a few members of her family.

Grandma and Grandpa didn't come—too far for them to travel.

Mom and Dad didn't come. Who knows why and who cares?

Uncle Charles and Aunt Georgia didn't come. I don't think they were even invited.

When she bothers to introduce me, Sylvia tells people that I am Bryan's adopted sister.

"He wasn't raised with her, though," she says, as if that makes any sense to anyone.

As soon as I can, I break away from her to wander the house. I go from room to room of sofas and chairs and tables. There are photos and knick-knacky things and plenty of dust over the surfaces, but no evidence of Bryan.

Between the kitchen and dining room, Leonard stops in front of me, deviled egg pinched between his fingers.

"Doing okay, kiddo?" he says.

"Sure," I say.

"Did you get something to eat?"

"I'm not hungry," I say.

Uncle Leonard frowns like it's impossible not to be hungry, and shoves the egg in his mouth, the whole thing sliding in, and he makes a big show of chewing.

"Is any of Bryan's stuff here?" I say.

He nods and chews, wiping his fingers off on his pants and

dipping his chin as he swallows. "Sure," he says. "I bet you'd like something to take home."

"I guess," I say.

"You bet," he says. "You can have whatever you want. The kids already took what they wanted." He puts a big paw of a hand on my shoulder and calls to Erin, who's over at the buffet. "Jen here wants to see some of Bry's stuff," he says. "Can you show her where it's at?"

Erin separates herself from the crowd of people, carrying a plate heaped with macaroni salad and bread. She's a younger version of Sylvia and Leonard, the perfect combination of bland.

"Sure," she says, forking salad into her mouth and tilting her head to tell me to follow.

Erin leads me up a flight of steep steps to the attic where a box is balanced on an old table.

"Here," she says, one hand holding her plate, the other waving at the taped-up box.

Rain hits the roof over us and I go to the big cardboard box.

"Thanks," I say. "You don't have to stay with me; you can get back to the . . ."

I don't know what to call this thing they are having—a party, a wake, an open house?

"It's okay," she says, leaning against the side of an old dresser and wiping her mouth with one hand.

I give my best go-away look but it's wasted on her. Erin's attention is back on her food, forking it into her mouth as if this is her last meal.

I take a deep breath and pull the tape off the box, that sound mixed with the sound of rain over us. This must be his stuff from college—books, records, papers. I pick out a red plastic cup that says THE UNIVERSITY OF OKLAHOMA on the rim. Inside is a heavy beaded necklace with a cross on the end. I pull up and up, and it's actually a rosary as long as my arm.

Erin bites into her bread and talks with her mouth full. "You can have those," she says.

"Really?" I say, eyebrows way up on my face. *Oh yeah, these really add up to my brother; I'll treasure them always.* "Gee, thanks," I say.

Erin's jaw slows on her chewing and her eyes watch me, not sure. She sets her plate down on the dresser and wipes her hands off on her jeans.

I do my best to ignore her completely and shift myself so my back is to her, hands over Bryan's things, papers, a cleaner he used for his records, a few albums.

Erin moves around so she can see what I do but she keeps her distance now, which is probably wise.

Along the side of the box is the edge of something and I fish out this photo that is at least 14 inches wide and long. The shot is a full-size of Bryan wearing a yellow T-shirt, face flushed and sweaty, and in the background is a chain-link fence around what looks like a tennis court.

I look over at Erin but she shakes her head.

"Why not?" I say.

"Because," she says. She reaches her hand between us but I pull the picture away.

"Why?" I say.

"It's mine," she says.

"You had this stuff all packed," I say.

"So?" she says.

"So Uncle Leonard said I could have something," I say.

"You can," Erin says. "You've got the rosary."

"But I want this," I say.

"No," she says.

"Why?" I say.

"Because it's mine," she says.

We stand there, the two of us, the sound of rain on the roof.

"Look," I say, my voice calm and low, "I'll take it, make a copy and send it back to you."

There's no give in her though and she shakes her head.

"It's my picture," she says, "you can't take it."

The way she's being makes no sense at all and if I was myself, I'd just sneak the damn thing, steal it if I had to but right now, I'm not myself and I feel like tearing the photo up in a hundred pieces just so she won't have it either.

She looks at me and I look at her, all this around in my head and I take a deep breath. I put the photo down on top of the box of Bryan's things and leave the room.

My heels make the only sound on the wood steps, louder than they should be, but I don't care. Without looking at anyone, I go through the dining room, living room, and then out the front door.

The gutters are rusted through and rain splatters onto the edge of what seems to be a porch. It's more like a leaning bunch of boards that give a little relief to the house.

I'd do anything to leave right now, but it's dark, I don't have a car, and I'd be soaked to the bone after 30 seconds in that rain. I feel wet already and I'm just on the porch. I lean against the house, arms crossed over myself, and the sticky-sweet smell of this place is all around.

The front door opens and I hold still. Leonard steps out on the porch then, his weight moving the whole thing. He looks into the shadows.

"All alone out here?" he says.

I don't say anything and Leonard goes back, flips on the

porch light, a bare yellow bulb with black threads of a broken spider web hanging around the bottom of the fixture.

"There you are," he says, walking to where I'm at. He digs down into his pockets and pulls up a pack of cigarettes. "Did you find anything you wanted?" he says.

"Yep," I say.

"Good," he says, lighting up and then taking a drag that makes his round face pull in at the cheeks.

I look down at my black shoes and my toes feel wet inside. "There was a photo," I say. "But Erin says she wants it."

He blows smoke into the night. "Yeah," Leonard says, "well, Erin and Bryan were pretty tight."

"Really?" I say.

"Oh sure," he says, voice upbeat and happy.

"You know," I say, "when Bryan was at my wedding, he told me a lot of things, but he never mentioned Erin."

Leonard looks my way and narrows his eyes behind his thick glasses. The good thing is, the man doesn't know me at all, so I make my eyes go wide open and innocent.

"Hmm," he says, looking out at the night again, "that's funny."

The rain hammers the fiberglass roof over the porch and he stays quiet.

Since I came here yesterday, I've waited for Leonard to tell me he's sorry about my brother's death, to say how he and Sylvia might have let Bryan down but that hasn't happened. Instead, I've listened to him talk like an expert on the investigation of Bryan's death, the police reports, the specifics of what happened and when. He says a lot but says nothing at the same time. He doesn't know the actual day Bryan died, or even the day he disappeared and he didn't go to where they found his body so he doesn't know what the land looked like. Still, in his know-it-all way, he says he's not convinced it was suicide despite the fact that the case is closed.

Now, I can't even look at Leonard without the question in my head. What the hell went wrong, why is my brother dead and I know I can't leave this place without asking.

"Can I ask you a question?" I say.

"Shoot," he says.

"Why do think Bryan didn't do it?" I say.

Leonard snaps to attention, his whole face still.

"You are direct, aren't you?" he says.

It's not really a question, so I don't answer. I just stand there and wait.

"Motive," Leonard says then. "There's just no reason for it." He moves his tongue around on his lips, spits out a bit of something, maybe tobacco.

"Is there a suspect or some evidence of another person involved?"

"Well," he says, cigarette between his fingers, looking at something under his fingernail, "the roommate was a little off, but no, there's no evidence." He looks off into the night. "At least that's what they tell me."

"Who?"

"The police at the university."

"Did you meet his roommate?"

"No."

"So how do you know he's off?" I say.

He looks at me again and squints. "Peg told me you were going to go into journalism," he says.

"I might," I say.

He nods, watching me, but he doesn't answer my question. "That's nice," he says, looking away from me.

I shift my skirt around my hips, smooth my sweater, and the rain slows down over us. I want to ask him again why the roommate is off but I don't know how. I don't really care about his suspicions, I'm just trying to make my way to the question I can't get out of my head.

"Why did Bryan come here?" I say.

"Excuse me?" Leonard says.

"When he came to the wedding in August, he told me that he had a choice," I say. "I just wonder why he was with Aunt Georgia and Uncle Charles but then left. Why did he decide to pick you guys? I mean he was from Carson and all."

Leonard looks at me the way you do when you want to figure something out, one eye closed, lips pressed together in a kiss.

I try as hard as I can to look confused and maybe a little dense, and finally, Leonard looks away and moves his foot over the edge of the porch.

"There was a pact," he says, "between your dad and me."

"A pact?" I say.

"You know, the kind of pact brothers make?"

I lean my shoulder into a post that holds up the roof for the porch. "No," I say, "I don't know about that kind of a pact."

Leonard flicks his cigarette off the edge of the porch. "Well, back when we were kids, we swore, if anything happened to either of us, we would take care of each other's kids."

"Really?" I say.

"You bet," he says.

The rain slows from a downpour to a shower and the wind blows from cool to warm.

"So Bryan knew about this pact?" I say.

"Well, he didn't at first," Leonard says, "but I told him about it."

I take a deep breath in, the air thick and too sweet.

"I'm a little confused," I say.

Uncle Leonard has both his hands in his pockets now and he shifts his weight so we are face to face.

"Maybe I can help?" he says.

I look for a way to be polite and gracious, at least to be fair, and then I take a deep breath. "If you made a deal, why didn't you take me too?"

Leonard's face is a wide-open fill-in-the-blank look, like a lie before it's told.

"Well, ah," he says, "because. Well, you see, you kids didn't get along—that's why."

I want him to tell me about the lie, how I supposedly accused Bryan of having sex with me. I want to know if Leonard is the asshole who started that rumor or if he was just the one who kept it alive.

"But you made a deal," I say, "right?"

"Well, yes, it was a deal," he says.

"And it seems that if you made a pact, well, it wouldn't matter what we thought; we were kids."

Leonard adjusts his pants around his round middle and steps back from me. "I don't think I like your tone," he says.

"I'm just trying to understand here," I say, standing off the post. "I'm trying to get a picture of two brothers who made a pact and how it was important to take Bryan, and to tell Bryan this story, but this is the first I've heard of it."

"Maybe you can't understand some things," he says. "Maybe you're not supposed to."

"Maybe you don't want me to," I say. "Or maybe you're not telling the truth."

"Now you're out of line," he says, finger up at me, voice stern like a father on the brink of punishment. "You're obviously upset and confused."

The rain stops, just like that, and the quiet is so strange compared with all the noise of before.

"Look," I say, "my brother is dead and he's all I had left. I don't think wanting to know what happened makes me confused."

The wire of Leonard's glasses press in at the sides of his bald head, making indents at his temple skin as if they are too small for his head. He moves his hand over his jaw then, adjusting his glasses on his face.

"We did our best with Bryan," he says. "He made his own choices."

"So what now?" I say. "Are you changing the theory that it wasn't suicide?"

Leonard shifts his weight on the porch, a red stain of color up his neck and face. "This conversation is over," he says.

"What conversation?" I say. "You haven't told me anything."

Leonard doesn't say anything else though, a posture of outrage that gets him over to the door, pulling it open in a huff, and then going into the house without looking my way again.

I stand there, alone, the sounds of people in the house talking and I wonder if Leonard is filling everyone in on what a terrible person I am, confused, upset, pissed off.

Laughing at myself, I shake my head and wipe the moisture off my face.

What am I going to do now?

I lean against the house, moisture from the siding pushing through my skirt and hose, and I look up at the green fiberglass roof, bits of leaves and twigs stuck up there.

As much as I hate it, I'm the survivor, like Aunt Georgia likes to say, the one who stands alone watching the twisted, burning wreckage and wondering, Am I lucky or am I really being punished by my survival?

I close my eyes, and in my head are Bryan, Leonard, Sylvia, the truth, the lies, and, before this, Mom and Dad and more lies, and before that, my own parents and what terrible mistakes were made that led to a path that ends here in a place that smells like death when it rains.

I'm not going to get any answers from these people, from anyone in my family, when am I ever going to learn and the frustration of that reality makes me feel like I'm lost, like I don't know where I'm going or even how to go on.

The rain starts up again, small drops slapping on the fiberglass roof and I open my eyes to this life.

You will go on, I tell myself, you're going to get out of here, get away from these people and put as much space between you and them as possible. You're going to do something with your life, something important and all you have to do is get out of here and do it.

The yellow of the lightbulb makes a circle of yellow light near the door and through that light, the rain sparkles like small jewels just before it hits the ground to become mud. I cross my arms over my stomach, such a hard feeling in me, like I'm turning to stone right here on the front porch.

PART SIX
CAREER

SIX

SPOKANE, WASHINGTON ❧ 1988

"Hey, over here," a guy says. "Come wish our buddy a happy birthday."

"Yeah," another guy says, "interview him."

At the back of the banquet room is a table of guys who have on tuxedos, and it looks like they're having a party. The guy who calls to us has a beard and glasses; the other guy is bald and his cheeks are red. They laugh and slap at the back of this younger guy, clean-cut with dark hair.

Show up somewhere with a television camera, and people can't wait to make asses of themselves. It happens every time.

I hold the camera tripod in both hands and because I have on sunglasses, no one can see how I roll my eyes.

Lyle stands with his camera in one hand, flat out ignoring the table of guys and looking around the room.

"I'm going to shoot up there," Lyle says, curly hair and bushy eyebrows.

"Try not to lose anything."

"Ha, ha," he says, taking the tripod away from me.

The guys are still at the table but I flip open my notepad to look like I'm deep in the business of writing.

My story was on a drug operation in Idaho but it fell through after Lyle lost a fuse to his camera and we had come back to town. Now we're stuck covering an art benefit, what I call fluff news.

"Come on," the beard says, hand reaching in my direction, "it's the guy's birthday."

I look their way again and the birthday guy is pretty cute, this movie-star quality to his face, wide smile, straight nose, and just looking at him makes me feel better somehow, less angry at how Lyle blew my story.

"Sorry," I say, shrugging one shoulder, "we don't cover birthdays."

All the guys laugh at that, drinks held up, cheers.

Part of me is drawn into their fun and camaraderie. I envy them in a way, but I'm not here to have fun. I have a job to do.

A year after Bryan died, I became beat-reporter covering crime and investigation. I've worked at three different stations from Montana to Washington, have moved seven times, and have been divorced from Lance for over a year. I put in 60 to 80 hours a week—half my money comes from overtime.

For a personal life, I have a long-distance thing going with a guy in Boise, a great apartment here that overlooks a park, and a dog, this little cocker spaniel I call Carmel.

Compared with the fun these guys are having, though, my life depresses me.

Lyle has his camera balanced on his shoulder, takes a wide shot of the room, and I put more space between myself and the table, looking one more time at the birthday boy.

He has on a pressed white shirt, cuffs unbuttoned, sleeves rolled to his forearms, and he's laughing at something someone said, his head back, not a care in the world. As if he knows he's being watched, he shifts his eyes to me. They have a shimmer to them, like light on water.

I could pretend I'm not looking his way, but I don't. Instead, I smile and mouth the words *Happy birthday.*

His smile lifts a little at that and he nods like he understands.

About two months after Bryan's funeral, I went to the house at Twelve Mile to see Grandma and Grandpa.

They were there like always, in the basement, Grandpa with the remote control in his hand, flipping through the channels, Grandma with her legs curled under her body, reading a paperback romance.

I sat at my old spot at the end of the green plaid sofa and it felt like nothing had even happened.

Grandma, Grandpa, and me talked about nothing, really—the weather, which had been unusually hot; Grandpa's golf game, which was a little off.

Since the funeral, I had been in a strange funk, as if all the deaths in my family were rolled into this one, forcing me to a complete stop. I got sick with some lung infection, didn't have the energy to keep up with school, dropping out midterm, and even Lance was getting pissed off at me.

"Why don't you just snap out of it," he said, "you didn't even like the guy."

Grandma and Grandpa were already over it, there was no sign Bryan's death was taking a toll, at least none I could see. In fact, I noticed almost immediately they had put away his photo that had been on top of the TV all these years.

Was that the trick? Put away the photos, forget, move on. Are you really supposed to just snap out of it? And if you are, why can't I stop feeling so bad?

"Can I ask you guys something?" I said, a slip in my voice that Grandma took for tears. She took their box of tissues off their big table and handed it my way.

"Of course you can," she said.

I shook my head to her offer of tissues and leaned forward on the sofa, elbows on my knees. I was way past tears.

"Leonard says he took Bryan because of a pact between him and my father," I said. "Is that the truth?"

"If Leonard told you that," Grandma said, "I'm sure it's true."

Grandpa nodded his agreement.

"Why?" I said, "why is it true just because he says it?"

Grandma held the box of tissues in her lap and Grandpa shifted forward in his chair.

"Jenny?" Grandpa said, "what's on your mind?"

I licked my lips then and took a deep breath.

"I don't believe it," I said, "I think he used that story to get Bryan away from Georgia and Chuck."

Grandpa frowned then, a little crease between his eyes just above his glasses and Grandma moved her hand around the collar of her tropical print dress like she was checking for something.

"Bryan chose to go with Leonard," Grandma said.

"Or maybe he was bullied by loyalty," I said, "we all know Bryan worshipped Dad."

"Jenny!" Grandpa said. "What's gotten into you?"

They both looked at me like they didn't know who I was.

I didn't know every detail of the story but it was coming into focus. I talked to Aunt Georgia and Uncle Charles after the funeral and they told me about the battle over Bryan. They knew all about the pact. In fact, it was the pact that made Bryan's decision for him. Before that story, he was going to stay in Carson with Aunt Georgia and Uncle Charles. He was going to sign the custody papers.

"If he'd stayed with Georgia and Chuck," I said, "maybe he'd still be alive today."

Grandpa watched me for a long time, a tick in his jaw, and Grandma looked from him to me, hand still at the collar of her dress.

"You cannot blame anyone for what happened to Bryan," she said in a low voice, "It's something we can't understand."

"Why?" I said.

"Why?" she said.

"Why can't I blame someone," I said. "Why can't anyone take a little responsibility? Why can't we even talk about it?"

"That is enough," Grandpa said, shaking his finger at me just like Leonard had done in Oklahoma.

"Why?" I said. "Why is it so wrong to want to understand this?"

"You don't want to understand," he said. "You want to blame people."

"I want the truth," I said.

"The truth is, we did what we thought was right for you kids," Grandpa said. "Case closed."

Grandma started to cry then, nose going red, tears rolling down her face. "After all we've done for you," she said, shaking her head, "to blame us like this." She pulled a tissue and held it to her nose. "We did the best we could," she said, pushing a tissue up behind her glasses.

"That's not what I mean." I reached to her but she pulled deeper into her chair.

"Grandpa?" I said. "Come on—why can't we can talk about this?"

As still as stone, Grandpa watched Grandma, his whole face still in that frown, and then he looked over at me. "Maybe you should just leave now," he said.

"What?" I said.

He moved his whole hand over his face, not looking at me at all.

"Just go," he said.

I left that day, this feeling in me that there was nothing between us after all. It was fine when I was the good girl, the one who didn't ask questions, the one who smiled and refilled their cocktails but when it came to the truth, there was no room for me anymore.

I told myself it didn't matter if Grandma and Grandpa didn't love me anymore, I'd lost everything anyway.

Not long after, they moved from Mom and Dad's place to California to live near my Aunt Carol and Aunt Mary Beth. A few years after that, they died.

Grandpa went first, Grandma died a few months later.

On the fourth day of June, I sit in a bar called Cyrus O'Leary's with a bunch of late-shift coworkers. There's Lyle, a producer named Ava, another camera guy named Allen, and the guy who does weather.

Why I hang around with these people, I don't know. They don't like me, and honestly, I don't like them. Still, we always end up together after work at some bar, a motley crew of late-nighters who debrief over a beer.

Bernard Shaw is on CNN reporting about a bombing in Israel, and I sip at my beer, gone warm now. Everyone at my table watches CNN and I wonder how you get a job there.

A guy walks past our table, looks our way, my way, and there's something familiar about him.

He sits at a table against the wall and I look at the door of the bar, waiting for a woman to come in and join him, but the door stays closed.

When I look over at the table again, he's still there, alone, and he orders a beer from a waitress. How do I know him?

Leaning across the table, I push at Lyle's elbow, and he looks my way with his glass blue eyes.

"Two o'clock," I whisper, head tilted. "Who's the guy?"

Lyle raises his bushy eyebrows as if he's curious and looks at the guy, who is still alone. He frowns for a minute and then leans back to me.

"Ballet Art Auction," he says.

"When?" I say.

"A couple weeks ago," he says. "Birthday boy."

I pick up my glasses, unfold them, and put them on my face.

The guy sips at his beer, looking up at the television.

"Go for it," Lyle says, and laughs, smirk on his face. "God knows you need a good thrashing."

I give Lyle my best fuck-you look, and Allen, watching us, laughs and shakes his head.

As I take off my glasses, Lyle's words sting, even though I'd never show it. He always says I'm uptight, too serious, but I don't give a shit what he thinks.

"Excuse me," a voice says from behind me, and it's the guy, close enough to touch, his beer in one hand.

"I think we've met," he says.

"Really?" I say, clearing my throat, surprised.

"Yeah," he says, combing his hand through his hair, nervous, maybe. "It was my birthday a couple weeks back, and you were there, with that guy, I think."

I look over at Lyle, who lifts his eyebrows, *I told you so,* and

I turn around to face the guy completely, my back to everyone at the table.

"I'm sorry," I say, shaking my head but I'm stalling. I remember his movie star smile and those eyes that shimmer like light on water and I remember how he was part of something with those other guys, something that I wanted to have but didn't.

"My friends were giving you a hard time," the guy says, "and you had on this suit with black and white checks."

He zigzags his finger over his chest as he describes the suit I wore, and that makes me laugh.

"You have a good memory," I say.

This close, I see how his eyes are blue with flecks of gold.

"I never forget a pretty face," he says.

"Oh, that's good," I say, looking over my shoulder at Lyle, but he's not even watching anymore.

"Is it okay if I join you?" he says.

"Me?" I say. "You want to sit?"

"Yes," he says, "if that would be all right."

I roll my lips together, trying not to show how flattered I am.

"You bet," I say, pushing out an empty stool at the end of our table.

The summer after Bryan died, Lance and I moved to Montana. He got a promotion to a store in Billings and I finally snapped out of my funk about Bryan, bought myself a little dog, and got back into college.

At first, things were good for us. Lance was a successful manager, we bought a house, and I was hired as a reporter in my senior year of college.

I wanted to be the next Barbara Walters or even a foreign correspondent, and Lance thought that was just great—at least that's what he said. Somewhere in there, he also talked about kids again, reminding me that I did agree to have a few after we were married four years. I nodded—*Sure, sure, kids; yeah, four years.*

I don't know if it was our jobs or that I didn't really love him the way you should love a person you are married to, but Lance and I pulled apart. Right after I started to work, we started to fight about everything, but mostly about how Lance wanted me home when he was home.

Lance took a transfer to Seattle, saying a move to a new town would cure our problems.

"Seattle?" I said. "No way."

"Come on," Lance said. "We can't pass this promotion up. Seattle is a great opportunity for me, for us."

"But Lance," I said, "we just bought a house."

"We'll sell it."

"But the guy at the bank says you shouldn't sell before you've been in a house for at least five years."

"What does he know?"

"What if it doesn't sell?"

"It will."

"What about my job?" I said.

"You'll get another one, a better one."

"I can't get a TV job in Seattle," I said. "That's a huge market—I don't have the experience."

In our three years together, Lance had changed in so many ways. His muscles had all shifted to a spare tire and his wound-tight quality was now an overconfidence that wouldn't consider failure. He prided himself on being a great salesman, said he could sell ice cubes to Eskimos, and that day, he sold me on going to Seattle.

Turned out, though, I didn't get another job, we didn't sell our house, and we went deeper into debt paying Seattle rent and a Montana mortgage. Worse, Lance finally admitted a truth he had been hiding since we met. He didn't want me to work at all—he never had—and now that I was unemployed, he wanted me to have those four kids and consider myself lucky.

I left him on Christmas Eve 1986, and our divorce was finalized on the third anniversary of Bryan's death in 1987.

Lance got everything, the debt, the house, our stuff, the money in the bank. I got my name. Not Duemore, but Lauck. I was Jennifer Lauck again.

The cute guy turns out to be Steven Roy Dorsey, born and raised in Spokane, graduated from high school in 1980, a ski bum in the winter and a farm worker in the summer who is just about to graduate from college even though he's 27 years old.

He's funny and boy-next-door good-looking but edgy too and a little dangerous. His hair is combed up and back, James Dean style, and he's into car racing and restoring old cars. He says the women in Spokane bore him to death because they just want to get married and have a bunch of kids, and after all, there's plenty of time for that. He loves the idea I want to go to New York and eventually become a foreign correspondent with bullets zinging over my head from a bunker in Beirut.

"I bet you'd look great in a flack jacket," he says.

"You think so?" I say, laughing.

"You bet," he says.

We close down Cyrus O'Leary's that night, talk about everything for three hours, and before we say good night, I do two things I never do when I first meet a guy.

I give him my home telephone number and I kiss him good night.

✦ ✦ ✦

After the divorce, Mom went nuts I didn't take Duemore back as my name, said she was insulted and that I hurt Dad's feelings. I wanted to laugh out loud at the idea of Dad having feelings and her being insulted. I figured they'd both be glad since I was nothing to them anyway.

Still, it turned out to be this big fight where she hung up on me and refused to take my calls.

Once I moved near home again, they did subtle things like never coming into town to see my new place and never watching my reports on the television, but then they would invite me out to the house for dinners and get all upset if I said I was too busy.

It was the same game: *We love you but we're going to treat you like shit.*

When I did get together with them, the house was a mess, the yard was full of weeds, and amazingly, Kimmy did no chores, had her own car, and was being sent to a high-end private school despite the fact that she wasn't even a C-level student.

God, it made me so angry, I could barely hold it in. I couldn't stop comparing, I couldn't stop being bitter. All the years I lived with them, cooking their dinners, ironing their clothes, taking care of Kimmy, keeping the house spotless, the yard weeded and not one 'thank you,' from them, not one, 'hey, you're doing a great job.' I was a slave for them and they got paid for me.

I stopped making the effort to go out to the house and I did a little personal investigation. It's amazing what you can find when you're persistent and pissed off.

I got ahold of all the years of Social Security benefit information—the VA even sent me some paperwork—and then I called Mom and Dad on the telephone to have a heart-to-heart chat.

"Remember that money you guys promised to save for my college?"

"What money?" Dad said.

"What money?" I said. "You cannot be serious."

"There was no money," Dad said.

Mom was breathing on the other line and I heard her catch her breath.

I was in my apartment with papers from the Social Security and the Veterans Administration all over the coffee table and the floor. It was my own little evidence hearing, with Carmel the cocker spaniel as my jury.

She padded over the papers and sat close to me the way she always did when I was home.

"Is that the story you're going to stick with?" I said.

Dad was quiet, and then he said it again. "There was no money!"

I balanced the telephone between my ear and shoulder and moved my hands over the papers, comforted by the feel of facts. I shook one report loose and held it up.

"That's funny," I said, "because I'm holding a bunch of information from the Social Security and the VA, and you know what? This says there was money, and interestingly, there's a part here on an interview Mom gave to a man from the VA. Can I read it to you?"

Carmel watched me, brown eyes the color of milk chocolate and as round as marbles. *Go on,* those eyes said. *Read it.*

The VA report, dated 1975, is the transcription of an interview in which at the age of 12, I told the man I was going to college and Mom said they would "conserve" at least the VA benefits and possibly some of the Social Security benefits.

"That doesn't mean a thing," Dad said. "So what?"

I dropped the VA report on the floor and sat up, my voice like a lawyer in my apartment.

"So do you admit there was actually money?" I said.

"It was for us, not for you," he said.

"And you never said you would save a bit of it?"

"Hell, no," Dad said.

"Dick," Mom said from the other line, "she knows, all right? She knows."

Dad mumbled his old line about how lucky I was, how if it wasn't for them, I'd be in a ditch in L.A., and I looked up at the ceiling.

He hung up then, and Mom took over, clearing her throat. She said it was true, that they did make a mistake of sorts.

"We all did," she said.

"What mistakes did I make?" I said.

"There's no use in pointing fingers," she said. "What's done is done."

"Well, that's convenient," I said.

"Look, I don't know what else you want from us," she said.

I looked at the floor, at the papers and lost my train of thought completely. What did I want? The truth was, I didn't care about the money at all, I made it just fine without their help. I guess I just wanted to finally hear her say that she had never loved me, to admit the thing I always knew was true and maybe admit the real reason they agreed to take me.

"Why can't you just admit that the only reason you took me was for the money?" I said.

"That is not true," she said, her voice angry now, a nerve hit hard, "you have no idea how hard it is to raise a child, how expensive it is. Social Security money didn't even cover the telephone bill."

"I wasn't even allowed to talk on the telephone," I said.

"You know what I mean," she said.

"No, I don't." I said.

There was a long silence on telephone then and she cleared her throat.

"There is no use going over all this, we did our best and if I do say so myself, I think you turned out pretty good."

The nerve of her taking credit for my life, as if my time with them made me who I was.

"You did your best?" I said.

"Yes, Jenny," she said.

I cleared my throat then and spoke my words so carefully into the telephone. "Remember when I first came to live with you," I said, "and you told me stories about my mother?"

"Yes," she said, sounding a little confused.

"Remember how you said she was such a good person and that you felt you were friends with her, best friends?"

"Why yes," she said, "and I still believe that."

My apartment was full of afternoon sunlight that cut through the tops of the trees and made patterns of light and shadow on the carpet. Carmel, bored now, put her face on her paws and closed her eyes.

"What would my mother think of the way you've treated me?" I said.

Mom got quiet then, dead quiet, and I thought she might not answer, but then she did, in a voice so low, I barely heard her.

"She wouldn't be pleased," she said.

It was the most truthful thing she had ever said to me, so truthful I couldn't think of another question to ask.

Three months later, I meet Steve, the birthday boy, and meeting him changes the texture of everything.

Colors are brighter, food tastes better, jokes make me laugh harder, and life is just good. Steve is a breath of clean, crisp, perfect air with a great sense of humor and a mystic understanding of my body that he credits to *Cosmo* magazine.

I pull Steve into my world with both hands.

It doesn't matter what time I get off work or what days I can see him, he's always there, ready to go. At midnight, he'll go running with me. Without any notice, he'll jump in the car for a weekend at the beach. Day or night, just say the word, and he throws off his clothes to fool around in the middle of the living room, on the sofa, or anywhere the spirit moves him.

Three months after we meet, he moves in and not much later, he declares his love in this sweet, drunken midnight announcement: "I love you, I mean I really love you."

It's magic to be with him, the kind of thing you read about and hope for, but I can't feel what he feels, I even blow off his "I love you, man," as if it's no big deal. I don't want to get serious with Steve and tell him that being in love is great, but that I've been married before, that it's highly overrated, and that the most important thing is my job.

Steve listens when I talk like that, smiling and nodding like he understands, but deep down, I don't think he really gets it.

A little over a year later, the fire between us settles a little, but not much, and we talk about it as if it's some mystery to be solved. I think it's lust but Steve says lust doesn't go on and on this way. He says it's more like being on a drug, like we're addicted to each other.

Steve works full time for an auction company now, clerking in the office and traveling to these car auctions on the weekends.

I've been submitting my work for awards because awards

look great on your résumé, and one of my friends says I might think about getting an agent before jumping to a bigger market.

I'm still reporting nights and weekends, putting in 60 hours a week, and I've been on a story for the last week that has led the news every night.

This 17-year-old kid disappeared from Spokane. The authorities think he might have been abducted and there's a big hunt for him. On Saturday my cameraman is Allen. On the basis of some reports, we drive west to look around. We stop in these little farm towns, asking casual questions of the local folks in gas stations and grocery stores, and eventually find the kid ourselves at this farm.

It's a big deal to find him the way we do, but after I talk to the kid, who wasn't abducted at all, I think it's wrong to put him on television. He's young, he ran away from home, and he's all mixed up.

It's still our exclusive story but instead of staying and taking video of the tearful mother-and-son reunion, we did a low-key story that says he's safe and that the hunt is over.

My boss, this sourpuss guy, comes unglued that we didn't force an interview on the kid and his mother, calls me at home Saturday night and tells me to get my ass into the office on Monday morning.

Come Monday morning, I have this speech all worked out in my head, a defense for Allen and myself: "It was the right thing to do—I'd do it again." But my boss isn't even in.

While I wait, I look over my phone messages and open my mail, trying not to look as nervous as I feel.

The sounds of the newsroom are a mix of police-scanner static, automatically typing wire reports, and the sharp voice of an assignment editor who argues with someone on the telephone.

Using a letter opener, I slit the back of one envelope and pull out a sheet of paper that says SOCIETY OF PROFESSIONAL JOURNALISTS on the letterhead. I read over the announcement, and it says I've been nominated for five awards.

I look around the newsroom but these people are day-shifters, and I work the night shift. The only people who would be impressed are Lyle and maybe Ava. Steve too. But none of them are here.

I look at the sheet again, reading the words over and over.

"Lauck!"

Looking up, I see my boss is on the other side of the newsroom, hands on his hips, and he waves me over.

I take a deep breath, pulling back the pieces of my own defense, and once he hears about this, he won't be so mad, I'm sure of it.

"Check this out," I say, crossing the newsroom, "five nominations from SPJ."

I shake the letter, the paper rattling.

"Great," he says, no real expression of good or bad on his face.

He holds the door of his office open and does this little head tilt, like *Go on in.*

My boss has never been angry at me; in fact, he pretty much ignores me unless my stories lead, and then he comes by my cubicle and says, "Good work, Lauck."

He closes the door and comes around his desk, sitting down. "Sit," he says, motioning to a chair.

Behind his desk are a couple of framed awards and shoved way behind his computer is a dusty photo of his family, a wife and a couple of daughters, all blondes with big smiles.

With my letter in my hand, I sit on the edge of a chair covered with scratchy gray fabric. Being in here is trouble—I can feel it.

Bits of my speech come back to me, morality, judgment call, and through the walls of his office, the newsroom sounds are far away.

"We're letting you go," my boss says, matter of fact.

I let out a little puff of air—so much for a defense.

"Letting me go?" I say.

"Right," he says.

"You mean I'm fired?" I say.

"Fired is an ugly word," he says.

There is a strange feeling down my neck, a thousand tiny pins pushing into my spine at the same time.

My boss talks about how it isn't personal, but they want to make a change, that I don't fit into the team anymore, and how this weekend proves I'm not right for hard news after all.

He goes on and on but his words stay outside of me.

If anyone asked, I would say I am my work. It is everything, my entire identity, and until this moment I've never imagined anything else for myself.

As my boss talks on and on, it's as if he is unplugging me from the wall.

The failure is all over me.

How do I walk out of here and look at all those people who still have their jobs? How do I get another job after being fired? How do I pay my bills? How do I even move after something like this?

It's so humiliating, the worst possible thing that could happen, and I can't even think. With my thumb and first finger, I push between my eyes and my boss finally shuts up.

In my lap is the letter with the announcement, and before, it was good to be nominated, but now, it's the thing that rescues what little pride I have left. Like a quick little pep talk, I tell myself that being fired is bad, but it could be worse—I could not be nominated at all *and* be fired.

I fold up the nomination announcement and slide it back into the envelope. Clearing my throat, I look over at my boss, a man I barely know who is going bald and always wears wrinkled shirts and ties that are frayed around the edges.

"Is that it?" I say. "Are we done?"

"We have taken the liberty of closing out your paycheck, through the weekend, of course," he says, passing an envelope my way, the familiar check inside. *Gee, thanks.* I take it from the desk and lay it with the other papers on my lap.

He stands with his hand out like he wants to shake or something.

I look at his hand and then at his face.

I've never been fired before but I'm sure you don't shake hands with the asshole who cans you.

I turn around, open the door, and go to my desk to clean out my stuff.

"The guy actually stood there and wanted to shake my hand," I say. "What a prick."

"Gee, Jen," Steve says. "I can't believe it."

"*You* can't believe it?" I say. "What about me?"

Steve and I are on the sidewalk in front of the building where he works. I drove right over, just to tell someone. Steve combs his hand through his hair, looking around.

"Well, shoot," he says, "what are you going to do now?"

"What am I going to do?" I say.

"Yeah," he says.

Right now, I need someone to lean on. I actually thought he

would be that person, but the way he looks, more lost than me, I know he's not.

It's cold out here on the sidewalk in the shade of the brick buildings, and I feel more alone than I have in a long time, probably since Bryan died, the kind of alone that feels like a bottomless hole you could fall in and maybe never crawl up from.

I can't believe I got fired.

Tears burn out of my eyes and I look down so he doesn't see, except it's too late.

"Gee, Jen," Steve says, moving closer then, hand on my shoulder. "I'm really sorry."

I flick the tears off my face.

"Forget it," I say, shaking him off. "I'm fine. Just forget it."

I look past Steve at the street, the traffic, the whole day in front of me with nothing to do. "Well," I say, lifting my shoulders with a deep inhale, "you've got to work, so I'll talk to you later." I dig into my pocket for my keys and open the door of my car.

"What are you going to do?" he says.

I get in and roll down the window. "Maybe go work out," I say.

"No," he says, "about your job." Steve leans down to look at me sitting in the car, his hand on his knees, clean-cut hair combed back, not a care in the world.

In the year we've been together, I've met Steve's family, a mother and a father and a sister who live out in the valley, in the same house Steve grew up in. He has aunts and uncles, grandparents, friends, a history he can always turn back to, people who are there for him to lean on and right now, I'd give anything to have his life instead of mine.

"Don't worry about it," I say. "I'll figure something out."

Making my face into a smile, I start up the car. "See you later," I say.

"Sure," he says, standing away from the car. "See you later."

My job was like being on the freeway going 100 miles an hour; being fired is like crashing against a wall and having to walk the rest of the way.

At the grocery store, in restaurants, even out for a walk with the dog, the eyes that used to recognize me now look down and away. I'm sure everyone in town knows I've been fired, and my failure makes being in Spokane like poison.

I have to leave.

A friend in New York says she'll put in a word for me, another friend says I could come back to Montana, and Lyle, who was just promoted to a station in Portland, says he'll put the word in for me there.

Of all three, Portland seems like the best but instead of waiting around, I hire an employment agency and take the first job they find, which turns out to be as a secretary for a financial planner.

Less than a month after I lose my job, I tell Steve that I put notice on the apartment, called a moving company, and even have a line on some rentals in Portland.

"And you're moving?" he says, looking around. "Just like that? What about me? Where am I going to live?"

"Steve," I say, "I've been telling you that I can't stay here; I have to do something."

We are in the living room, him on the sofa with Carmel, me on the floor, knees pulled to my chest.

Steve takes a deep breath in and out, shoulders sagging, and he combs his hand through his hair.

"I didn't think you'd just up and leave," he says. "It's a little impulsive, isn't it?"

"I guess it's a little impulsive," I say, shrugging my shoulders, "but how about this? Come with me."

Carmel is at attention, watching us with her big milk chocolate eyes.

"I can't just leave," he says.

"Why not?"

"I have a job."

"Steve, you're a clerk for an auction company. Big deal. Is that what you are going to do with your life?"

Steve rubs his face with his hand, not sure what to do.

"Come on," I say, crawling over to where he is, my hands on his knees. "Come with me. It will be a fresh start, an adventure."

I would never admit it but I need Steve to come with me. That need is what I use to convince him. He listens while I make promises I can't keep. I sell him on how cool Portland is compared to Spokane, how there is so much opportunity in a bigger city, that a smart guy like him will get a great job in no time at all. Way back in my memory is how Lance did this to me once, how it was a disaster, but I shake it off, telling myself this will be different.

Portland is called the city of bridges for the 13 bridges that go back and forth from east to west, and off in the eastern sky, you can see Mount Hood and what's left of Mount Saint Helens.

Steve and I get a place in a high-rise called the Parkside Plaza. I walk to work every day and, to help cover expenses, take a second job teaching aerobics at a snooty club on the waterfront.

It turns out being fired is a badge of courage. Anyone worth shit in the business gets fired at least three times. I interview at all four stations in Portland and even though nothing is open yet, people say they are interested.

Steve gets a job leasing cars but it doesn't work out and then he takes two part-time jobs, one at a ski shop, another folding towels at the health club where I work.

That first year in Portland is not good.

I get sick with some strange lung thing that's worse than after Bryan died, and then, after I get better, my skin breaks out in a rash that is itchy and ugly and apparently, a medical mystery.

I hate being a secretary, I hate the guy I work for, and I'm so broke, I miss payments on my student loans and credit cards, calls coming in from bill collectors at all hours.

Steve isn't happy either, says he made a mistake moving to Portland, that there isn't any work for him, and I know he blames me. We fight all the time, so much that Carmel spends most of her time hiding out in a little space in the closet, and Steve finally gives up on us completely.

"You're making me crazy," he says. "I can't take it anymore."

"Don't call me crazy," I say. "You're the one who can't get a goddamned job."

"It's not my fault I can't get a job, it's not like I haven't tried."

"You haven't tried hard enough," I say, "because you don't know what you want to do. Do you think you just graduate from college and then they all line up to hand you a briefcase and keys to an office? What the hell do you want to do anyway? What are you going to do with your life?"

Name the day and the way we fight is always the same.

Steve paces around the living room, combing his hands through his hair like he's holding his head together, and I talk fast with logic that makes sense to me but not to him. Finally, he goes completely silent, not even defending himself, which makes me furious.

"So go!" I yell at him. "Get your shit out of here and leave."

"Fine," he says, hands up in surrender and just like that, he packs up a few boxes and walks out the door.

At first, I don't believe he's gone. It's an act, a bad fight we both need to cool off from. He'll be back that night, the next day, by the weekend, or even the following Monday, but after a while, there is no sign of him, no call, no letter, nothing, and I know he's gone.

I start to really miss him. I miss hearing the sound of him in the apartment, I miss his stuff hanging in the closet, and I even miss fighting with him.

When he was here, I had someone else to talk to, but now, it's just me, and I never did like my own company.

About a month after he leaves, it's a Saturday and I can hardly take the quiet of being alone. I go to the spare bedroom to coax Carmel out of the closet.

"How about a walk?" I say, kneeling down and petting over her soft fur.

Sometimes, I think she's all that keeps me sane these days, brushing her blond fur, making sure she's walked and fed, keeping her nails clipped back.

"What do you say, sweetie?" I say. "You and me, a little stroll?"

Her milk-chocolate eyes are sad and a little wary.

"Come on," I say, "it will do us both some good."

She gets up then, stretching herself out like a cat, long shakes of her back legs. I scoop her up under my arm and hold her like a football, warm little dog body against my side.

The park blocks of town are all grass with tall trees and the light that comes through is broken by the branches. Park benches line the sidewalks and one man is asleep on a bench, arm hanging off the side so far that the back of his hand is against the sidewalk.

Carmel sniffs his way but I steer her to the opposite side of the park.

I wonder what Steve's doing this morning, if he's missing me, but I know he's not. Of course he's not.

My shadow lies on the sidewalk in front of me, connected at my feet but angled off on its own direction. I follow behind Carmel, and my shadow goes ahead.

A couple walks toward me on the sidewalk, hand in hand, and the woman says, "Isn't that a cute dog?"

Sunglasses on my face, I smile like everything is great but they probably can see how I'm this lonely woman walking a dog, no man to hold hands with or to share her Saturday. I rub over my arms, broken out with a fresh rash that itches whenever I think about it. I scratch at myself and watch them walk away, still hand in hand.

Carmel is intent on sniffing the base of a tree, so I look around. Across the street is a New Age bookstore called Forces of Nature. Portland has a lot of those places. Steve and I used to joke about the whole New Age movement, how it was just a bunch of whiny granola eaters stuck in the '60s.

I stand there for a long time and after Carmel finishes her sniff, I pick her up and cross over.

Inside Forces of Nature, strange music plays, this combination of flute and wind chimes, and the air smells musty, like incense.

A woman at the counter has on a sunburst tie-dye dress and this serene expression on her face as she says, "Welcome."

I smile, keeping myself to myself, and move around the edges of the store. I look at the shelves of books on everything from meditation to Buddhism to angels. Under Self-Help are titles like *Healing Your Inner Child, The Wounded Child,* and *Healing the Child Within*. I thumb through one, then slide it back on the shelf just as quickly.

Past the books is a wall of glass shelves, crystals and beads and little rocks with sayings carved in them like "Calm" and "Peace." I move my hand over the one that says "Peace," and it's smooth and cool on my fingers. Turning it over, it says six dollars—yikes, six bucks for a rock.

I drop it back into the pile with the other rocks and move on to a bulletin board with the names of all sorts of people, psychics, tarot card readers, and hypnoregression therapists.

It's like browsing in a record store, almost overwhelming unless you know what you want. Where do you start with something like this, and how do you ask?

Hi. I'm completely screwed up, my ex-boyfriend thinks I'm insane, and other than that little blond dog out there, I have no successful relationships. What would you recommend, a deck of tarot cards or just some crystals?

Outside, a woman squats by Carmel, petting her, and I watch until she gets up and moves on.

I scratch at my itchy arm again and take a deep breath, looking around at all the strange stuff that seems to promise something I can't quite figure out.

Can a rock that says PEACE and a little incense help move me forward or at least shift me in that direction? I almost laugh at the whole idea, so stupid and simple, and yet, what do I have to lose?

Twenty bucks later, I walk home with a bag of New Age goodies, the "peace" rock, some incense, and a tape of ocean sounds, Self Help 101.

At home, I check my messages, and of course, he didn't call. What did I expect? But that's fine; I don't need him.

I put on the tape of ocean sounds, light a stick of Nag Champa, put the "peace" rock on my nightstand, and even though everything stays exactly the same, I do feel a new idea come on.

Maybe I just need a fresh start, a clean slate, and if I just get rid of any evidence of Steve, I'll stop thinking about him.

It's not the best rationale, but it's something to keep me busy.

I make a pile of photos of Steve, souvenirs I picked up when we were together and gifts he gave, and that leads me to a sweep of my whole apartment, where I sort and organize and clean.

For the rest of the day, I toss out old clothes, shoes, magazines, photos, and as I work, I tell myself I'm going to be fine, there isn't anything wrong with me, I will meet someone else, I will find a good job back in TV, and I will get through this. I will. I will make myself get through it.

Carmel sleeps on the sofa, ocean wave sounds fill up the apartment, and the incense is almost burned down when I get to the spare bedroom closet where I store my old pink trunk.

Carmel made her little bed right next to this, a place to hide out when Steve and I would fight, and I don't want to see her in the closet ever again.

I pull the trunk out, and the pink metal is dented on the top now, with deep scratches in the pink and silver paint. I open the lid, and it's like it has always been, a time capsule of a child; pink princess bedding, faded daisy sheets and a pile of stuffed animals and running trophies.

The ocean cassette tape snaps off and I hold myself so still, no feeling in me at all.

I take a deep breath like I'm going under water, holding myself from thinking about what I'm doing. As quick as I can, I take out my parents' wedding album, the velvet bag that holds just her pearls now because I lost the wedding ring when I was with Lance, and put both things on the top shelf of my closet. There's no way I can throw away books, so I dig those out too, *Grimm's Fairy Tales*, the *Little House* series, *Ferdinand the Bull*. Then, I put the bedding, stuffed animals, and trophies back inside, close the lid with a thump, shove the crooked lock closed and carry the whole thing down to the Dumpsters.

Over the next six months, things don't get better; they just get different.

I do get a job back in TV as a part-time producer, thanks to Lyle. I move out of my apartment and to cut down on expenses, I move in with a woman I met at the health club. I even sell my parents' old dining room set as a way to lighten the load and help pay off a little debt.

I start dating a rich kid from New York who is nice enough but smokes too much pot and has no idea what he wants to do with his life.

I try to figure out what's wrong with my skin, talking to doctors and even a few natural healers, who give advice about diet, eat citrus, stop all dairy, try marigold cream, and then one man, a throwback to the '60s, complete with the headband and long beard, says my problem isn't my skin.

How I ended up in his store, I don't know, but there I was in this place that sold everything from dried mushrooms to dandelion heads, and the guy took one look at my rash—not even a close look.

"Your skin isn't the problem, man," he said.

"Excuse me?" I said.

"You gotta go deeper," he said.

"Deeper?" I said.

His dark brown hair was longer than mine, parted down the middle, and tucked behind his ears. His eyes were the color of dry dirt.

"This is old energy working its way out," he said, stepping back from me then, an expression on his face like he was almost disgusted I didn't get it. "You have a therapist?" he said.

Putting my hand on my chest, I laughed. "No, of course not." That got me an even more disgusted look.

"If I were you," he said, "I'd get one." He went behind his counter then, pulled out a clipboard, ignoring me, and I scratched at my itchy arms, broken out with a fresh rash that looked like a burn, so ugly.

I didn't need a therapist. People who saw therapists were on the streets talking to themselves, screaming at the sky, head cases who thought they were Napoleon in another life.

What I had was an allergy or something simple that could be fixed with a pill or an herbal concoction but here was this guy saying things I couldn't even imagine.

What did he know that I didn't and how could I ask?

I stood there for a long time, waiting for something to happen, and finally, he looked up at me, like *You're still here?*

"Isn't there anything you would recommend?" I said, looking around at the walls of jars with all their herbs inside. "I mean, surely there is something I can try?"

He shook his head then, a fast push of air out his nose.

"Bee pollen," he said. "You might try some bee pollen."

I bought the bee pollen that day but it didn't work. In fact, my skin got worse and that's what pushed me to break down, out of ideas and natural healers, just flat out of energy to even search for help. I was on the floor of my apartment crying, desperate, so sad without knowing why. My life felt like a punishment but I couldn't figure out what it was I had done or how to atone.

From my spot on the floor, I looked up at the ceiling while Carmel looked worried at me from her spot on the bed and I asked myself what I wanted most in life. If there is just one thing you want Jennifer, what it is it and so fast, almost too fast the word "peace," came into my head. It wasn't like some New Age thing either, it was a desire for calm that could live inside my soul. I needed to find my way to peace.

Another six months went by and I stopped dating the guy from New York, took some freelance work with this woman who needed someone to write audio scripts and one day, at a recording studio where I was working, I met a man in a wheelchair.

Jay was a musician in town from San Francisco, this mystic guy who was paralyzed from the chest down after he went on an acid trip in the '60s and did a swan dive out the window in order to avoid being drafted into the military.

In his van, all equipped for him to drive, we went out to dinner a few times and just hung around together at the recording studio, talking about everything. He was into astrology and meditation and Carl Jung and when he gave me a book that was published by the Foundation for Inner Peace, I felt like it was a sign.

He used to say that he chose to stay in this life and learn all of its lessons. When Jay jumped out of the window and lifted out of his body that was crumpled on the sidewalk, he knew he had a choice; live and be paralyzed for the rest of his life, or give up and potentially face the possibility of reliving this life again.

Before Jay, I never considered that life was full of lessons. I never thought about the possibility of other lives, karma, the universe, and collective consciousness.

Everything changed just by talking to Jay, who listened to my ideas, so silly compared with his, so superficial in a lot of ways.

It was Jay who told me I had a very big head and a small heart, which he didn't say to hurt my feelings but more to show that I thought about things too much and didn't feel enough. He was also the second person to recommend a little therapy, promising it wasn't just for the mentally disturbed.

From Mr. Bee Pollen to Jay and then to a bunch of great books on every subject from Buddhism to astrology to psychology, I put myself on a mission to find this peace I wanted.

I didn't do therapy, I wasn't ready for that, but I did take in so many new ideas that I could feel a change, a slowing down, a softening. My skin wasn't completely better, but it healed a little and then, Steve called.

The Convention Center is near the river, twin towers of glass that point to the sky like rockets. On the south side, Silver Collector Cars holds its auction, which is a parking lot of cars, people milling around eating hot dogs and popcorn, and a staging area where cars are driven, one by one, to be auctioned to the highest bidder.

Steve is the one on stage with a microphone in his hand, the fast cadence of selling in his voice and through the room. Hands go in the air, the bidding strong.

"Sold," Steve says, pointing at a man in the front row. "Number fifty-two, you bought it right there!"

On the phone, he told me he was an auctioneer now and that he wanted me to come see him.

I walk along the edge of the place, blending in, and part of me is happy to see Steve again, maybe too happy, but then, there's how he left a year ago without calling one time. What will happen with us now? Will the year have made him stop caring about me? What will I feel for him?

A red Mustang pulls up on the stage and Steve says, "Now that's a great car," into the microphone.

I lean against a door that has an exit sign over the top in green letters.

Another guy describes the Mustang and Steve takes a sip of bottled water, looking around the room and then stopping when he sees me.

He squints like he's making sure first, then so fast, he smiles that movie-star smile that I remember so well, that shimmer in his eyes like light on water.

Goose bumps run a race over my skin, up my arms, meet between my shoulder blades, and I lift my hand in a wave.

After the auction, we go to a restaurant called Casa U Betcha and order margaritas.

"You were so good up there," I say, my hand flat on the table between us, not sure what to do, touch him or just keep to myself.

"I've got a long ways to go," he says, "but thanks."

"I mean it," I say. "You were wonderful. I'm so proud of you."

He looks a little embarrassed but past that is something else, a flinch inside his blue eyes.

"I guess I did amount to something after all," he says.

Just like that, we are at the exact place we parted and I can still hear my own angry voice yelling at him, "What are you going to do with your life?" What was the matter with me? Why was I so hard on him?

Looking down at my glass with its salt around the rim, I feel terrible.

"I'm really sorry about that, Steve," I say, looking at him again, eye to eye.

"No," he says, waving me off in this brave, *It doesn't matter* way. "You were right. I didn't know what I wanted."

I've been the way he's being now, acting tough about things that really hurt me, and I can see right through to the truth. I hurt him more than I know—and more than I can live with.

I reach across the table and put my hand on top of his, the feel of him familiar against my own skin. "No," I say, "I wasn't right and I mean it—I'm sorry."

He looks like he might dodge me again but doesn't. He holds my eyes and nods like he understands.

Over dinner, we cross back and forth through the year we were apart, his story of becoming an auctioneer, mine about Mr. Bee Pollen and Jay, and in our talking, we pull back together, the same in a lot of ways, but different too.

I know he wants to try things again, it's right there in his shy smile and the way his blue eyes move over me like a touch. Even though I can't make any promises that I will be easier this time around, I do take him home with me that night, and after Carmel greets him with licks and her funny little welcome-home dance, I pull him back into my life with both hands.

Less than two months into being together, Steve says he wants to get married, and in fact, it's the only way he'll stay with me.

"I want to have a house and maybe some kids," he says. "I want to do those things with you but if you don't want to do them with me, I'll understand and move on."

I don't want to be married but I don't want to be without

Steve either and so, we get married that October and buy an old house that needs a complete restoration.

I finally start searching for a therapist.

After a short stint with a woman who made me hold her hand while she chanted, "Om," and another woman who wanted me to interpret my pain with objects from the natural world, I found Howard Waskow, a white-haired, white-bearded man with a taste for cotton shirts with tropical prints.

Howard has his office in the attic of an old house that was converted to office space. The walls are painted white, the carpet is a warm brown, and two wicker chairs with mashed-down pads, face each other. He has a side table of blond wood with little carvings of animals, a pad of paper, and a box of tissues; a leggy plant over by the window; and on the wall over his right shoulder are two photos of still water, one from the mountains, the other from the sea.

On our first day together, I sit with my hands gripped on the armrests of a wicker chair, eyes on the photos of water and piece together a story. I start with Steve and being married even though I never wanted to be married again and how I love him so much but don't feel like he really knows or understands me. Then there is my family, a mother and a father I can barely have a civil conversation with, whom I haven't actually seen in years, and of course, there is all that moving around I've done, my work in TV news that used to seem so important but now feels shallow and empty, the divorce from Lance, the death of my brother, and the years of guilt because I know I should have done something to help him but didn't.

As I talk it out, I check in with Howard, looking past his wire-rimmed glasses and into his brown eyes for some sign that he's being plowed under by my story but he just nods and listens, hands folded together over his round stomach.

I look at the photos of water again and go on, telling him

everything as fast as I can, just to get it out before the hour is up. I tell about my evil stepmother, living almost homeless in L.A., the death of my father, and I end with the death of my mother.

There're still 30 minutes left on the clock when I finish and I'm worn out by myself but Howard doesn't look tired at all. He watches me closely, as if he can see something with every gesture and inflection, asks if that's it, which makes me laugh.

"Isn't that enough?" I say.

He laughs too, nodding, and in his eyes is a look something like admiration. "Actually," he says, "you've done remarkably well."

"Remarkably well at what?" I say.

"Living a normal life," he says.

I laugh again and roll my eyes, restless with his calm, restless with my own story laid out between us, restless with myself. I shift in the wicker chair, elbows on my knees, and look at him eye to eye.

"So you don't think I'm crazy?" I say.

"No," he says, "of course not."

"And you think you can fix me?" I say.

Howard smiles and it's a nice smile, the kind that makes his round face even more round. "You don't need to be fixed," he says.

"I don't?"

"No," he says.

After that, we talk a little more about what it is to see someone like him, the cost, the amount of time we'll be spending together, and how in the end, it's a process in which I'll learn who I am and even a new way to look at things.

Maybe it's the way he seems so sure nothing is actually wrong with me, maybe it's how I feel safe being in his attic office, or maybe it's the calm that comes from his words, a calm that I want to feel. When our hour is up, I write him a check and make a regular appointment to see him every Thursday at three o'clock.

"I don't know if Howard is going to be the right person," I say, "but he's better than the others."

In the kitchen, I wait for the water to run from a rust color to clear at the sink, and Steve takes a bottle of wine out of the refrigerator. On the radio, a station plays the whole *Rumors* album of Fleetwood Mac, which Steve turns up because he spent a good share of his adolescence fantasizing about Stevie Nicks.

"He did say I didn't need fixing," I say, rolling my eyes. "What do you expect for fifty bucks an hour?"

"It's true," Steve says.

"What's true?" I say, filling a pot and turning off the faucet.

"You don't need fixing," he says.

Wine bottle wedged between his knees, he tugs at the cork, and I put the pan on the one burner on our stove that works, turning the power on high.

"How can you say that?" I say, "I am thirty-two years old, in therapy, burned out on my career, unemployed, and ready to have a major fight with you over what color to paint the house."

He pops the cork then and smiles that movie-star smile of his but I keep going, hand up to tick off what's wrong with me.

"I have no family and no friends. All I have are you and that little dog over there."

Carmel lies on a little rug that's in the doorway between the dining room and the kitchen, watching everything with her milk-chocolate eyes.

Steve pours one glass of wine and then another.

"You're too hard on yourself, Jen," he says, bringing a glass of wine to the stove and then moving his hands around my waist.

It's something he always does when I cook. He comes up behind me, pulls me against his chest, and presses his chin into my neck.

"If I'm not hard on myself, who will be?" I say. "Someone has to whip me into shape. I mean come on, I'm a loser. Do you know I used to have a plan?"

"Shhh," he says against my ear. "Listen."

The water comes to a boil and I stir noodles in, more things in my head that are wrong with me.

"Are you listening?" he says.

"To what?" I say.

"This song."

"What is it?"

"Shhh," he says.

On the radio is a song I've never heard before, just a voice and a piano and the words *"For you, there will be no more crying. For you, the sun will be shining."*

"Have you ever heard this song?" he says.

I hold my breath then, looking at the wall, steam from the noodles lifting into my face.

"I've always known that song; it's been in my head for years," he says against my ear. "And when I met you, I immediately put the two together."

I put my hands over his arms then, holding on to him holding on to me, and I stop thinking about things that are wrong with me.

"It's what I've always wanted to give you—you know, happiness."

I turn in his arms then and look up at his face, blue eyes

with gold flecks that look like light shimmering on the surface of water. When we are close like this, it's such a nice fit, almost perfect.

He doesn't understand all the shadows that move through me or the therapy but he doesn't tell me not to go and he doesn't complain about the cost, which is more than we can afford.

I don't understand him all the time either but I do know Steve is a good man who wants me to find whatever it is I'm looking for, and if that's not at least a path to happiness, I don't know what is.

The song on the radio, "Songbird," ends with the woman singing the words *I love you,* and I press my ear to Steve's chest, the beat of his heart so strong I can almost feel it in my own body.

I am at the top of a ladder, 30 feet off the ground, with a dust mask over my face, belt sander between my hands. The sound of the machine is like rocks in a can, even when you aren't sanding.

Steve works in Las Vegas today, a regular Thursday auction where he flies out in the morning and comes home late at night.

I've given up TV news completely, taking on a little free-lance work here and there but all my ambition goes to the house now.

Over the last five months we painted the inside and have now turned to the outside, scrape, sand, and prep, doing the work ourselves to save money.

Laying the sander on the side of the house, I grind down the old paint, the sound in my head so familiar now I don't hear it at all.

My mind wanders around the way it always does, restless thoughts.

Steve and I are talking about having a child but I don't think it's the right time. The house isn't ready for a baby, we aren't earning that much money, and deep down, I don't know if someone like me should have children. Talking to Howard is one thing but having a child is serious business.

White paint flecks off the house and against my face. I pull the sander back and smooth away the dust.

Still, I am 32 years old, not that much time left to have a child, and I think my mother was about my age when she died.

I flip the button of the sander to off and the sound is a car driving by on the road in front of the house and a couple of birds who fly from our fence and up into the branches of the magnolia tree.

For the last couple of weeks, Howard and I have been talking about my mother and trying to sort her away from the person I've been calling Mom for 20 years.

We talked about the Duemore adoption, how it never felt right and how they don't treat me like a daughter at all.

"At least with my first mother," I said, "I felt loved."

"Well," Howard said, "how about thinking about her more?"

"What do you mean?" I said.

"I mean take her back into your heart as your mother and let—what's her name?"

"Peggy," I said, laughing because I wish I could forget her that easily.

"Right," he said, nodding. "Let Peggy go."

Since the conversation about the money and if they loved me or not, Mom and I never got back to a normal relationship. She would do the silent treatment, refusing to take my calls or if we did talk, there were long silences filled with tension. I knew she didn't love me, that she never would love me but, like a crazy illness I could never recover from, I just kept trying. I sent nice birthday and Christmas presents, I called on the telephone, all the while believing that there was something about me that made her heart so hard rather than the fact that she was just that way.

What Howard said seemed so simple—just let her go—and once I tried, it wasn't that hard to do.

After that, Howard and I talked about my mother. I even showed him the photos I had been dragging around for 25 years and admitted, for the first time in years, how much I missed her and that I even felt that I had failed her.

"When I was little, she used to say we would all forget her," I said, "and in way, she was right—we did. My father remarried, then died, Bryan and I were split up, I got adopted, and then, life just took me away. I forgot."

Waves of despair moved over me in his attic office, tears that felt older than time and I held my hands over my face, crying like a little kid.

What seemed like an hour went by before I stopped crying, and Howard was there, waiting, like always, concerned and understanding and calm.

"But you see, Jennifer," he said, leaning toward me, the sound of the wicker moving under his weight, "you didn't forget her—you just survived."

Two gray pigeons land on the roof close to where I stand on the ladder and then fly off when they see me, their flapping wings lifting them off in a hurry.

Talking about my mother is like painting this old house. You go back to the original surface, one layer of paint at a time, learning about who lived here before you ever came, how for years it was neglected to the point of dry rot and peeling paint, how further in, there is a layer of lime green that someone took the time to put on, and then before that, a sturdy layer of white that has held up in some places since 1923.

Now her memory is out in the open, I realize I want to know more, I need to know more.

How old was she when she died?

Where did she die, how, and why?

Questions lift like dust, one after the other, scattered all around. I climb down that ladder, go into the house, get a drink of water, pick up the telephone, and dial directory assistance for Los Angeles.

I'm not a reporter anymore but it's just like riding a bike. You make one telephone call that leads to another. You talk to this person, get put on hold, talk to that person, and sometimes you even get cut off. That's fine. Dial again, start over, never give up.

Her death certificate is the first piece of documentation that comes in and it shows she died when she was 34 years old at UCLA Medical Center. The cause of death was respiratory arrest.

Next, I write to UCLA Medical Center for the complete file of her medical history.

"You might want to look at this," Steve says, waving a white envelope in the air.

I'm up a ladder again, this time painting a dark green color on the trim that frames the front of the house.

Steve stands in the driveway, the rest of the mail in his arms, and he has paint spatters on his face and in his dark hair.

"IRS?" I say, rubbing at my nose with the back of my hand. "Did they finally catch up with me?"

"Ha, ha," he says, looking at the envelope in his hand. "It says 'UCLA Medical Center.' Were you waiting for something from them?"

I've told Steve the barest details of what I am doing but it's hard to explain something I don't even understand. Still, he's being the way he always is, helpful and supportive and even a little curious.

We go into the house and sit at the table in our old kitchen, and my hands shake as I tear open the envelope, papers rolling apart as if they have to stretch and be free, a pile 50 pages thick.

"Wow," I say, flattening the papers with my hands.

Steve moves his chair around to look at them with me and I split them up, giving him half.

"So what are these?" he says.

"My mother's medical records," I say, "at least part of them."

"And you get this stuff?" he says. "They just send it to you?"

"I'm the only surviving child," I say, nodding. "Legally, they are mine."

I skim over the lines of official language, my mother's name at the top of each page, the names of different doctors, different procedures, and all of them are emergency reports.

"Listen," I say, reading out loud. " 'This is the first admission for this thirty-two-year-old white woman who is thin, chronically ill, with a complete loss of motor movement in her lower spine.'

" 'This is the second admission due to a three-day history of vomiting and diarrhea.'

" 'This is the third admission of a woman who took an overdose of Seconal and Valium.' "

I stop then and read that last line again. *This is the third admission of a woman who took an overdose of Seconal and Valium.*

"Oh my God," I say, my hand over my mouth and it's a heavy curtain pulled back, bright light into my brain, too much light.

"What?" Steve said.

"Oh my God," I say, looking at him and then past to a spot of the wall, white paint that's cracked and peeling.

I push the papers to him then, giving over the story that's too much to read right now, and besides, I was there.

Steve reads my story and then licks his lips, laying the pages on the table again.

"Do you remember this?" he said.

I nod my head, trying for a smile because after all, it was a long time ago, but I can't.

It takes almost a year to piece together the story of my mother and her 10-year struggle with illness that went back to before Bryan was born.

Janet Ferrel Lauck, my mother, had scarlet fever when she was seven, her grandfather was a Methodist minister, and she grew up in Boise, Idaho, with her brother, Charles; a younger brother, Steven; a mother, Rowena; and a father, Ivan.

She met my father in college who was on his way to being an accountant and always said he would be a millionaire or broke by the time he was 40.

She said he was the best kind of good-looking, boy next door mixed with drop-dead handsome.

Before they married, she had this pain in her back, but she didn't talk much about it; she didn't like to complain. She took aspirin instead, 2, 5, 10, and eventually, up to 30 a day.

When she was 23 years old and seven months pregnant with Bryan, she got sick, vomiting blood from ulcers worn into her stomach by all that aspirin.

After Bryan was born, they found an 11-inch tumor twisted into the nerves at the base of her spine.

Most of the tumor, called a benign growth, was removed and for the first two years of Bryan's life, she slowly recovered.

She couldn't have more children—it would kill her—and so, when Bryan was three, they adopted me.

She called me her special gift, said I was a sign that she was going to live, and for three more years, she was in the best health she would ever be.

We lived in the house on Mary Street with a willow tree out front and a fence made from white rails and brick posts. Our living room was sunken and she let the mint grow wild around our back porch.

My parents had a philosophy for living back then: If you made $15,000 a year, look like you made $30,000. If you made $30,000, live like you made $60,000. Somewhere along the line, they missed a payment on the medical insurance, and were dropped from their policy.

When I was four, her back started to hurt again. She took up with the aspirin but didn't tell anyone about the pain until she started coughing up blood again. The tumor wasn't as big this time, but it was back, pressing on the nerves for her legs and digestive system. She lost a kidney, had a whole range of internal infections, from her blood to her bladder, and was on so many medications that sometimes, she went into what seemed to be schizophrenic hallucinations. No one knew for sure if she was mentally ill or if the combinations of pills was the problem, but my father, trying to make his million and shoulder the medical bills without insurance, was undone by the possibility of mental illness.

In 1969, he committed her to a mental hospital in Sparks, Nevada.

According to Aunt Georgia and Uncle Charles, this was the first serious blow to the Ferrel and Lauck families, since the Ferrels were furious that my father would commit her and the Laucks were convinced she needed psychiatric care. My father apparently committed her after asking the advice of Grandma Lauck.

The medical reports show she was released to her father, Ivan. According to Uncle Charles, the fight between the families is why my father moved my mother, Bryan, and me away from Nevada.

In L.A., he went to work in a firm with another man and put us in a two-bedroom apartment with a view of the ocean. It was our job to take care of her. My father was gone for days at a time, sometimes working, sometimes seeing another woman.

Within two years, my mother went to the emergency room at UCLA six times for different infections—bladder, bowel, blood—and one for the overdose.

I don't think she wanted to die. I think she found out he was seeing another woman and wanted to get his attention. For the second time, he committed her to a mental institution, this time without telling anyone in either family.

The patient, Janet Lauck, was functional and able to return home to her family, but her husband is adamant and refused. It was his decision to commit his wife to the Olive View Mental Hospital in San Fernando.

She came back from the Olive View Mental Hospital almost a year after her overdose, went to the emergency room three more times after that, and died on Bryan's tenth birthday.

Three months after her death, my father moved us in with a new family, a healthy woman who was in a cult called the Freedom Community Church. They too had a philosophy for living: If you made $20,000 a year, live like you made $40,000. If you made $40,000, live like you made $80,000.

She had three of her own kids and spent money like it was going out of style.

My father, who said he would be a millionaire or broke by the time he was forty, died of a heart attack when he was 39 years old. He left no will, and other than a couple of insurance polices, his estate was debt.

The house is pretty much done, just the kitchen left to go, and it's almost perfect: hardwood floors, walls painted warm yellows and creams, pieces of furniture from the Mission era. Everywhere you look, there is something lovely to see, a nice piece of art, a pretty vase of flowers, curtains I made myself from rich velvets and see-through chiffons.

Looking at it now, it's hard to believe all the work Steve and I put in. It's not just a house anymore; it's a home we carefully brought back from years of neglect and now know, understand, and even respect.

With the story I was meant to uncover, sort out, and finally, tell, I've been restored too. I'm not the unwanted and unloved Duemore girl who is lucky not to be hooked on dope or a prostitute or even dead. I'm the daughter of Bud and Janet Lauck, two people who had so much but lost it to illness, pride, selfishness, and a few bad decisions.

My father was the golden boy, the promise of his family, who drove himself to only fulfill that image of success. My mother let him run her life without once picking up the telephone to call anyone for help.

My fear that I will never amount to anything comes from my father and my inability to reach out and ask for help comes from my mother. Still, knowing all my parents' failings doesn't change how they were *my* parents and that I love them both right now as much as I did when I was a little girl. A truth that took me 20 years to find and accept.

✦ ✦ ✦

On a Thursday afternoon, my last Thursday with Howard because I've asked to take a break, I get ready to go see him, putting my wallet and keys into my purse.

Howard agrees this might be a good time to stop and says I'm welcome to come back whenever I want. He does like to remind me that there is one person I haven't spent much time on. I tell him I'll get to Bryan later, after I've cleared my head a little.

In the bathroom, I comb my hair, grown out so long it's all the way down my back, and I smile at myself in the mirror. In the reflection, my own dark eyes look at me, and from a place that doesn't think, I know it's time.

Like our old house, I was all broken down and messed up and out of order, but now, things are in place again and there's an empty room in my heart that's waiting to be filled with life.

The telephone rings then and I put my comb away, turn off the light, and get it by the third ring.

Steve is on the line, that sound of the cellular connection and the other far-off sounds of the Las Vegas airport.

"What are you doing?" he says.

"I'm so glad it's you," I say.

"Uh-oh," he says. "What did you buy?"

"Ha, ha," I say.

I carry the telephone from the TV room to the kitchen, double-checking my purse. "I was just in the bathroom," I say, "you know, getting ready for Howard, when something hit me."

We've been married for three years now, almost three, anyway, with a big anniversary trip planned for Hawaii, but I feel silly right now, embarrassed even.

"Do you want to hear?" I say.

"Sure," he says.

"I think it's time for a baby," I say.

Steve is quiet on the line but I still hear the airport behind him.

"Hello?" I say, and I can't help smiling.

"It funny," he says. "I was just thinking that this morning, when I left for the airport."

"No, you weren't," I say, laughing.

"I'm serious," he says.

"I must have read your mind, then," I say.

"Or maybe I read yours," he says.

PART SEVEN

BRYAN

SEVEN

JANUARY 2000

Missouri in January is low-rolling land that runs to the very edge of the sky and all there is to break the horizon is the random farmhouse surrounded by a windbreak of naked trees.

It's a lonely-looking place with acre after acre of fenced in fields. Most of those fields are filled with gray stalks of corn that hunch down to the earth, broken.

After a hundred miles of this sameness, there's a farmer on his tractor, tiller blades cutting down the old corn and churning the stalks into the black soil. Maybe he's tired of waiting for the winter to end or maybe the season is about to change and I just don't see it.

I'm headed for Conception.

Conception, Missouri.

"All life begins at Conception," Father Samuel said on the telephone when I called for directions. He laughed at his own joke, seminarian humor, I guess, and I laughed too, even though I thought Conception seemed a pretty strange place for a Catholic seminary, considering no one is supposed to have sex there, let alone give birth.

Father Samuel invited me, said I should come be in the community if I want to understand why Bryan spent three years of his life there.

I follow his directions, right and left my way through an alphabet soup of roads to something called Route VV and stop at a three-way intersection.

Off to the right is a sign that reads CONCEPTION, ONE MILE.

Pulling over, I shift the car from drive to park and just sit idle at the side of the road with my thumbs hooked over the bottom of the steering wheel.

This place is right out of a Hitchcock movie. I can see Cary Grant running through cornfields with a crop duster chasing after him. It's not a place I can see Bryan at all—too dusty, too dry, too far from the ocean.

I push my hands through my hair and look in the rearview mirror, no one behind me, no one in front, just flat land and cornfields.

I found the roommate he borrowed the gun from, the guy Leonard once said was off. I found Bryan's best friend from the seminary years, a guy named Chris—Father Chris, with his own parish in Denver. I've gotten death certificates, high school and college transcripts, newspaper clips, and a little bit of a police report covering the two-week investigation when Bryan was a missing person, and I've talked to so many people that all the information has to be filed in categories just to keep it straight.

Some things you can't figure out by staying home, though, and now, I've decided that to really find the truth, I have three trips to make, one here to Conception, one to Denver to meet the roommate and Father Chris, and the last one to Oklahoma, where Bryan died.

The plane tickets have been booked and paid for, Steve is taking care of things at home, and I've committed myself to this journey, but still, sitting here in a car in Missouri, part of me doesn't want to go on, almost resents that I've done this much for a brother who really wasn't much of a brother to me.

Steve, a total convert now, says it's the right thing to do, especially because I was changed so much by learning the truth about my parents.

"It seems scary now," he said before I left this morning, "but I'm sure it will be worth it."

"Worth what?" I said.

"Peace of mind," he said. "Truth. You know—the truth will set you free."

He wanted to come with me, for moral support, but we both agreed it wasn't the right place to bring a child, and so he's home with our little boy, Spencer, who will be three this May.

Spencer, with his impossibly soft skin, the curve of his head that fits just so in my palm, lovely beyond lovely, ten fingers, ten toes, brown eyes the same dark color as mine, and this small pea-size birthmark under his arm. Someone called it a mark of royal blood.

My little prince, a gift from the gods, whole, like hope.

When he was 15 months old, bouncing away in his Johnny Jump Up, I swear, in his dark eyes, I could see Bryan as the little boy he once was.

Around my neck is a locket with photos of Steve and Spencer cut out in tiny ovals to fit and now it sits over my heart so that as I go into the past I will remember what I have for the future.

I put my hand over the locket then, the feel of the metal against my hand and chest at the same time, and I look to the right again.

CONCEPTION, ONE MILE.

I shift the car to drive again and turn on my signal.

I've come this far; I might as well go one more mile.

Conception Seminary rises like a dream from the farmland. There are all sorts of brick buildings with copper-roofed spires and a big church called the Basilica of the Immaculate Conception.

I drive past the church and around to the guest parking, then make my way to the room assigned to me with little time to spare. I'm going to something called vespers at five-fifteen and then meeting Father Samuel for dinner.

My room is this spare little place with a twin bed and yellow shag carpeting that hardly inspires devotion.

Church bells ring out then, right on time, and I toss my bags on the bed, wash my hands, and get myself to church.

As the winter sun sets, there is such a stillness to the air here, calm before the storm. The campus is tiny with just four buildings and one main walkway that leads to each. My community college in Spokane was bigger than this school.

Over by the church are a few men, five maybe and they are in black robes, hoods over their heads.

I adjust my coat around myself, tightening the belt at the waist. I've never been so aware I am female and wonder if my mere presence will cause a distraction or at least the turn of heads but none of the men look my way.

They line together and go through a side door, one by one, heads bent over, hands clasped in prayer.

From information I was sent, I know this college is part of a Benedictine monastery and that the men who live here practice the Rule written by St. Benedict in the sixth century.

Inside the church are more men in black robes, heads bowed, hands together, and they shuffle in a line to the altar, a strange off-key chant between them.

The heels of my boots are loud on the stone floor and I walk on tiptoe to the pews. Three other regular people are here, one woman and two men, and they are way up front, heads bowed in prayer too.

The church is bigger from the inside than it looks from the outside—the ceiling must be three stories high—and there are a bunch of complex biblical scenes painted on the walls. It's the kind of place that takes God seriously and being here makes me feel small and almost unworthy, which says everything about why I don't miss being Catholic or going to church.

The men stop chanting then and a hush fills the church.

They sit down and the other people sit too.

I sit, cross my legs, and wonder where Bryan sat when he was here. Did he have a favorite spot or did he mix it up? While he sat in here, did he pray or daydream or even stew in his own rage? Was he hating me for that terrible lie he thought I told about him? Was he asking for forgiveness or salvation or just guidance?

Over the altar are paintings of eight men with yellow lights around their faces, probably saints, but I couldn't tell you who's who. I do know Bryan's eyes looked up at those faces, probably hundreds of times, but what did he think about?

I take a deep breath and let it back out again, adding my own sound to this huge place of prayer. With my mother and father, at least I know how they died, but with Bryan, it's a mystery I may never solve.

No one in my family is interested in the mystery and a few refuse to help.

For years, there have been rumors through the Lauck family grapevine about the cause of Bryan's death and they come down to three possibilities: foul play, homosexuality as motive, or insanity. I want to prove all three wrong.

Aunt Georgia and Uncle Charles have been helpful, answering any question I ask, but secrecy lies over my father's side of the family like a fog.

For a little while, I had a telephone and e-mail thing going with Leonard, and in that same know-it-all voice I remembered at the funeral, he talked about the time Bryan came to live with them, saying that Bryan didn't care about anyone else but himself, that he took but didn't give, and that he had to relearn acceptable behavior.

"I had to be tough on him. I had to round off his sharp edges," Leonard said. "He had a heck of an adjustment."

Then Leonard altered history a little, saying Bryan wasn't wanted by Aunt Georgia and Uncle Charles, which is why Leonard and Sylvia took him to begin with.

"Chuck said he didn't have room for Bryan and basically kicked him out," Leonard said.

In 16 years, Leonard had dropped his story about the pact he shared with my father and now had this new story.

"That man is lying," Uncle Charles said over the telephone, giving me the name of the attorney they worked with to get legal custody of Bryan and the name of a real estate agent who had been helping to find them a larger house so they would have the room.

"We wanted him desperately," Aunt Georgia said, from the other line. "I just hope Leonard never told Bryan he wasn't wanted. That would have been devastating."

I tried to speak with Leonard again, to hear his side based on the evidence but he ducked out of sight, refusing to talk, and now, through the grapevine, I hear he thinks I'm crazy too.

The prayers stop, a strange silence in the big church, and I look at my watch—five-forty.

I'm supposed to meet Father Samuel at five-forty-five.

The monks move out of the church together, heads down, hands clasped in prayer, and after they leave, I wander a little through the church and then the halls of a building called St. Josephs, where there is an oversize photo of this year's class, students with smiles on their faces, not much different than any small school. They all wear suits and have their hair combed neat and tidy. Some are very young and some are older, in their forties and fifties.

I go down a steep flight of stairs, following the sounds to where food is set out, cafeteria style, and there are a few people eating down here, a couple of priests and the people who were just at vespers.

I lean on the edge of a table and wait, trying to look as if it's the most normal thing to be standing around a seminary cafeteria.

When Father Samuel shows up, he's an average-size man in a black robe belted at the waist, wire glasses and thinning hair.

He's polite enough, shaking my hand and saying he's sorry to be delayed. "Let's eat," he says.

He waves me to the buffet as if he has dinner with women who travel from long distances all the time, so I act casual about it too.

Dishing up salad and taking a slice of bread, I chitchat, sizing him up. *How long have you been a priest? Oh, that long, wow. You must really enjoy your work.*

Sitting across from each other, complete strangers really, we eat together with that feeling between us.

"So you used to be a reporter?" Father Samuel says.

"That's right," I say, picking at my salad, "television news."

"That must have been exhilarating," he says.

Father Samuel smoothes peanut butter on a slice of white bread and I can tell he's not really that interested in my former television career, just making small talk in the same way I was. Sizing me up.

"For a while, it was exciting," I say, setting my fork next to my plate, "but the business isn't what it seems. I got out while I still had my soul."

Peanut butter bread balanced on his fingers, Father Samuel considers me differently, a small smile on his mouth.

"If you're not careful, you can lose your soul just about anywhere," he says.

"Even here?"

"Especially here," he says, moving his eyes around the cafeteria. "This place isn't what it seems either; there's as much sin here as any other place."

He eats his peanut butter bread then and his eyes watch me. There's a straightforward quality to him, a person who doesn't need to be charmed or dazzled and so I bypass any more chitchat and he does the same.

Father Samuel says the school is pretty small, there is a high turnover, and in the years they are here, each student goes through an intense process of reflection that includes personal counseling and spiritual guidance as well as college studies.

Even though he can't divulge the contents of personal counseling, and those records were already destroyed anyway, Father Samuel did ask around. Bryan was considered a model student who got almost perfect grades and didn't cause any trouble.

Of course, Father Samuel didn't know Bryan himself, so it's a hard conversation to have. Instead, he talks more generally about what it is to be here and how the four years of preparation lead to something called discernment.

"What's that?" I say.

He wipes his mouth with a napkin, puts it back into his lap.

"The call of God," he says. "Four years is enough time for most to know if they are called, or as we say, to discern."

"Called by God?" I say.

He nods like it's so simple, a calm on his face and I want to start laughing. It doesn't seem that simple to me, and more than that, wouldn't it be awful if you weren't called? Talk about rejection.

"How do you know who's been called?" I say.

"We can tell," he says with an insider's confidence.

"How?"

He looks at me and I look back at him, eyes steady. It's something I've learned over the years. When you ask a question but don't get the answer you want, ask again with fewer words and hold your ground.

Father Samuel moves his tongue around under his lips, frowns a little. "We call it a fire in the belly," he says. "Once you see that in someone, it's really unmistakable." He picks up his fork and moves the rest of his food around on his plate.

Sitting back in my chair, arms crossed over myself, I'm flat out of questions.

The other people who were here are gone now and I didn't even hear them leave. I look around and it's just me, Father Samuel, and this woman who collects the dirty dishes and covers leftover food.

Father Samuel takes a long drink of water, wipes his mouth with his napkin one last time. "I've arranged for you to speak with someone who has that fire," he says.

"You have?" I say.

He nods. "His name is Brother Jude," he says, "and he knew your brother."

✦ ✦ ✦

Father Samuel deposits me with Brother Jude, makes introductions and then good-byes.

"I know it's been a long time," Brother Jude says, after Father Samuel leaves, "but I was very sorry to hear about your brother's death."

He wears a black robe belted at the waist, hood making a cowl around his neck, and he offers his hand.

Almost by instinct, I want to correct him and say I wasn't Bryan's real sister, but I don't. Instead I just shake his hand. "Thank you," I say.

Brother Jude sits and moves his hand to an empty chair close by. He's not quite as tall as me, has a beard that's closely cut to his face and these round glasses that give him an owlish look.

We are in a big room with wood paneling on the walls, chairs positioned around for conversation. Heavy curtains are over the windows and warm light comes from table lamps on end tables.

Brother Jude says he didn't know Bryan that well, but he does talk through what he remembers, how they shared a few classes, how Bryan was serious and intense, and then he laughs at one memory of a Halloween party where he went as Superman and by coincidence, Bryan showed up as Clark Kent.

"Bryan and I kidded around about the coincidence of our outfits, but I thought it was quite ironic," he says. "Here I was, a short, average-looking guy, and Bryan was just striking. I should have been Clark Kent and he should have been Superman."

Brother Jude is an everyday man, shy with a great laugh and a warm personality, and maybe it's how down to earth he is that makes me comfortable and even brave. After he tells me all he knew about Bryan, I ask him more general questions.

I tell him how I grew up Catholic but it just faded out of my life after Bryan died. I lost faith in Catholics, maybe God too, blaming both for Bryan's death, and now, I wonder how one can find faith without religion getting in the way?

Brother Jude watches me talk, and his eyebrows lift behind his round glasses, surprised, and that makes me stop.

"That's all," I say, laughing at myself.

Brother Jude is quiet for a long time but I can tell by the way he nods to himself and holds his hands together that he's not offended at all; rather, he's just thinking.

"I can understand the loss of faith," he says, "and that you might think this place and even the Church were part of what led to your brother's death."

I put my hand over my heart. "I'm not saying it was anyone's fault."

"Of course not," Brother Jude says, "but when something like this happens, it's natural that all of us would look inward to see where we failed Bryan. Even those who didn't know him well. If we don't consider these questions, how can we learn anything?"

We look at each other and it feels as if truth moves around, invisible like the air and yet so tangible.

He talks about the Catholic Church and how it needs to change to meet the needs of modern followers, especially women. He says it has changed some but not fast enough for many.

It's such a different response from what I would have expected and he is so sincere that I realize what Father Samuel meant by the *fire in the belly.*

Brother Jude tells me that the journey to faith is a personal one, that each of us must listen to our own hearts to find the way, inside or outside of a specific religion.

The light from the table lamp makes a circle on the carpet, a warm feeling to this place and this man.

"Can I ask you one more question?"

Brother Jude smiles at that and I guess he's already figured out I have a million questions.

"Do you think suicide is a mortal sin?"

Brother Jude tilts his head to the side and frowns. "The Church no longer holds that to be true," he says. "There is just no way to know what happens to the soul." He puts his hand on his own chest then. "I personally cannot accept that a loving God condemns anyone to hell," he says.

He has the calm of someone who has spent a great deal of his time with questions like mine and has actually arrived at the answers. What would it be like to feel that way and how do you get there?

I stand up then, thank him for his time and his honesty, and Brother Jude rises too, holding my hand with both of his. "I hope I helped," he says.

"You have," I say. "More than you know."

I cross the seminary campus alone now and there are no city lights to ruin the night sky. I stop to look up and my eyes go to what is familiar, the Big Dipper, Orion's Belt, Little Dipper. The sky is so black, the stars are so bright. Arms around myself, I just look at all of it, so huge above, me so small down here.

What a conversation, what a place, so different from what I would have thought, and yet, what did I expect?

My own questions of faith and God and religion surprise me, but I know deep down, I want to believe in something too. I like to think I have it all figured out, my defense against things that don't make sense. I even try to believe there are little signs that pop up in my own life that say I am going in the right direction, like how my son was conceived on the anniversary of my mother's death and then came on her birthday, somehow a sign that my search for her and then the choice to have a child were the right things to do.

Is that God or something else, a force in the universe that connects all things, or is it just something that's personal to each of us? Maybe it's just coincidence, like the existentialists who believe that the universe has no intrinsic meaning or purpose and each of us is responsible for our own destiny.

Millions and millions of stars blink from every possible direction of the sky, and I can almost feel Bryan around the edges of this place. Not in some haunted-house way; it's more like there are pieces of him left behind that have been waiting for whoever would come looking.

Are you up there, Bryan? Are you watching and am I going in the right direction now?

I look around but I'm alone out here in the night.

The path that leads to the other campus buildings has these small lights along the sidewalk, circles of light that barely touch each other, the shadows of the night just beyond. I watch my feet walk slow steps on the sidewalk, feet in the light, my head full of Brother Jude and Father Samuel and the stars and Bryan.

The next morning, I'm on my own in the library. I look up back issues of the student newspaper, admission handbooks, and the student annuals. In the upstairs stacks, I sit on the concrete floor with the student annuals, 1980 to 1983 on my lap.

A rectangle window shows the sky and the day but around me in here is just a strange silence.

No one is in the library today. It's lit up and open but I looked and couldn't find one person.

Surrounded by books, I flip open to page 1 of 1980 and as if he were waiting for me, Bryan practically pops off the page.

He's in the back row of a group shot staged in front of the basilica and he's a head taller than everyone else.

"Hey," I say, my own voice the only sound and it's stupid to be relieved but I am. That's the interesting thing about death. You know it with your head but the actual death is something you never truly take into your heart. It's just like the person went away rather than died and you are always looking for the impossible, that the person will reappear. In a way, seeing him on the page feels like magic, another piece of evidence that this person existed.

That evidence is in all three of the annuals, Bryan as a freshman, a sophomore, a junior, all photos the same, serious expression on his face, dark hair parted to the side, and that little mole over his lip.

I used to tell myself that there was no way Bryan could be a priest, and even since driving here yesterday, the landscape felt impossible. But as I make my way through his years here, I realize I was wrong. He was here, and he looks fit, healthy, and happy. On the last page of the last annual is a photo that even shows him in this momentary place of peace.

He's with two other guys, the three of them wrapped in white sheets for a toga party. It makes me think of Brother Jude, who said even seminarians like to have a good time. The other guys are goofballs hamming it up but Bryan has such a serene expression on his face, as if caught with his guard down. He has one arm up and leans against the door frame, his other hand on the shoulder of his friend. He's in this classic Roman god pose, only it's not a pose—it's who he is, this naturally beautiful man.

It reminds me of the photo my cousin Erin wouldn't let me have all those years ago, this single moment captured when he was just being himself and in his eyes is all the potential of what he could have been if he had held on.

So many different feelings move through me in the quiet of the stacks. I'm restless and sad, and there's even that old anger. *How could you leave me here all alone, Bryan?*

I look up at the window, a rectangle of blue sky, no clouds.

I read somewhere, a psychology book I think, that when you have a conflict with someone, it never goes away until it's resolved. You have two choices: resolve the conflict or separate yourself from the other person with the understanding that when you see or speak to the person again, the conflict will be there, waiting. It never goes away until it's resolved.

That's how this feels.

Bryan and I have a deep conflict and even though he tried to talk a bit about it at the wedding, we didn't cover enough ground. I didn't know how, and now, with his face looking up at me from the photo, it's just the same.

He hurt me in ways I can barely think about. Not just with arm-twisting and Indian burns but with that look in his eyes that said I didn't count, the mean way he told me I was adopted.

"You're not one of us," he said. "You're not real."

God, I wish I could get over it but it's right there, between us. What can I possibly do now? Scream at his picture, spit at him, get up and walk away, pretending not to care when the truth is, I loved my brother and I'm trapped by his death, a conflict that will go forever unresolved?

I look at his photo again, that face I know so well, that little mole over his lip and it hurts all over again, the kind of hurt that aches deep in your bones.

To shake Bryan back down to a memory that was safe in the shadows behind my heart, I put on pair of sneakers and snap my headphones over my ears, running off the grounds of Conception and up a two-lane farm road with Sheryl Crow singing in my head. I pass a row of what looks like student dorms, all the windows facing out to the fields.

Off to the left is a field of brown and white cows eating dried grass. One of them looks at me with slow eyes, jaw moving on the grass she eats.

"Moo," I say.

The cow stops chewing and watches me run to the top of the hill, turn around and run back down the way I came.

I don't know why I still run since I hate it. When Bryan and I were kids, Deb made us run all the time, eight miles a day for training, competitions on the weekends, the dream of the Olympics in our future. I hated it then, swearing I would never run if I had half the chance but here I am, running, telling myself that the reason is how I don't want to get out of shape. Deep down, I know it's my own personal form of abuse. Why do I do it to myself anyway? It's bad enough I was abused into doing something I hated but now that the abuser is out of my life, it's like I can't help myself. I have to go on with the abuse, as if this is all I'm good for, as if this is the best I can expect.

The seminary is far away on the horizon, the spires lifting out of the farmland and I stop running and start walking, a hard wind blowing my clothes against my body.

It's the same with Bryan, I keep beating myself with the old abuse of how he wouldn't let me be his sister, even though he already told me he was sorry. There's this part of me that can't let it go, won't let it go, like a hook caught deep in my heart. When will I be free?

Back on the seminary grounds, I wipe my face on the sleeve of my shirt and at the top of the steps that lead up from the guest parking lot is a man in a black robe and he waves.

"Are you Bryan Lauck's sister?" he calls out.

I nod and take the steps two at a time to where he is.

"Did Father Samuel tell you I was here?" I say.

"No, I saw your name on the sign-up board."

"My name?" I say, a little out of breath.

"Lauck," he says.

He reaches his hand to me then. I wipe my right hand on my shirt and shake his hand.

"I'm Father Albert," he says. "I used to be one of Bryan's teachers, and when I saw your name on the board, I knew you had to be related."

Father Albert has an easy smile, almost childlike and a kind of clumsy way of moving that's very likable. He asks all sorts of questions about why I'm here and who I've talked to, leading me to a sitting area.

I sit on one end of this beige sofa, wagon-train design in the fabric, and Father Albert sits at the other end.

"Everyone really liked Bryan," he says. "He was a sweet kid with a remarkable work ethic."

He describes Bryan as a student who worked hard to get straight A's, who asked for extra-credit work on a regular basis. All this time I thought Bryan was naturally brilliant, like our father had been.

"His enthusiasm was as intense as his focus and his focus was as intense as his despair if he was unable to achieve his goal."

"Did you know his parents had died?" I say.

Father Albert adjusts himself on the wagon-train sofa, shaking his head. "No," he says, "I found out about that much later. Before his death, I thought he had family somewhere here in the state, but none of them ever came to the college for family visits."

"Is that unusual?" I say.

Father Albert frowns and nods at the same time.

"Families are encouraged to come as a show of support for

the student," he says, "but some don't, either because they can't afford it or for personal reasons."

The sweat from my run is dried on my face and my muscles are stiff. "What does that mean?" I say. "Personal reasons?"

"Some families aren't supportive," he says, shrugging. "It happens."

Far off, bells ring, time for vespers already, and I've been here exactly 24 hours.

Father Albert says he's going to search through his papers tonight for anything he might have saved of Bryan's and then invites me to a special mass he's going to say tomorrow.

"It's at Mount Clyde," he says, "about ten minutes from here."

"Mount Clyde?" I say.

"It's a convent," he says, "Benedictine sisters. If I'm not mistaken, Bryan spent a fair share of time there."

"How did he spend time there?" I say. "Is that allowed?"

"Oh sure," he says. "They have a wonderful chapel and the grounds are very inviting."

We walk down the hall together, stopping at my room, and he shakes my hand in both of his, just like Brother Jude did, like an embrace.

"Think about it," he says. "I know the sisters would love to have you."

The next morning, Sunday morning, I get out of bed at seven A.M., with a headache behind my eyes.

A retreat group arrived last night, adults studying to be confirmed, and a couple of them slept in the room next to mine. They both snored so loud, it was like they were in my room and not their own.

I get up, take a shower, and get ready for church.

Last night, I had a long talk with Steve, trying to tell him what it's like over here, monks and priests and prayer six times a day, a throwback to the sixth century.

"It's very different from what I thought."

"What did you think you'd find out there?" he said.

"I don't know," I said. "A secret society, maybe, a bunch of sexual deviants—you know, all the stuff you hear on the news, but it's not like that. They are really nice, at least those I've met."

"So why did he leave?" Steve said.

"I'm not sure yet," I said. "It looks like he fit in, everyone liked him, he was a great student. Maybe he didn't hear the call of God."

"God calls?" Steve said, his voice with that joking tone to it, part cynic, part clown. "Is that on the phone or in a lightning bolt?"

I laughed with him then because I thought the same thing.

After that, I told him about how Sylvia and Leonard never came to the seminary to see Bryan. That it might have been because they were broke, although they lived within driving distance, or because they didn't agree with his decision or just that Bryan never invited them. I wasn't sure.

In the background was a high howl and then Steve put Spencer on the line.

"Mom? Mom? Hey, Mom?" he said, his way of getting our conversations started.

"Yeah," I said, smiling, "it's Mom."

"Come home, Mom," he said.

"One more day, honey," I said.

It got quiet on the line then, just the sound of his breathing, and I knew he didn't understand *one more day.*

"Come to the airport and get me, okay?" I said.

"Okay!" he said, dropping the phone then in a loud clatter. Steve picked it up.

"Hate to tell you this but he misses his mom," Steve said.

"I got that," I said.

"I miss you too," he said.

"I'll be home tomorrow night," I said.

"Good," he said. "Single parenting is no picnic."

For a moment, I felt a pang of guilt for being away on this self-absorbed journey, one that might never yield any fruit. We said our good-byes without talking about that, though. He told me to do this and without his support, I don't know if I could have come this far.

Mount Clyde is a 10-minute drive, a little paradise built into a low groove of land with buildings made from light-colored stone, like sandstone.

The grass is green, the flowers are tended, and the bushes are perfectly groomed. Bare branches of the winter trees arch over the sidewalks that lead to the chapel.

In contrast to the stark world of Conception, Clyde feels like beauty, and for the first time this weekend, I'm not hyper-aware of being a woman.

I walk alone over the curve of the walkways, under the trees, past the bushes, and bells ring over the small chapel.

Inside, the chapel is painted deep reds and yellows, gold trim around the pillars and the arches. There are statues of saints, mosaics, and murals, and even pillars made from a deep green marble.

Pulling off my gloves, I unbutton my coat. A woman walks up to me, white hair and the darkest brown eyes.

"Welcome," she whispers and offers a single white sheet of information about today's mass.

"Would you be too frightened if I placed you in the stiles?" she whispers.

I don't know what a stile is so I just shake my head like I'm not afraid of anything. She puts her hand on my elbow and leads me to where all the nuns sit.

Maybe this woman thinks I'm a nun and I almost laugh out loud. I take off my coat and act normal, and all around, nuns have their heads bowed in prayer, some old, some very young. The older nuns wear the habits with the veils but the younger nuns wear black slacks, black sweaters, black skirts.

The bells stop ringing and a group of nuns stand to sing. One of them has a voice that lifts higher than the others, a voice so sweet it almost hurts, and when I find the source, she is a tall woman with gray hair cut short around her head. As the women sing, two altar boys and Father Albert walk up the aisle between the stiles.

The mass goes along the way I remember from childhood, prayers, singing, readings, and then Father Albert says, "Let us offer each other the sign of peace." A couple of nuns step to me and shake my hand, their fingers so soft and delicate, and the ones who can't reach where I sit hold up peace signs straight out of the '60s.

From across the aisle, the woman who showed me to where I sit comes over and offers her hand too. "Peace to you, lovely lady," she says.

I put my hand into hers, a brief touch that is over in a moment but is so kind and sincere I feel like crying. I've been here 20 minutes and this place is such a comfort it feels like home. I wonder if Bryan felt that too. I wonder if that's what brought him here time and time again. I wonder if he battled with his feelings about women here or maybe resolved them enough to go out into the world again.

The mass continues on but I'm still thinking about the contact made with these women and the feeling of safety and kindness and comfort, holding on as long as I can before it all slips away.

✦ ✦ ✦

The Benedictines have this tradition of treating visitors with the highest respect; it's one of their rules. In this tradition, the sisters invite me to have breakfast with them and won't take no for an answer.

"Have some coffee and help yourself to some of Sister Ann's wonderful sticky buns, fresh out of the oven."

Father Albert comes in then and says I might as well relax and enjoy, because the sisters won't have it any other way. They all laugh, some of them the same age as I am, others younger, still others who are much older.

Father Albert has a bowl of cereal and talks with some of the sisters about this and that. At the other end of the table, I ask questions about Bryan, but none of them can remember the young man; he was here too many years ago.

"Do you have children?" says an older nun who sits close to me. She has a black veil bobby-pinned to her white hair, blue eyes, and she's a tiny thing, bent with age. Around the table, all the nuns look at me, and I put my hand to the silver oval of my locket.

"One," I say, snapping it open to show my boy sitting in a big rocking chair, a guitar balanced on his lap.

The way women do, they point and coo and say, "My goodness, he's a big boy for two."

"What's his name?"

"Spencer," I say.

"Spencer," the older nun closest to me says. "What a nice name."

"This must be your husband," one of them says, pointing to the other photo in the locket.

"Oh, he's so handsome," one of them says, and the other women laugh at her. I smile and close my locket then, Spencer and Steve against my heart, and the older nun who sits close to me puts her hand on my arm.

"Do you plan to have more children?" she says.

I shake my head. "I don't know," I say.

"Oh, you should," she says. "Children are such a blessing."

She has her other hand over her own heart and the look in her eyes says she has first hand experience that goes way beyond what I know. I've only just started this work of being a mother, am still caught up in how hard it is sometimes, how scary it can be and the idea of another child is as far away as the moon. The way she smiles and nods at me though, I can also see beyond the work and into how I've been changed by being a mother. It's the kind of love for another person that cracks open even the hardest heart.

I take a deep breath, my hand still over my locket and smile at her.

"You are right," I say. "They are a blessing."

I leave Sunday afternoon as quietly as I came Friday night, and as I drive, I listen to a CD I bought from the sisters at Clyde. They have a whole world of their own where they bake communion wafers for all the churches around the United States, house a huge religious relics museum, and burn their own CDs.

The music is flute and piano mixed with the sounds of nature, things like rain and wind, and it fills the car.

Who would have known so much was out here in the middle of nowhere?

After Clyde, I had breakfast with a couple more monks, nice men who remembered Bryan as sweet, quiet, intense and who offered more condolences about his death.

One man named Brother Thomas said that Bryan's death was a time for deep reflection at the seminary, all of the staff looking inward to see where they might have failed him. It makes me wonder why such reflection never happened in my own family.

I drive the same way I came, past the same barren fields, trees and houses, but it's not so lonely for me now. It's just a place, like any other place, not perfect, not terrible, and I think Bryan had a few years of real peace here. Three years of a 23-year life.

The music on the CD fades from flute to the sounds of rain, and a little thunder too, and as I drive east to Kansas City, the weather outside is clear and sunny.

EIGHT

DENVER, COLORADO

Two weeks later, I get off a plane in Denver, Colorado, pulling my luggage up the exit ramp.

Chris Hellstrom is supposed to meet me and I'm nervous to meet him face to face. Chris was Bryan's best friend from the seminary, and we've talked so much on the telephone, I feel as if I known him for years. He has a deep voice, is very smart and a dry sense of humor I don't always get.

Steve even noticed how much I like Chris, made a little joke about it when I left home this morning. "You are coming back, right?" he said, "this isn't some kind of *Thorn Birds* thing, is it?"

A lot of men couldn't handle the kind of journey I've been on for what seems like forever now, but Steve isn't a lot of men. He's the kind of guy who tells me that I have to go and then holds the door wide open when I get back. It must make him so afraid sometimes, but he never says it in so many words, and it makes me love him that much more.

"Of course I'm coming home," I said, kissing the side of his face. "He's a priest, for heaven's sake."

✦ ✦ ✦

Off the plane, I look around and Chris is easy to spot, the only person here who wears all black with the white square at the base of his throat. He's very tall with blond hair and a neatly trimmed beard and a mustache. He's also very slim, not scrawny or skinny, just lean.

I walk to him full of the confidence of our many conversations. "Hello, Chris Hellstrom," I say.

Chris stays absolutely still, the beginning of a smile he holds back in an effort to be serious.

"That can't be you," he says, deep, slow voice just like on the telephone.

I let go of my pull-around luggage, put my hands out to the sides.

"It's me," I say.

He shakes his head. "Absolutely not," he says. "Your photos don't resemble you at all."

"That's a joke, right?" I say. "Your Midwestern humor?"

He laughs at that, a little self-conscious, and reaches for my luggage.

We make our way from airport to car, talk about the flight, the weather, and I try to adjust myself to Chris as whole person and not just a voice. His eyes are a pure blue color bordering on violet, and he has an easy way of moving, controlled but elegant.

On the drive to Denver, it's dark out, a long ribbon of freeway banked in by fresh snow that's a few inches deep. The road is clear though, a skiff of snow dancing over the surface, fresh snow falling against the windshield and then away to the night.

We talk about nothing really, the snow, the airport, and how the last time I was in Denver, the airport was Stapleton.

"When were you in Denver?" Chris says.

"A couple years after Bryan died," I say, crossing my arms over myself. "My ex-husband's brother worked here."

"You were married before?" he says, looking my way and to the road again.

"Yes," I say.

"What was your married name?" he says.

After I tell him, Chris gets quiet in a strange way, narrow face with these hollows under his cheekbones that pull inward and make their own shadows. Maybe he's just focused on driving in the snow, maybe I shouldn't chitchat so much, or maybe it's the divorce thing. Catholics aren't big on divorce.

A couple of cars are along the side of the road and one has skidded in the median where the snow is deep.

I look at his profile again and wonder what he's thinking about.

He pulls the car off the highway, looking my way.

"Have you ever had plum wine?" Chris says, dead serious.

I laugh and shake my head. He pulls his car into the icy parking lot of a strip mall, parking in front of a Chinese restaurant and turning off the ignition.

"Then you haven't lived," he says.

Inside the restaurant, a man, woman, and two teenagers sit in a corner booth.

"Uh-oh," Chris says, "parishioners."

The man waves at Chris then and Chris bows his head.

"Quick," he whispers, "hold your hand up so they see your wedding ring."

"Ha, ha," I say.

"I'll meet you at the table," he says, unbuttoning his coat.

I take off my coat too, sit down at the booth, and when Chris comes back, he leans forward, elbows on the table.

"I told them you were my sister," he whispers.

"And we look so much alike," I say, putting my purse on top of my coat.

He sits back and takes the menu up. "I think so," he says.

The direction of our conversation, on the border of flirting, is a little unsettling. I think about Steve again, his saying, "This isn't some *Thorn Birds* thing, is it?" I bite my lip and look at my own menu.

The waitress comes over and she's a tiny woman with black hair. Chris holds his fingers up like a peace sign.

"Two plum wines," Chris says, "right?"

"Right," I say.

"Bueno," Chris says. Chris puts his menu down and looks at me and I'm not sure what to do—keep joking around, push right into memories of Bryan, or just be still and wait.

The waitress breaks in, thank goodness, plum wine in two tiny wineglasses, and after she leaves, Chris raises his glass in a toast.

"To Jennifer," he says. "Welcome to Denver."

The wine is too sweet for my taste but not bad, and after we order dinner, Chris and I move into conversation about Bryan.

They started at Conception in same year, 1980, and their friendship evolved from a shared taste in music. They both had a room in Saint Michael's Hall, and sometimes, after classes or in the evening, Chris would end up in Bryan's room, where they would drink a Coke, talk and listen to Alan Parsons Project, Rush, Toto.

"Guys don't just sit down, talk for three hours and become friends," Chris says. "We need something exterior to ourselves that's emotionally safe and when we talk through that, we find out things about the other person. That's what happened."

Bryan never discussed his family or his past but Chris knew something was going on at a very deep level. He saw it in how Bryan used music as an escape, locking himself away in his room, headphones on, music cranked loud, and later, when the two took up playing racquetball.

"If he missed a shot, the guy just became furious," Chris says, "stomping around, calling himself stupid."

The waitress takes away our plates then, boxing up the left-overs, and Chris pours tea for us in these small dragon cups.

"Was he mad at you?" I ask. "I mean, were you afraid of him?"

"No, no," Chris says, pushing a cup my way. "He was self-punishing about it, as if holding himself to superhuman standards, and several times I asked directly why he got so mad, but Bryan would never answer. He would just go, 'Ahhhhh,' and that was it."

Chris gets quiet, elbow on the table and his face leaned into his hand. "Now, I probably wouldn't let it go so easily," Chris says, "but then, I was naive about those kind of things and I just hoped his anger was getting worked out somewhere else."

Chris tells me how each student goes through Character Formation, where they talk about personal issues with specific priests or monks.

"Do you think Bryan ever talked about his stuff?" I say.

Chris frowns at his tea, turning the cup around and around on the table.

"We shared a lot of things, the ups and downs of classes and grades," Chris says, "but the very fact that Bryan never went into the deep struggles while talking to me—I mean never—makes me think he may have been incapable of going into it with anyone."

Chris says what I've already thought about. The fact that no one at Conception knew anything about Bryan's personal life shows he was good at blending in and looking normal. Only the rare person who got close to him would know about the currents under his smooth surface.

The tea is gone and the conversation pulls to the present, where we are back to being Jennifer and Chris, two people from such different worlds, a little spark of something between us that feels like intimacy. Is it our shared history with Bryan, the connection of the living after the shock of such a death, or just that magical thing that happens with some people who connect from the very moment they meet?

I don't have the words to talk about it, too strange and awkward, and so I pay for dinner and small-talk through the rest of our first evening.

The next morning, the Rocky Mountains are out my window, a bank of snow-covered peaks that stretch north to south as far as I can see. Chris picked this hotel, promising a room with a view, and he wasn't kidding—it's spectacular.

At our pre-set time, Chris picks me up at the hotel, and it's good to see him, all the same feelings between us despite a good night of rest and the light of day.

We go for a cup of coffee and a bagel, bumping into more parishioners, a common phenomenon, considering he's the main priest for the biggest Catholic church in Denver, but still, Chris seems a little embarrassed to be caught out with me. This is . . . a friend? The sister of a friend? Just how do we explain me, anyway?

Just like at the seminary, I'm so aware I'm a woman, self-conscious about the fit of my black sweater, the way my hair is twisted up and clipped back, a few strands loose around my neck, the perfume I put on this morning.

I'm also aware of Chris. How he wears the collar again, his black shirt and slacks, how he smells like soap when he stands close to me on line.

He's a great-looking guy, just a couple years older than me, and I wonder what kind of attention he gets from the mere female mortals in his parish.

"Oh, I'm just an old man," he says, laughing when I ask.

"Don't kid yourself, Chris. You're . . . what? Thirty-eight? Thirty-nine?"

"Thirty-eight," he says.

"See?" I say. "You're just a pup."

He laughs, embarrassed at how I tease him, and I doubt he gets much of that around here.

After we finish our coffee, Chris gives me the grand tour of his parish, the parochial school across the street, and then his house, which is a tiny place with hardwood floors and walls painted an off-white.

We settle in his living room, me on the sofa, him with one leg crossed over the other in a chair, we pick up where we left off last night, talking about Bryan and how they became friends and then about the one time Chris met Leonard and Sylvia back in 1982.

"Bryan was polite with them but very closed off," Chris says. "They didn't seem close."

"Did that surprise you?" I say.

"No," he says, "not really. What did surprise me was the poverty they were living in. The whole time we were there, we ate soup, an ongoing soup that was very good because they let it go down and would build a new soup on top of that, so you'd get all the old flavors mixed with the new."

I almost ask if they were too broke to come see Bryan, but I don't. I look down at my own lap, my hands, my wedding ring.

I don't know anything about poverty, I've been pretty lucky that way, and maybe that's why they didn't go to support Bryan, not because they didn't want him to be a priest, but because they were broke or even embarrassed by their poverty—or maybe Bryan was embarrassed for them and didn't encourage a visit.

I take a deep breath—so many ways to consider a question.

"Did you ever see them again?" I say, looking at Chris, "after that one trip?"

Chris is quiet, thinking about it and then nods.

"Well, at the funeral, of course," he says.

"You were at the funeral?" I say.

"Yes," he says.

I squint my eyes then, trying to see him in the past and he smiles.

"You don't remember, do you?" he says.

"No," I say.

"I'm not surprised," he says. "You were very solitary when you were there; that's why I remember you."

A pile of papers is on a small table next to where Chris sits, and he leans over, picking through and taking out this small rectangle of paper. He hands it across to me and inside are the words *In memory of Bryan Joseph Lauck,* that incredibly stupid poem "Treasured Seasons." *For everything there is an appointed season, a time for sharing, a time for caring.*

Chris leans forward, elbows on his knees, chin tilted up. "Turn it over," he says.

I flip the paper over and on the back is my married name and the address of my first apartment in Spokane, written in my hand.

I look at Chris again and memory is so tricky. I can almost see myself writing all that information down and giving it to a younger version of him but it's like a shadow of a memory.

" 'In case you have any information,' " I say. "That's what I said, wasn't it?"

"You were starting your search even then," he says.

I sit back against his sofa again, the slip of paper in my lap, and my shoulders let go, as if I had been holding some weight there.

When you see someone you met and spoke with 16 years earlier, when you hold a piece of evidence of that meeting and then look into their eyes, everything changes.

"I completely forgot about this," I say.

"I did too," he says, "until I was going through all this old stuff and saw your name, your married name, which you told me last night."

I look down at the paper again. "You've kept this all these years," I say.

"That's right," he says.

He's quiet for a moment. "Maybe I knew you would come back into my life," he says.

It's just so unexpected, so odd, and yet, another sign of sorts, as if we were meant to talk one day.

"You know," he says, clearing his throat, "I did keep in touch with Leonard and Sylvia after the funeral; that is, I spoke with them on the phone a couple times."

"Really?" I say.

"Sylvia told me something," he says, "something I never got out of my head."

He rubs his hand over the whiskers of his chin, looking up for the exact words. "She said Bryan blamed himself for his mother's death," he says, shifting his eyes to me. "Did you ever hear that?"

"No," I say, a flash of new anger at Sylvia. They may have been poor but what a thing for her to say and I wonder if that is something that was said to Bryan: "You know, your mother died because of you." Did Leonard say that to Bryan, or maybe Sylvia, in a moment of anger, one of those opportunities they chose to smooth his rough edges?

They are the kind of thoughts that bring on a whole new wave of anger that sparks the same old anger that has burned in me since the day I found out Bryan killed himself. What the hell happened to him while he was living with Leonard and Sylvia anyway?

I put the program on the coffee table then and look at my watch. In an hour, I have a meeting at a coffee shop with Bryan's old roommate, but more than that, I'm tired of this talk.

"Well," I say, "as much as I hate to say it, I should go."

Chris looks at his watch too.

We both stand up, kinks in my back and legs, Chris stretching his arms over his head.

"Is that what it's like to be married?" he says. "Talking all the time?"

There's no way to describe marriage to a priest—too weird—so I just shake my head, *No, that's not what's it like.*

"Dinner later?" I say. "Or are you tired of me yet?"

"Of course I'm tired of you," he says, tucking his black shirt into his black pants, trying to keep his face serious.

I pick up my purse and put it over my shoulder. "That's more humor, right?" I say.

He nudges against my shoulder with a fist, big-brother style. "You are quick," he says.

Chris has confessions to take this afternoon, so we make plans to meet at six, his promise of a good dinner for my last night. He drops me at my hotel, tells me to be careful, and drives away.

✦ ✦ ✦

For about two months, Martin Louis was Bryan's roommate at the University of Oklahoma. He owned the gun Bryan used and it's a miracle I found him, let alone that he lives just 30 miles outside of Denver.

The first time we spoke, I was so surprised it was actually him that I didn't know what to say. Martin wasn't surprised at all.

"It was just a matter of time," he said.

"Why?" I said.

"I knew Bryan had a sister; he mentioned you lived in the Northwest," he said. "I figured you might try to find me and ask a few questions."

"Has anyone else in Bryan's family contacted you?" I said.

"No," he said.

Over the phone, Martin seemed intelligent and serious. He didn't seem "off" to me, but this afternoon, in a Denver Starbucks, I meet him face to face, just to be sure.

Martin Louis is a small man, and I mean *small*. I bet I outweigh him by at least 20 pounds. We shake hands and even his hands are small, almost delicate. He has wire-rimmed glasses, eyes a midrange blue and brown hair going gray at the temples. He wears khaki slacks and a dark green fleece jacket.

I order a double Americano but he says he doesn't want anything, a stiffness to the way he sits at our table with his hands held together.

I've already told him I'm not angry in any way but I can tell he's here out of duty and not because he actually wants to talk.

In 1983, Martin was an older student, 26, when he came to UO as a freshman. Bryan was 23 and a senior. Martin describes Bryan as polite but reserved and calm. While the two didn't have a friendship, Martin knew basic things about Bryan—distant family in Oklahoma, how he was a former seminarian, a philosophy major, and that he planned to go into the military when school got out.

"It seemed odd for a former seminarian to be going into the military," Martin says, his hands still together on the table in front of him.

"Why?" I say.

"Ethically, they are opposites," he says, as if it should be obvious.

I hold my cup between my hands, warming my palms. "Did you guys talk about his ethics?" I say.

"One time, in a very superficial way, we talked about the idea of heaven, Bryan's view of heaven," Martin says, pushing up his glasses with one finger and then resting his hands together again. "Back then, I had a scientific 'there is no heaven' viewpoint, but since, I have discovered God exists, and he has a wicked sense of humor."

"Why do you say that?" I say, sipping at my coffee.

Martin, in his quirky way of talking, mouth barely moving as he speaks, says Bryan's death was one in a long line of failures that weren't directly his fault but were associated with him through bad decision making. "Whenever it seemed to count, I'd always fail," he says. "For example, in the military, I got caught with a Baggie of marijuana that wasn't mine."

He adjusts his glasses on his face again.

"Bryan's taking my gun and killing himself was just another failure, something I refer to as the 'hammer of God.' It either makes you stronger or it kills you."

It's a strange kind of logic, but what lies under that logic is what interests me. Under Martin's words is this feeling of accountability for what happened, more accountability than I have been able to get out of my own family.

After that, Martin gives me the whole story of how he

showed Bryan the gun one day, as a courtesy but made sure not to show him where he kept his ammunition. He kept the two separate as a kind of insurance that the gun wouldn't accidentally hurt anyone.

Martin says Bryan didn't seem interested in the gun at all.

Over spring break, Bryan got sick and kept to the room for several days.

Near the end of the break, Martin noticed Bryan was gone but didn't think anything of it until campus police showed up at the room.

"It was a short conversation because I didn't have any information," Martin says. "Only after the police left, I had the thought, maybe a hero fantasy, that Bryan might be in trouble, and that was when I went to check my gun, and it was gone."

Around us in the coffee shop, other people talk, cups and saucers rattle, the coffee machine makes a hissing sound as the Barrista steams milk.

Martin says after Bryan had been missing a few days, the police came back to say they found the gun and one spent bullet, ammunition that was different than the type Martin used, something called +P ammo.

"I told them I didn't use that kind of bullet," he says. "It would tear up my gun."

Martin tilts his head side to side, like he's loosening himself up a little, and then he wraps up the story, says Bryan's family came to collect his things from the room and that he stayed clear the entire time, never meeting Leonard or Sylvia or anyone until me.

The police didn't question Martin again; in fact, they gave his gun back, and that was when he decided to pack up and go to California. Martin doesn't say he was kicked out of the school, but I get the feeling he was, or at least suspended.

"As I was packing, I turned over a drawer where I kept miscellaneous junk," Martin says. "I was picking through this pile and found two stray bullets that were the same type of bullet the police said Bryan had used, +P ammo."

Martin squints a little then, like he's in some kind of pain or maybe just searching for the memory. "That's when I remembered that I did have three stray rounds, loaners from a guy I knew," he says. "Bryan found the third."

Martin is different now, shoulders giving way a little bit under his jacket, but he stays so still in his chair, those hands still on the table.

"Did you tell the police about it?" I say.

He looks at me then, the smallest flicker of defeat in his eyes.

"No," he says, shaking his head. "I was just devastated it was my gun *and* my ammunition. I was always so careful about keeping them separate."

Even though the coffee shop is in a strip mall off Colorado Street, there is still a view of the mountains just past the traffic. The winter sun sets on the top edge of the Rocky Mountains, makes the snow a bright white at the peaks, but the slopes are shadows.

I know the rest of Martin's story, how after Bryan's death, he went through a profound depression of his own, almost took his life with the same gun, only he institutionalized himself and now lives this life of self-imposed exile, little to no contact with people, no wife, no children.

We stand up then, shake hands, and he says I'm welcome to call or send e-mail.

"I'm sorry this happened to you," I say. "I'm sorry my brother chose your gun. I guess I'm sorry you had the gun in the room to begin with."

Martin shrugs and then makes a small kind of grin, probably relieved to be done.

"Remember," he says, zipping his jacket all the way to his chin, "God has a wicked sense of humor."

I push my hands into the pockets of my jeans. "I'll remember that," I say.

I stay behind, watching him go out the door of the coffee shop, get into a white car and drive away. After he's gone, I sit down again, pressing my hand on the side of my to-go cup, not so warm anymore. Being here reminds me of all the years of reporting and how interviewing all types was part of the job. Once, I sat knee to knee with a man charged with the stabbing death of a hitchhiker. Allegedly, he stabbed her something like 30 times and later was convicted on DNA evidence that made the odds of his not doing it like 30 million to 1. As I sat across from him and looked into his eyes, he was just a normal person who talked in complete sentences and was actually pretty charming. I walked away from that interview thinking, *Well, maybe he didn't do it.*

Even though I'm on a quest for truth, I realize it is such an inexact process. I have sat with Martin Louis and looked him in the eye and I know with a kind of certainty that he had nothing covert to do with Bryan's death but I can't prove it. All I have is a feeling and since when did a feeling stand up in a court of law?

Your honor, my intuition says he didn't do it.

I'm not in a court of law, though; I'm in the classroom of my own heart and soul, trying to understand and learn how my own instincts can lead me from dark to light, immoral to moral, wrong to right.

My gut tells me he didn't do it and my gut tells me that this whole murder angle is a way for Leonard to keep Bryan's death away from himself, a boundary between him and any personal accountability. That's his burden, not mine.

Outside the sun is almost gone behind the mountains, high clouds that zig and zag pink across the sky. I put on my coat, walk out into the cold of the evening and back to my hotel.

Chris and I end up at this Italian place he knows about in Cherry Creek, panels of glass for the walls and inside, all sorts of trendy people drinking wine and eating pasta. We sit in a booth with a candle on the table that makes shadows on the white paper laid over a linen tablecloth.

"So," he says, "more questions tonight?"

"Absolutely not," I say, smoothing my hands over the table. "Let's talk about sports or the weather or whatever you want."

"Perfect," he says.

He does all the work of ordering, glasses of wine, some pasta dish in a cream sauce, then this amazing dessert of chocolate and cream and ladyfingers soaked in brandy.

All through dinner, Chris tells stories about living in Italy that make me laugh, and by dessert, I'm tired, sitting all slouchy with my elbow on the table, face in my hand. "I'm glad I made this trip," I say. "I've mostly enjoyed meeting you."

The candle flickers in its little glass globe, the shadows moving around on the table.

"Why, thank you," he says in deep voice. "The compliment goes both ways." He pushes his plate away, elbows on the table, hands together. "I wasn't going to tell you this," he says, "but now I've met you, it seems appropriate."

I roll my eyes to the ceiling. "Nothing serious, please," I say.

"Well," he says, putting his hands out, palms up, "it was just a matter of time."

That makes me laugh.

Chris holds his hands together again. "I don't want you to take this the wrong way," he says, "but I think your soul is going through some deep changes right now."

I sit up in the booth, self-conscious again.

"That's humor, right?" I say. "You're making a joke."

"No, I am serious," he says. "Here I am, a priest, dressed like a priest, and you are not intimidated at all."

I sit extra still, hands on the plastic of the seat.

"Why should I be?" I say.

"That's my point," he says. "You're not; you are open, you are searching."

Chris has a strange kind of mystery to him, to his voice and he clears his throat. "Do you remember the first time you called?" he says.

"Sure," I say. "It was September, I think."

"Right," he says, "and it was really out of the blue, that call. I was surprised to hear from you."

"I remember," I say.

Chris clears his throat again.

"Well, a few days after that call," he says, "I was giving a mass at my church and I had a deep sense Bryan was lifting."

The sounds of the restaurant are around us, people's voices, silverware on glass plates, glasses hitting together.

"I hope you understand what I am trying to say. It's not like I'm psychic or anything but during prayer, sometimes you feel things," he says. "I had a very strong sense that Bryan was released from purgatory and went to heaven."

I sit back and let go of the breath I was holding.

"You think Bryan has been in purgatory?" I say.

"I do," he says.

With anyone else, I'd wrap this conversation up as fast as

possible but this is Chris, a man I was almost destined to speak with and so, I look at him, person to person.

"Okay," I say, "define purgatory for me."

He smiles a slow smile and moves his hand over his mouth. "Do you ski?" he says.

"Yes, I ski."

"Okay," he says. "You are a skier and you are up on the mountain, say, skiing between the trees."

"I don't ski between the trees."

"Say you do this time and when you are up on the mountain, you run into a tree and break your leg."

"See?" I say, trying to joke my way out of where he's going. "That's why I don't ski between the trees. Too dangerous."

"Listen."

"Sorry."

"It's a bad break," Chris says. "Your bone is completely coming through the skin."

"Yuck," I say, shaking my head. "I get it."

"Say a doctor comes along, a doctor who says he loves you, and says, 'Well, I love you, so I'm not going to set that bone, because it would be too painful.' Now you are crippled for life. That's not really love. Who wants to be crippled for life?"

Chris stops then. "Are you with me?" he says.

I nod my head.

"Purgatory, in my mind, is where God is the doctor and He says, 'I love you and I'm going to set this bone right so you can walk again, but it's going to hurt—a lot."

He's quiet then, letting his words sink in, and they hit a deep nerve in me, deeper than I even know or even want to show.

"I've upset you," Chris says.

"He killed himself to stop the pain," I say, holding myself so still.

"But you see," Chris says, elbows leaned over the table, eyes such a pure color of blue, "if Bryan is in heaven, it means he's next to God and he isn't in any pain at all."

I shake my head. *How can you prove that? How do you know?*

"There's more," he says, reaching across the table, like he's trying to get my attention, but his hand stays flat on the white paper between us.

"For Bryan to be in heaven with God, he has to love you the way God does, without reservation."

I look at Chris and he looks at me.

"You don't have to say that, Chris," I say. "I know it's not true."

He looks at me with those eyes of his and then smiles with an inner confidence. "But if it is," he says, "imagine how it would feel."

I can't look at him, can't even let myself imagine such a thing. Maybe Chris just feels sorry for me and is trying to give me something to hold on to.

The idea of that makes me mad all over again.

I don't need Bryan to love me. Fuck him. But there it is, that anger that holds on like a fist, only who is it hurting now? Bryan? Chris? God?

I turn my hands in my napkin, my thoughts around and around, the feeling of Chris watching me.

This anger of mine is alive and sometimes feels like a wild poison ivy that covers my entire heart. I know there is a power to anger, the kind of power that helps you survive, the kind of power that pushes you to find the truth when everyone else just thinks you're crazy, but through this moment in a Denver restaurant with Chris Hellstrom, I see that there can be wisdom in letting it go, or at least, pulling it back in order to make more room for the good things like love and understanding and joy.

When I look up, Chris just smiles at me, as if he read my thoughts.

"You are a very wise man, Chris," I say, smiling back at him, "no matter what they might say about you."

He puts his hands together then, resting his chin on them, a smile all the way up into his deep blue eyes.

"That's humor, right?" he says.

I nod and laugh a little.

"Yeah," I say, "that's humor."

My last day in Denver is Sunday, and even though Chris has promised not to ruin our friendship by trying to convert me, he did ask if I would like to come to mass at ten.

I don't really want to go to church but I can't miss seeing him do his job.

I tell him that I'll walk from my hotel to the church and meet him there.

Before I leave the hotel, I call home. Spence is the one who answers the telephone.

"Hi, Mom," he says, little-boy voice on the line, and I can almost see his skinny body in his polar bear pajamas, short brown hair, big brown eyes.

"Hey, there you are," I say. "What are you doing this morning?"

"French toast!" he says.

"Wow, French toast—that's great."

"Mommy come home?"

"That's right," I say. "I am coming home."

"Okay," he says, "bye-bye."

The phone bangs on the floor, Steve saying something about being careful.

"You there?" Steve says.

"Still here."

"Good trip?"

"Intense trip."

"You expected that."

"That's true."

"Ready to come home?"

"More than you know."

"We'll meet you at the airport."

"Perfect."

Walking to church, the snow is crust on the dead grass, the sidewalks are dusty with salt pellets, and this part of Denver is ugly strip-mall development and dirty asphalt.

Last night, after Chris dropped me off and said goodnight, I cried for this wave of new feeling inside of me, the possibility that maybe I could be free of my old anger and that, if Chris was right about all this, Bryan could now feel a pure kind of love for me that could erase all the years of bitterness between us.

I felt like all the work I had been doing to find the truth about why he died was my own form of purgatory, a baptism through fire that was teaching me lessons that would last a lifetime.

Being alone now hurts in a new way, a sharp pain that used to be dull, and maybe it's that concrete idea that my mother, father and Bryan are all together in heaven but I'm still here, trying to figure this all out.

Can they see me down here? Can they see how hard it is sometimes?

I walk past a sleepy neighborhood of brick houses built close together and my step is the familiar one of the survivor, long, fast strides, head up, shoulders back, *Don't fuck with me,* and this morning, I hate the survival part of me. I don't want to power my way through this life anymore but how do I stop doing something I've gotten so good at?

Up ahead is St. Vincent de Paul and the bells ring for mass.

When I come to the corner, I don't cross. Instead, I just stand there, that familiar feeling of being on the outside of things.

An older couple goes in, the man holding the door for his wife, and then it's a young family, a man who holds a little boy in his arms, a woman hand in hand with a little girl who has on shiny black shoes.

"Why aren't you a Catholic?" Chris said last night.

"Why should I be?" I said.

"Because you are," he said. "You are so obviously a Catholic in everything you say and do."

"That's not true," I said.

"It is," Chris said. "You just don't see it." He was kidding the way he does but it was a joke with a meaning on the other side. I don't know if I agree with him. My family has been Catholic for years and look how it's turned out for us.

Crossing the street, I go inside and the winter sunlight is broken beams of pink and blue and green through stained glass. The familiar bowl of holy water is by the door, and I put in my first finger out of habit and respect and then I touch that finger to my forehead, just my forehead.

This church is nowhere near as lovely as Clyde, nowhere near as imposing as Conception. It's a family church with sensible brown carpeting, wide aisles, and a cry room in back for the babies that will undoubtedly cut loose mid-mass.

The place is packed with what Chris calls "the flock," and I sit off to the side, pull out a prayer book, and by habit, turn the pages to January 30. Some things never change.

The choir starts up then, the flock rising, all eyes on their songbooks.

Altar boys dressed in white come up the center aisle and behind them is Chris whose thin body is covered in layers and layers of green and white robes decorated with gold.

He's so serious, the father, the leader, and for the first time, I see him as a priest first, a man second.

Chris does a nice job up there, talks in his clear deep voice, readings from the books of Deuteronomy, Corinthians, Mark. Chris moves his arms in these big impressive gestures and the people look up to him for words of inspiration and guidance.

Wouldn't it be nice if someone stood up and said, "Excuse me, Father but I really don't get this Deuteronomy thing. Can you break it down for me?" But that's not the way the Catholics work—they are quiet listeners—and maybe that's why Chris is wrong about me. I want to roll up my sleeves and debate a thing; I want to ask questions.

People stand around me then and I stand too, looking down at the prayer book where the responsorial psalm reads: *"If today you hear His voice, harden not your hearts."*

If today you hear His voice, harden not your hearts.

Chills lift over me, running down my legs and around my back and it almost makes me laugh at myself. The words are just words, but they touch a different place in me, almost like God saying, "Hello—pay attention now; don't be too hasty."

I look up and over the heads of the rest of the followers, looking at Chris up there, and I wish I could wave this book around and show him those words. He's busy with the ritual of preparing communion, but it doesn't matter, I know in my heart what those words mean, and once again, maybe Chris is right about me.

On the ride to the airport, Chris plays an old Toto tape Bryan made for him back when they were in seminary together and the music sounds dated and old.

"I can't believe how fast the time went," I say.

"You should've stayed longer," Chris says.

"As if you could handle me for another day," I say.

"That's true," Chris says, voice with that tone he gets when he jokes, but between us is a strange quiet, like regret.

Out the window, it's office buildings and fast-food restaurants and gas stations.

I look over at him again, long, narrow face, blond hair, and even though part of me can't wait to get home, another part of me wants to hold on to what we've shared together.

"When's the last time you saw Bryan?" I say.

Chris takes a deep breath in then, and squints his eyes.

"May 1983," he says, "when he left the seminary." He looks my way and smiles a sad smile."I helped him pack his stuff."

"Did you guys talk about why he was leaving?" I say.

Chris shakes his head.

"Like so many things, we didn't talk about it directly," Chris says, "but I don't think he had the calling."

I shift in my seat to watch him as he drives.

"How did you say good-bye?"

Hands at 2 and 10 on the steering wheel, Chris looks my way for a second and then looks at the road again. He clears his throat.

"Before he got into the car, I gave him a big hug and said, 'I hope things go well for you,' " Chris says. "In typical Bryan style, he gave me this big bear hug that he broke off quickly, like *Okay, it's been great—off we go,* and he was just gone."

As Denver speeds by, Chris is quiet for a long time, eyes on the road. "I had this sense I wouldn't see him again," Chris says.

I put my elbow on the door and lean my head into my hand,

looking ahead too, and the freeway is dusty from being salted for the snow and ice.

Over the telephone Chris had told me about the day he learned of Bryan's death, how one of the monks pulled him from class to break the news. Chris told me that he took the rest of the day off and just stayed in his room, at first crying and being angry and then feeling afraid for Bryan's soul. Chris told me that he prayed for Bryan that day, begging God to have mercy.

The tape plays a song, "Goodbye Girl," about a breakup between a guy and a girl, with the words "It's so hard to see the truth with the sun in your eyes."

"Great song," Chris says, "Bryan really liked those lyrics."

We ride the rest of the way in silence and once we're at the airport, there's a mix-up about my flight, the departure is wrong on my itinerary and we have to make a run for it.

At the gate, I check in and Chris stands back, wearing a black coat that is such a contrast to his fair skin and blond hair.

"It's just like a Lauck not to have time for a decent goodbye," he says.

I hug Chris fast, my cheek to his blond whiskers.

"The difference is that you will be hearing from me again," I say.

"Oh sure," he says, waving me off. "That's what they all say."

The woman at the gate tells me that I have to board and I look at Chris again.

"I mean it," I say, squeezing his hand. "I'll call next week."

I go to the plane and halfway down the ramp, I look back to see if he's still there or if he left, but Chris is still there, arms at his sides. I wave one more time and he lifts his hand too.

NINE

NORMAN, OKLAHOMA ⁂ MARCH 2000

On the anniversary of a person's death, everything feels different. You are more moody, more cynical, more thoughtful. You find meaning in simple things like the weather, the landscape, a song on the radio. You remember bits about the person who died, snippets of memory triggered from almost nothing. You feel a new wave of grief that's like last year's grief, only a little different. It's like how the sky looks as the sun goes down: Each moment of descent changes the texture of the colors, but so slowly, you almost can't tell.

Somewhere along the way, I learned I wasn't supposed to grieve. When a person died, you packed up their stuff and moved on, and it's a good trick, at first. After a while, you forget the person was ever there, you stop listening for their footsteps, stop hearing their voice, and you even forget the look of them. You think, *That's it, I'm over it.*

If I look back when I was the most miserable and life felt almost impossible to cope with, I see it was always around the anniversary of a death, my mother's, my father's, and even

Bryan's. I left Lance on Christmas Eve; the anniversary of my father's death is in December. Steve and I broke up in September, right at the anniversary of my mother's death. If my skin is going to flare up, it's always in March, the anniversary of Bryan's death.

It's like the body has its own calendar and the heart its own rhythm and no matter what your head does to convince you otherwise, the body and heart go their own way.

This year, instead of pretending there isn't a death to remember, I make a point to go to Oklahoma on the anniversary of Bryan's death.

Like Missouri, Oklahoma is flat land that runs to the edge of blue sky, and as I leave Oklahoma City headed for Norman, there are billboards advertising everything from diesel fuel to DNA testing. "Do you know who the daddy is? Come see us today."

The weather is supposed to be sunny and hot and so I rented a convertible. With the Midwest wind blowing my hair around my face, I drive to Norman, check into a hotel and then go to the University of Oklahoma, which is at the center of town.

At the main entrance of the campus, I parallel-park my rental car and fill a meter with quarters.

It's a big school with stone buildings, sprawling grounds, and winding sidewalks. The main entrance is called the North Oval, and down each side of the street are buildings from every architectural school: Gothic Revival, French Renaissance, Ancient Greek.

At the far end of the Oval is a copper statue of a man who looks off to the horizon. Engraved in stone at his feet are the words *The University of Oklahoma exists for the students but the*

University cannot give you an education, it can only help you acquire one for yourselves.

I wonder if Bryan considered those words or if he just walked by with his head down.

In his three years at seminary, he was almost a straight-A student, but in his time here, he fell below a B average, as if he had given up on being a good student.

I walk the entire campus, just to get a feel of the place, and it's a fine-looking school even if, compared to seminary, it feels pretty impersonal. I wonder if it felt that way to Bryan too and if somewhere inside, he missed the routine of Conception and his friend Chris.

At the far edge of campus, I cross the lawn to the UO police station, a cinder-block square of a building with a narrow run of steps to the front door. When I get there, a tall man in pressed khaki pants and a plaid shirt comes out the door.

"Lieutenant Harp?" I say, shading my eyes.

"That's me," he says.

We shake hands. He has a tidy haircut, a mustache, and a badge clipped to his belt that says UNIVERSITY OF OKLAHOMA POLICE DEPARTMENT.

"Welcome to Oklahoma," he says.

"Thanks."

Even though I am all alone and relatively defenseless, he's like a hundred other police officers I met on the beat as a reporter, so when he waves me in the direction of a small white police car, I get in without being that worried.

Inside the car, I buckle my seat belt, and Lieutenant Harp hands me a thick pile of papers stapled at the corner.

"I figured since you came all this way," he says, "you'd probably like a copy for yourself."

At the top of the page it says *University of Oklahoma Police De-*

partment, Case No. 03-84-0884, DO NOT DUPLICATE. It is the report of the police investigation of Bryan's death, the whole thing.

For more than two months, I wrangled for these with a university lawyer, a nightmare of paperwork and telephone calls that ended with my getting just one page of the report and a legal letter that said it was policy to keep the investigation sealed. Of course, I called on the phone, explained this was my brother we were talking about and if it was a suicide, why keep the investigation sealed?

"University policy," the woman said, her voice such a brick wall, I gave up hope of seeing the full report. Having the pages in my hands now is as good as hope restored but instead of singing hallelujah, I just smile at Lieutenant Harp, all cool and collected, like it's not a surprise at all.

"Thanks," I say. "Thanks a lot."

"No problem," he says, driving out of the lot and toward a water tower painted a bright white.

"I thought we'd go right to the scene," he says, "if that's okay."

I nod my head, normal smile stuck on my face, my hand shaking a little as I turn the pages.

"Sure," I say, clearing my throat, "no problem."

"Turn to the back of the report," he says, "and you'll see a diagram of the scene."

On the last page is a simple drawing with a series of *X*'s, some circles and numbers that mark distance between landmarks. There is a crude drawing of a bike and a stick man labeled "the victim," and my elation about the police report is gone in the face of the reality of what we are about to do.

Lieutenant Harp stops at the intersection of two roads, Monitor and Merrimac.

"If there is going to be any trouble on campus," Lieutenant Harp says, "this is where it usually goes down."

He drives across Merrimac and onto a dirt road that circles behind a water tower. "Kids like to come back here and do drugs, party, get into fights," he says.

The road comes to a dead end against this stand of thick overgrowth, a combination of bushes and trees and long grass.

"If you decide to come back here later," he says, "let one of my officers know, because it's pretty dangerous, and we wouldn't want anything to happen to you."

I nod and Lieutenant Harp parks the car.

"This is it?" I say.

"This is it," he says, opening his door. "Hand me the report, and I'll pace it out for you."

I hold the pages with both hands and without breathing, give them up.

Lieutenant Harp walks off with my report and I rub my empty hands together, telling myself to calm down. *You'll get them back.*

I open my door and get out of the car too, boots on the dry dirt of the road.

It's not even noon but already it's hot out.

I shut the car door and on the ground are flattened beer cans and fast-food paper wrappers. Off a ways is an old mattress torn down the middle. A tall chain-link fence separates this place from what looks like a four-lane highway and far off is the sound of traffic.

I cross my arms over myself, rubbing my hand up and down on one arm, not sure what to do.

I've been at a crime scene before, have even seen dead bodies. This shouldn't be that big of a deal but it is. This is Bryan and the place he died and just standing here makes everything feel different, the sun hotter, the sounds louder, the light brighter.

Lieutenant Harp walks past me with these big steps, counting out loud. "Twenty-five, twenty-six."

A bird caws loudly like a crow and I look up, hand shading my eyes. In the bush is a black bird with white on its tail feathers and he rustles around in the top of the bushes.

Lieutenant Harp stops a few paces away, looks up at the water tower and then down at the report again.

The bird caws again, this *Go away* sound in his call.

"Okay. His bicycle was leaned here," Lieutenant Harp says, pointing at the edge of the overgrowth, "and your brother was found about six feet from the bike, which must have been inside the bushes there."

Coming to where he is, I squat down to look where he points. Past the tangle of branches is a clearing where sunlight filters through.

"Were the bushes this big back then?" I say, looking up at him, one eye closed to the sun.

"Sixteen years ago?" he says, "probably not as tall, but still enclosed like they are now."

"Is there a way to get in the middle?"

"Let's see," he says, going wide around the bushes.

I stand up again, the heels of my boots sinking in the red mud.

"It's pretty dense," he says, circling back the other way.

I watch him go back and forth in search of an opening and I look into the bushes again. The branches don't look that hard to push through.

Lieutenant Harp is gone around the other side, saying something about how he's not sure if we can get in.

I didn't come all this way to stand outside of things and I bend low, pushing through branches scratching my face and pulling my hair.

"Watch yourself," Lieutenant Harp says from the other side. "Don't get your clothes torn."

"It's okay," I say, readjusting my glasses on my face. "I'm fine."

Lieutenant Harp doesn't follow me in, still searching around for an opening and I go to the middle of the clearing, looking around and up at the sky.

It's so different from what I thought it would be, more like a fort than a forest, a hideaway where kids would play or lovers would make out.

The mulch underfoot is spongy and thick and I kneel one knee to the ground, the mulch soft like a pillow. I push my fingers down, the mulch cool on my fingers, and it's at least three inches before I hit soil, evidence that this place has been here and like this, for a long time.

I rub my hand off on my pants and the smell is dirt and decay and something bitter, like urine. What a place to die. What a place to be alone, and at the same time, it's so Bryan to find a place like this. He always wanted to be left alone.

There was a time when we were kids in L.A., just after our mother died and we had moved in Deb's big old house.

Bryan had his own room in Deb's attic and I went up there to get him for dinner. I remember calling his name and knocking on his door with the "Go Away" sign hanging on the doorknob but Bryan didn't answer.

I didn't want to go up there because it would make him mad but I went anyway. I remember how it was so hot up there, hot the way L.A. gets in the summer.

Bryan's bed was in the dormer part of the attic across from a small rectangle of a window and he was lying on his bed in a pair of shorts, eyes wide open with beads of sweat over his smooth, tanned face.

"Dinner," I said but Bryan didn't even blink his eyes.

"Bryan," I whispered, touching his arm with my fingers, this feeling in me that he was dead. "Bryan!" I yelled, and then he blinked and shifted his eyes to me.

"Want do you want?" he said.

"God, I thought you were dead," I said.

He sat up quick, bare feet on the wood floor and wiped the sweat off his face. He kept his hands over his face then, like he was tired or something. "Get out of here," he said.

Lieutenant Harp must have found a clearing, coming in without a scratch, his hair still neat and tidy.

What he must think of me right now, this strange person knee down in the mulch, dirt on her hands.

I put a smile on my face, back to business in my head and press myself to standing.

"You've read the whole report, right?" I say, shifting my shoulders around, trying to get myself back into myself.

"A couple of times," he says, handing the report over.

I take it in my hands, moving my thumb over the edge of thick pages.

"Okay," I say, "so tell me—does anything indicate that this might not have been a suicide?"

He watches me for a second, wire-rimmed glasses, blue eyes, official police expression on his face. "At the time, based on the evidence collected and the fact that there was no sign of a struggle," he says, "it was ruled suicide."

I push my hand into my pocket and move the mulch around with my foot, trying to scare up what a struggle would look like in this mulch. The soft mulch turns over easily, a different color on the underside.

"There's been a rumor in the family that this might have been murder, so that's why I'm asking."

"I understand," he says, adjusting his glasses. "It's not unusual in a case like this. Families have a hard time."

Lieutenant Harp is a big man next to me, tall and wide at the shoulders, but in his eyes, you can see a nice person.

"Do you do this very often?" I say. "That is, bring people to the scene of the crime?"

He smiles at that and nods. "Just last month, a couple came to see where their daughter had been raped," he says. "It's important for families."

"Do the people you meet wait sixteen years?" I say.

"One week, six months, sixteen years," he says, shrugging his shoulders. He puts his hands into his pockets, moves change around with his hand, and looks down.

"My brother died too," he says. "Not suicide but it was still devastating for me and my family. I guess I understand about needing to know the truth."

Far off is the noise of the traffic, and one more time, the bird makes its loud, sharp caw. I look up for the sound, sunlight coming through the tops of the bushes.

"What kind of bird is that?" I say.

"Bird?" Lieutenant Harp says.

"Making that sound?" I say.

He looks around as if he didn't hear anything and shakes his head. "I don't know," he says.

It's not that big a deal, the name of a bird, and I look around the inside of this place again. I want to stay here a little while longer, just to take it in and think, but I don't know how to ask Lieutenant Harp to leave me alone, and besides, what else could I possibly see? It's the middle of an overgrown bush, what looks like a juniper or maybe a cedar, and from here you have a broken view of the outside world, this feeling that you can look out but no one else can look in.

It's just a place but being in here gives me a small idea of what it was like to be Bryan, this person who saw out but wouldn't let anyone in.

"Seen enough?" Lieutenant Harp says.

I look around one more time and nod my head.

"Yeah," I say, "I've seen enough."

After that, I tour the campus with Lieutenant Harp and he points out all the landmarks, the library, Bryan's dorm 16 years ago, and, across the street from the dorm, a student bar that was a fixture on campus even back then.

Lieutenant Harp was actually a student here all those years ago, a sophomore when Bryan died but barely remembers hearing about it.

"See those flowering trees?" he says, pointing to a stand of wide-branched trees about to bloom with tiny pink flowers. "Those are Bradford pears," he says.

"Very pretty," I say.

"I may not know much about the birds here but I know a little about horticulture."

I laugh and he laughs too.

"I know only because I love the pears," he says.

The sun is high in the Saturday sky and I look at my watch—almost one P.M. Lieutenant Harp drives back to the police station and gives me his business card, says to call him anytime, to have him paged if I have any questions at all.

I put his card into my back pocket and hold out my hand.

"Thank you, Lieutenant Jeffrey Harp," I say. "It was nice to meet you."

He shakes my hand, professional and strong. "Good luck," he says.

✦ ✦ ✦

At the university library, no one pays any attention to me as I sit in a corner and read the story written in the police report.

It's all here, every detail, from the day Bryan was reported missing to the day his body was found and there is something so satisfying and tangible about the facts that I'm lost in them, my head in my hands while I read as fast as I can.

In 1984, from March 26 to April 11, the entire university police department was on the case.

Exactly as Martin Louis told me, Bryan was sick for a few days over spring break, disappeared over the weekend, and then, the Monday after spring break, was reported missing by a woman named Joann Kolstad, who was his supervisor. That same Monday, Louis's gun was reported missing too.

At first, an army recruiting officer says he actually spoke with Bryan that day, set an appointment for Wednesday, March 28, when Bryan was coming in to sign his enlistment papers. This puts the search on hold, but on Wednesday, when Bryan didn't show, the recruiter admits there was a mix-up in the scheduling, and the search for Bryan begins again.

There was an all-points bulletin, Bryan's bank account was checked for recent withdrawals, and in his room, police found his checkbook, credit cards, and a list of telephone numbers on a sheet of legal paper. Calling a few of those numbers, they learned from friends and relatives that Bryan had a history of depression. The police also find out that Bryan did have a girlfriend but that relationship ended back in the fall, and that he was last seen on Saturday night wearing a suit, but no one knew why.

Four days after Bryan is reported missing, Leonard arrived at the university and, in an interview with the police, denied Bryan ever had any depression and then says, as far as he knew,

Bryan was also heterosexual, even though no officer asked about Bryan's sexual orientation.

Pulling myself from the report, I sit back in my chair, a bright orange plastic chair and underline the words on the police report that say *Although no one had asked, as far as he knew, his son was heterosexual.*

Why would Leonard say such a thing? What compelled him to bring it up at all?

Far off is the sound of coins dropping and then a copy machine making a copy. I rub my fingers over my eyelids, it's right there, fresh anger that in another time, could take me completely except now, I won't let it. I take a deep breath and make myself focus on the report.

After two days, Leonard left the university, saying he had done all he could but the police didn't give up. They called all the hospitals, checked the bus station and went to all the retail outlets in town that sold handgun ammunition, in search of some evidence of Bryan.

On Monday, April 2, seven days after he was reported missing, he was found by a guy who was out for a jog.

The officer who first arrived at the scene wrote:

> Upon arrival I noted a red bicycle lying on its left side outside the tree line. When I looked into the trees, I saw the victim lying on his right side in a semi fetal position. I could find no signs of a struggle in the area. I also could find no signs of anyone else having been near the body. When I observed the body itself, I noted the general description fit that of the victim. Furthermore, I noted a mole over the left lip, which matched that of the victim. I further noted a S&W model 60 under the left

hand. What appeared to be a gunshot entry wound was present in the left temple.

Around are whispering sounds; overhead are fluorescent lights. I take off my glasses. Through me is the old feeling of defeat that stomps down the hope beyond hope that somehow there would have been a different ending to this story. It was all a mistake—they didn't find Bryan that day, it was some other guy, it had to be another guy.

On the page, it says: *I noted a mole over the left lip, which matched that of the victim.*

My mother called it a beauty mark; my father called it a birthmark, Bryan called it a mole. As far back as I can remember, there was always that mole over his lip, the mark that made Bryan Bryan.

When someone dies, you know it's true with your head, but your heart just can't believe.

I thumb through the rest of the pages then, just a few more left to go, and even though I don't want to read any more, I do it anyway.

Leonard doesn't come back to the university after they find Bryan, but on the telephone, he refuses to accept it's a suicide, calling for tests on Bryan's hands, for fingerprints on the bullet casing, and an autopsy. Bryan's body was exposed to the elements for too long for those tests and because there was no evidence of foul play, the medical examiner declines to do an autopsy.

After that Leonard has the police seal Bryan's checking account and his room, saying someone will come to collect his things.

The report closes with a final ruling of suicide.

Along the margins of the report, I make notes for myself, new names of people to call, the R.A. of Bryan's dorm, the woman who reported him missing, the army recruiter, and then the question of why Bryan was wearing a suit on Saturday night, when it says right here he was found wearing a windbreaker and jeans.

Why a suit? A date? Church?

There is always a mass on Saturday night and I make another note to get hold of the annual prayer book for March 1984; the sermon for that day may hold a clue.

All that I write is busy work to cover what I feel but it's not working.

I'm so pissed off at Leonard, I'm shaking. I can't believe he waited so long to come when Bryan was reported missing, that he would talk about Bryan's sexuality to the police, that he left so soon after, and that the last thing he did was make sure Bryan's checking account was sealed. I wonder how it felt for Leonard to spend Bryan's last $200?

I sit back from my papers then, hands fisted and then open again.

I'm not good enough at managing this anger yet and it's all over me, hatred for Leonard that digs deep. I'm angry as a mother who loves her son so much that if he disappeared, at any age, I would crawl on my hands and knees until I found him. I'm angry as a sister who was deprived of a brother. I'm angry as the only survivor of my family, angry for my mother and my father and for the way this crazy life of ours turned out. I'm angry that I'm all alone in a library in Oklahoma with a truth that doesn't change a goddamned thing.

I rub my hand over my face and I'm cold in here, as if my circulation has stopped. I push my papers in a big pile and leave the library in search of that bar Lieutenant Harp showed me. God knows I need a drink.

\+ \+ \+

O'Connell's is mostly empty tables, a bunch of jocks sitting at one, and a few people at the bar. The jocks eat baskets of french fries and there are pitchers of beer down the middle of the table.

I sit at one end of the bar, video poker machine by my elbow, and a young girl with a ponytail is behind the bar talking on the telephone.

At my elbow, the video poker machine plays a little song and stars shoot around, the words *Play, Win, Play, Win* on the screen.

The young girl finally stretches her telephone cord all the way to where I sit and tells whoever she's talking to to hold on.

"What can I get you?" she says, gum in her mouth, chew, chew.

"How about a Scotch," I say, because Chris told me that Bryan used to like Scotch.

"Rocks or straight up?" she says.

I roll my lips together. Who knows? "Straight?"

She puts the telephone back to her ear, a look in her eyes that says she's never been so bored and walks away.

Up and over the bar, two televisions are tuned to the same car race, NASCAR. Steve is the only reason I know NASCAR from Indy cars because he's into that kind of thing, very manly.

I wonder what they are doing right now, if Spencer is missing me half as much as I miss him.

The girl behind the bar isn't rushing to pour the Scotch, still deep in her telephone conversation and I lean my elbow on the bar, face in my hand, eyes on the cars going around and around. Even though the televisions are turned way down, I can just make out that engine sound of acceleration, downshift, acceleration.

When we were kids, Bryan loved the races too, even said he was going to be an Indy car driver when he grew up, the next Mario Andretti.

Who knows why but the idea of Bryan as a racecar driver made me so afraid for him. I couldn't have been more than three or four but I was so sure he would die in some car crash, I was actually convinced of it.

The girl comes back with the Scotch, puts the glass on a napkin and pushes it my way.

I look into the glass and through the alcohol, read the one word written on the bar napkin, *O'Connell's*.

I swirl the glass around and think how I used to be obsessed with death. If my father tried to get me on a sailboat, I screamed until he put me down; if he drove over the Golden Gate Bridge, it was another opportunity to flip out; and one time, when my father let Bryan drive Red, I was completely uncontrollable, screaming, "We are all going to die," at the top of my lungs.

I move my hand over the back of my neck—what a strange child—but still, I realize that all the times I feared death, Bryan was with me. Once we were split up, I never felt that same fear again.

I set the glass down on the napkin again, eyes up to the car race, and I guess it doesn't mean anything, but then again, it's odd. In his own way, Bryan gave off the feel of death. It was in the shadows that were always in his eyes, in the mean, moody, angry way of him.

Now I know the truth of how he was born, I realize that he knew death in a way I didn't. When our mother was seven months pregnant with him, she started to vomit blood from the ulcers in her stomach. She was hospitalized and given massive transfusions and with what I know now about babies, I'm sure Bryan's new self felt the shock waves. Then, to be born and, within the first few weeks of life, to have his mother go back to the hospital to have an 11-inch tumor taken from her spine. Why wouldn't Bryan end up a dark soul after such a beginning?

Looking back at his life from where I sit, it's almost impossible to be angry at him for being a shitty big brother. The guy had his own problems.

Reaching out, I lift the glass of Scotch and I take it all in one swallow, a burn that goes all the way down my throat.

I put the empty glass down on the counter and tell myself that I will never drink Scotch again. It was for Bryan, for the past, for this search that finally has me at the threshold of the truth and in a way, it was for Leonard. I know what happened now, I know what he did and what he said, I know what he didn't do too and in a strange way, it's enough for me. Leonard's silence didn't stop me.

The girl is off the telephone now, boredom still in her eyes, and she brings the tab, three bucks.

I pass her a five-dollar bill.

"Keep the change," I say.

The sun is on its way down but it is still too hot. In the car, I pull the handles for the roof and then push the buttons. The roof lifts up in the air, that hydraulic sound of the motor folding it down and back.

I start the car then, the sun on my shoulders, and drive in the direction of the water tower.

At the intersection of Monitor and Merrimac, I stop at the stop sign and remember Lieutenant Harp's warning. I know I should pay attention to what he told me but I'll be careful, hell, I won't even get out of the car.

I cross the intersection, drive the dirt road that circles just under the water tower and park exactly where we were just a few hours ago.

Putting my elbow on the side of the door, I lean my face into my hand.

I've come so far to get to this place and you'd think, after all the tears I've cried, that I would feel like crying now, but I don't.

In the rearview mirror, the sun sets down to the tops of the trees, and I can see myself in the mirror too, sunglasses on my face. I'm the one who has spent five years of her life searching for herself in the past and the one who now gets to live beyond it.

I should be thinking about Bryan as I look at the place he died but all I can think about is my son and home and getting to it, almost excited for what will come next, even though I'm not sure what that will be.

Maybe I'll have another child.

Maybe I'll start a new career.

Maybe I'll write all these memories down and try to make beauty from all the ugliness.

The questions of what I'll do now are almost as interesting as the possibility within the answers, and even though I'm still alone, I'm glad I survived and am here to ask those questions. I'm grateful for my life.

The sun is lower than the trees now, falling fast, and I look at the overgrowth one more time before backing up and then driving away, the place that Bryan ended his life at my back.

Portland is in bloom.

I push our red stroller through our neighborhood and to the park that's nearby, passing azaleas and rhododendrons vivid in their colors of purple, red, and pink.

The daffodils have spent themselves and the tulips are almost done. Lilacs come next, and then roses.

Spencer sings "The Wheels of the Bus Go Round and Round" in his high, sweet voice, and he doesn't have a care in the world, feet crossed, a Baggie of fish crackers in his lap. He's long-legged and lean, with dark hair cut like a bowl around his small head.

He tilts his head back, big brown eyes up to see me and I know from his view, I'm upside down.

"Sing, Mommy," he says.

"The wheels of the bus," I sing, and he sings with me, "go round and round."

When I came home from Oklahoma, I started a complex chain of telephone calls. The first to Joann Kolstad, the woman who reported Bryan missing. She had a great sense of humor and joy of life in her voice, but then told me how sad and sorry she was for Bryan's death.

Before he got sick, she heard that he had been rejected by one branch of the military—she thought it was the navy but gave me the number of another woman, Martha Finley, who would know better.

Martha Finley said it was the navy and that he was rejected right before spring break.

"Did he say why?" I said.

"No," she said, "he didn't talk about it at all. He was just pretty upset."

"How did you know he was upset?" I said.

She laughed over the telephone, a high sound. "He didn't say anything outright," she said, "but he was very quiet and serious. I knew he was disappointed."

Way back when I was a teenager, Grandma and Grandpa told me how my father wanted to be in the navy, had even enlisted when he was underage but Grandpa had pulled him out. The next year he was drafted into the army, and he hated it.

I called the army and navy recruiting offices in Oklahoma.

There is no record of Bryan but a navy recruiter told me that they are more stringent on who they take than the army is. The navy requires psychological testing and will reject a recruit right away if there is any evidence of depression.

After that, I tried to reach the actual army recruiter who worked with Bryan back in 1984 but spoke with his wife instead.

"My husband had nothing to do with your brother's death," she said.

"I know that," I said, "but he did help with Bryan's recruitment into the army. He had a chance to speak with him several times and I was hoping to ask him just a few questions."

"Well, I don't think that's necessary," she said and then hung up on me.

The park has a play structure of blue and yellow plastic, a Jungle Gym of bars and slides and ladders.

Spencer runs across the bridge made of rubber, and I reach for his legs, tickling the soft skin around his knees.

His whole face brightens with his smile, a light in his eyes because tickle is his favorite game.

"You can't get me," he says, running away.

"I'm going to get you," I say, ducking under the fire pole and around the back of the tic-tac-toe board.

We have this game on the play structure where he pushes his small fingers through the rotating blocks that are part of the tic-tac-toe board and then, from where I am on the ground, I reach to his hand and weave my fingers into his. We hold hands for just a moment before he pulls away, distracted by some other adventure.

Spencer does that then, pushes his long fingers through the rotating blocks, and on cue, I reach up and hold on.

✦ ✦ ✦

My next call went to Dale Gooch, who I found living in Kansas. He knew my name right away and was helpful, friendly, and, after all these years, still sad about Bryan's death. In 1984, he was the resident advisor for Bryan's dorm and was furious when he found out that Martin Louis had a gun on campus, said they all but ran him out because he wasn't that well liked.

"Louis was strange," Dale said over the telephone.

"Do you think he was capable of murder?" I said.

"I don't know," he said, "but I always thought it was odd for a guy like Bryan, who was a Catholic, to kill himself."

I told Dale how I met Martin Louis and agreed he was strange, but strange didn't necessarily imply murder.

"Let's imagine he was involved," I said. "How could such a small person get Bryan, who was six feet three, all the way down to the southern edge of campus without a struggle?"

It got quiet on the telephone line.

"It's true," Dale said. "Besides, Bryan wouldn't have had lunch with that guy—there's no way he would have been hanging out with him by the water tower."

"Did you know Bryan applied to more than one branch of the military?" I said.

"No," he said, "I didn't know that."

"Did you know his parents were dead?" I asked, "or that his mother died on his tenth birthday?"

"No," he said.

Like most people I'd talked to, Dale admitted he really didn't know Bryan as well as he thought. He says Bryan was a few years older, someone he looked up to and admired.

"He had this quiet way," Dale said, "a reserve that I always took for calm and even wisdom."

We were both quiet then, and he cleared his throat. "I guess it's like they say," he said. "Still waters run deep."

On the ride home from the park, Spencer's all set up with a juice box and a bagel.

I push the stroller on the narrow trail that runs through the park, and overhead, the branches of the maple trees make a canopy of green. We talk through all the things we did today.

"Swings," I say.

"Slide," Spencer says.

"Climbing," I say. "You are a very good climber."

"Hopping," he says.

"That's right," I say. "You are a very good hopper too."

He's quiet, eating his bagel, and I'm quiet too, just pushing him in the stroller.

The big question these days is if I should have another child, but I'm just not sure. Deep down, I wonder if the reason has something to do with Bryan and how he couldn't take me into his heart. It would be so hard to see my son reject his brother or sister for whatever reason. At the same time, it doesn't have to be like that, and maybe, if I make sure to be there to help them through the rough times of sibling rivalry and jealousy, they could depend on each other and even be friends.

I stop the stroller at the intersection, cars going back and forth, and Spencer says, "I want to push the button, Mommy."

"No problem," I say.

Backing up the stroller to the pole where you push the button for the Walk sign, I adjust the stroller so he can reach.

Spencer moves his bagel to his right hand and lifts up with his left, pushing the button with his thumb.

"All right," I say, "nice job."

Spencer smiles at his accomplishment and sits back in the stroller again, bagel in both hands.

My last call went to Chris Hellstrom and he told me how he's leaving his parish to take a new job as a spiritual advisor to seminarians.

"Interesting twist," I said.

"I know," he said, "and after all this with Bryan, don't think I haven't considered the irony."

"It's a good thing," I told him. "You can make a big difference."

Since my trip to Denver, I had started annulment proceedings for my first marriage, not because I was going to re-join the Catholic Church but just as a baby step in that direction and through it all, Chris had been there, not saying "I told you so," but giving me gentle advice like a good friend.

He was also there to help me sort through the mass that was given on the last day anyone saw Bryan, March 24. I tell Chris I can't prove he went to church that night, but deep down, I have this feeling he did.

Because all Catholic churches use the same mass and prayer schedule nationwide, probably worldwide, it's not hard to go back to 1984 and find the mass for that day. While Chris explained, I looked at my copy.

"In seminary, we learned to put special emphasis on the psalm, and because Bryan had three years of seminary, he would have done the same."

I read through the mass to the psalm and it reads: "If today you hear his voice, harden not your hearts."

Chills lifted on my arms and I put my hand over my mouth, but Chris kept on talking.

Chris said that particular psalm is a prayer that monks are invited to use every day and historically comes from the years when the Jews were led out of Egypt and needed to be reminded of God's existence.

"It tells us to keep our hearts open to God, even without proof," Chris said.

"This is God literally reaching off the page and saying, 'Don't do it, Bryan,' " Chris said. "Which makes me think he must have lost his faith somewhere along the line."

It got quiet between us, and finally, I took my hand off my mouth.

"Chris," I said, my voice very low, "do you know that is the same psalm I heard the day I came to your church in January?"

Chris got quiet then, and for the first time, I had the upper hand on him, one step ahead.

"That can't be," he said.

"It is," I said.

"Are you sure?" he said.

"Chris," I said, "me? Of course I'm sure."

For the first time since we'd met, Chris needed proof, a mere mortal after all. He told me to hold on while he shuffled through the pages of this year's prayer book. but I didn't need to look the way he did; I knew those words. I had felt them in my own heart on that cold day in January. They were the reason I was even considering my faith again. I just never told him that.

Chris started to laugh then, a deep sound over the phone.

"Well, I'll be," he said, "you're right."

From my Catholic days, I remember Lent as the annual event where you gave up something for 40 days and thought about the sacrifice Jesus Christ made by dying on the cross. When I was a kid, it felt like Lent lasted forever, this gray, bland time of the year, every year, where you ate fish on Fridays and just prayed for the end when you would be rewarded with a new dress, Easter eggs, and a basket of candy.

Ironically, Bryan took his life at the peak of Lent in 1984. I think he did it because he was upset about not being accepted into the navy, so upset it triggered a deep depression. His depression was sparked by failure, and failure feels like the link.

Bryan punished himself for any failure—on the racquetball court, in his studies, in every aspect of his daily life. He punished himself for failing to get into the navy, but I don't think he killed himself over the navy; I think he killed himself for failure.

Our mother died on his birthday, and if he blamed himself, that was the first failure.

Our father died less than two years later.

Bryan was sent from one home to another, yanked around like a yo-yo.

We were separated.

Sylvia was cold to him.

Leonard rounded off his sharp edges.

God didn't call.

The navy didn't want him.

Twenty days into Lent, with 20 more to go, the time to give up something precious and repent, on Saturday night, March 24, or Sunday morning, March 25, Bryan took that gun, found one bullet, rode his bike to the edge of campus, climbed into the center of those bushes, kneeled to the ground, and, probably very quickly, before he lost his nerve, took his own life.

It's not a simple conclusion and it hardly makes up for the tragedy of his death but it's a theory I can live with, a theory based on what I knew about him from the years of living together, on the hours and hours of conversations I've had with people who knew him and on my own intuition.

✦ ✦ ✦

Steve comes home from work at four, Spencer wakes up from his nap at four-thirty, and the three of us sit around the kitchen table trying to figure out exactly how you are supposed to color Easter eggs.

Spence is on his knees and leans over the table, brown eyes wide open, fingers touching everything—the white hard-boiled eggs, the little tablets that make the different colors, the little copper wire egg dipper.

The sixteenth anniversary of Bryan's death has come and gone like a whisper in the wind, and this year, my little dog Carmel finally died of old age.

I bought her three months after Bryan died and she died just a few weeks ago, as I was finishing my search for Bryan's story.

Her death was so hard on me, not just the death of a good friend and loyal companion but a death to the space between when I was completely alone, no man, no home, no child, moving from place to place, chasing a hollow career and always being on the brink of a breakdown. That little dog, blond with milk-chocolate eyes, was my best friend, and just recently I realized that her name, Carmel, was also the name of my mother's favorite place in the world, Carmel, California. I named her for a lost memory that linked me to my mother and her love.

"It says to add vinegar," Steve says. "One tablespoon."

"Give Daddy the measuring spoons," I say.

"I can do it," Spencer says, very big on doing things himself these days.

"Let me help you," Steve says.

"No," Spencer howls, frown on his face.

"We'll do it together," Steve says.

Just that fast, Spencer gets happy again and the two of them measure out tablespoons of vinegar into each of the six cups.

Steve and I have been married for almost six years and

Spencer will be three in another month. Finally, I'm not alone anymore, but in a way, I never was actually alone the way I thought I was. Everything that was important to me was just a memory away, and now, I have those too.

Spencer leans close to the cups.

"Be careful, buddy," Steve says. "That water is hot."

Steve puts his hand on Spencer's shoulder, eases him back.

All the months of talking to people, following leads, waiting for mail to come with bits and pieces of Bryan's story and I'm finally as far as I can go.

I do not have one more question to ask.

With my teeth, I tear open the package of dye tablets.

"You think these are safe?" I say.

"Should be," Steve says.

"Here you go," I say, handing the tablets over to Spencer.

"One per cup, Spence," Steve says.

"I can do it," Spencer says, little fingers taking up a red tablet, dropping it into a cup, the fizz of the red dye bubbling away.

"Look, Daddy," Spencer says, pointing his finger at the cup.

"Pretty amazing stuff," Steve says, nodding his head.

Spencer takes up a green pill, drops it into another cup, more bubbles.

"Wow," Spencer says.

Sometimes, when we are all together like this, in the moments of our life that come and go so fast you could never hold them, I try to hold on anyway. I try to be still and just see everything, and in that place, I feel so much love for what I have that I could cry.

Steve looks at me across the table then, movie-star handsome with a wide-open smile and eyes that shimmer like light on water.

"What?" he says, his smile going all the way into those eyes. "What are you looking at?"

I lean my face into my hand and just smile back at him because no words can say how I feel. Trying to explain would ruin the perfection of the moment anyway. He'll have to find this in his own way. It's the same with Spencer. I can lead him part of the way in this life but to understand how the heart really moves, eventually, he'll have to go it alone.

Spencer adds the last tablet to the last cup, a row of six different colors.

I scoot the bowl of eggs to the middle of the table and Spencer reaches out, grabs one in his small fist.

"Are we ready?" I say.

"I'm ready," Spencer says.

Steve laughs and puts his hand on Spencer's head, moves his hair around.

"I think we're ready," Steve says.

[illegible] this smile going all the way into those eyes.
[illegible] volume act?"

I [illegible] into my hand and just smile back at him because [illegible] can say how I feel. Trying to explain would ruin the perfection of the moment anyway. [illegible] have to find [illegible] in his own [illegible] with [illegible] If [illegible] can find any part of [illegible] understand [illegible] can't [illegible] will have to go it alone.

[illegible] to the [illegible] conv[illegible]

[illegible] the middle of the table and [illegible] the one in his small flat.

"Are we ready?" [illegible]

"I'm ready." [illegible]

[illegible] head [illegible] his [illegible] around.

[illegible] ready [illegible]

Still Waters

Jennifer Lauck

A Reader's Club Guide

ABOUT THIS GUIDE

The suggested questions are intended to help your reading group find new and interesting angles and topics for discussion for Jennifer Lauck's *Still Waters.* We hope that these ideas will enrich your conversation and increase your enjoyment of the book.

Many fine books from Washington Square Press feature Readers Club Guides. For a complete listing, or to read the Guides online, visit http://www.BookClubReader.com

Reading group guide for Still Waters

1. *Still Waters* begins with Jenny going to live with her grandparents. She loves the very precise routine of their days (golf, cocktail hour, supermarket on Tuesday, etc.). Many children would find such routine boring, but what is it about Jenny's background that makes her cling to these structured days?

2. When her grandparents tell Jenny that she's going to live with her aunt and uncle, she says, "I want to tell them I'll try harder, do better . . ." [p. 23] Do you think Jenny (and other children who are neglected, abandoned, or abused) feels deep down inside that she is to blame for her circumstances in life? Why do you think she tried so hard to "be good," and not to tell anyone when things were wrong, or say "no" to people who might hurt her?

3. Throughout her childhood, Jenny is fixated on certain possessions—her pink trunk, her Princess bedroom set—as the last vestiges of her life before her parents died. What symbolism do you think these particular objects hold for Jenny? Do you have similar items from your past that you have held onto as tokens of happy or significant times in your life?

4. When Jenny moves in with Aunt Peggy and Uncle Dick, she and Peggy initially relate to each other as friends

and confidants. Over the years their relationship changes, becoming highly adversarial. Why and when do you think this shift occurs between them? Do you think Peggy and Jenny have mixed feelings about each other, or are they very clear-cut?

5. When Jenny goes to stay with her cousin Sharon, Sharon's boyfriend molests Jenny. How to you think this incident fits in with Jenny's view of the adults in her life? Do you think it affects how Jenny relates to the men in her life?

6. The issue of telling the truth comes up a lot in *Still Waters*. In fact, it often seems like everyone around Jenny is lying or holding in their true feelings. How do you think Jenny learns the importance of honesty and openness, despite what she sees around her?

7. The intensity of Jenny's first relationship (with Luke) seems to frighten her. She says, "I get lost with Luke, with Randy, I know exactly where I am." [p. 164] Why do you think getting "lost" in a relationship is so scary for Jenny? Is this a normal adolescent reaction, or do you think it has more to do with her past?

8. Jenny repeatedly mentions the image she holds of her father in her head, "smiling, driving, wearing a sweater . . ." [p. 195] When children lose a parent so young, they often put that parent on a pedestal, remembering him or her as

unflawed. Think about the difference between what you thought of your parent(s) as a child and what you think about them now that you're an adult. What significance do you think this particular image of her father holds for Jenny?

9. Jenny's Aunt Georgia tells her, "You're a survivor, you always were." [p. 262] What makes someone "a survivor"? What traits does Jenny possess that help her get through this difficult life? How do you think you would have coped in her situation?

10. What do you think Jenny hopes to accomplish by visiting the seminary and college where Bryan lived—and the spot where he died? Do you think it's important to do things like this in order to truly understand and accept someone's death? In the end, do you think she has forgiven Bryan and other members of her family who treated her poorly?

11. Between her adoptive parents, her boyfriends, and her brother, Jenny is convinced that no one really loves her for her. By the end of the book, do you think that she finally discovers unconditional love?

A conversation with Jennifer Lauck

1. Have any of the members of the family you wrote about in *Still Waters* contacted you since its publication? If so, how did they react to the book and their characterizations in it—were they remorseful, angry, or did they own up to it?

I've not been contacted by any family from my father's side. Through extended family, that is cousins, I've heard there is a great deal of anger, resentment, even denial. One aunt reportedly said I was intent on bringing shame to the Laucks and this was a rather interesting comment. I believe the shame was already in the shadows and my telling the story simply brought it into plain view. Many in the extended family, who have first-hand dealings with Aunt Peggy, Uncle Dick, and Uncle Leonard, say I was extremely generous in my portrayal.

On my mother's side of the family, there has always been a tremendous amount of support and encouragement. I remain in close contact with Aunt Georgia and Uncle Charles and feel blessed that, finally, I have them in my life and in the lives of my children.

2. How did your view of religion change after you visited the seminary where Bryan lived? Do you think Bryan would have been a good priest?

The priests and monks of Conception and the sisters of Clyde showed me another side to Catholicism, a softer side. I appreciated the deep humanity that emanated from almost everyone I met and how they were searching for meaning in many of the same ways that I was. Most of my previous beliefs about Catholicism were based on a rigid structure of rules that you had to follow or else be condemned to severe punishment. I've learned that those beliefs are not in line with the true teachings of the Church. Although I am not a practicing Catholic, I do appreciate the power of spirituality through the door of Catholicism and how fulfilling it can be to have a community or even a church, to direct that spirituality.

On the question of Bryan, it is difficult to know what would have become of him. How deep was his depression? How intense was his pain? Could he have lifted through both depression and pain to heal others or would they have tainted his ability to give sound and loving advice? These are questions that I cannot answer. I would like to believe his soul was drawn to philosophy and faith so that, given time and maturity, he would have found true peace. Bryan's potential (and that of so many young men who struggle with inner demons) lies in those questions. That is the powerful tragedy of Bryan's life and death.

3. What can you tell us about the process of writing *Blackbird* and *Still Waters*? Did you find it cathartic?

Next to having my beautiful children, writing out my life has been the single most important thing I've done to heal.

4. How do you feel about what happened between you and your grandparents? They seemed to be the only people left in your family you felt close to, and they ended up letting you down. Did you ever forgive them?

Forgiveness has many faces but for me, it is the act of true empathy. My grandparents made very human decisions and mistakes. In writing about all this, I learned that their decisions were made from a foundation of hostile emotions and in most cases, decisions made that way always come back to haunt you. They may have let me down but, thanks to the writing, they have also become my greatest teachers.

5. How and when will you tell your son and daughter the story of your past?

Children are busy enough negotiating the maze of childhood. My past is my own but if I learn the lessons well, I can use my lessons to teach my children. That is primarily how I intend to tell my children about my past, in small, digestible bits that can help them along their journey.

6. On top of everything else you've been through, how has the fact that you were adopted played into your feelings

of being abandoned? Have you ever tried to search for your birth parents?

I haven't searched much for my birth parents. It's not something that seems very important right now.

I did feel very deeply for my birth mother recently though. It was the night my daughter was born. The doctor and nurses had left, my husband went home too and I was alone with this sweet little girl in my arms. We lay in the quiet dark room together, her sleeping in a tiny bundle, so warm and perfect in my arms. I felt so lucky and complete because she was here and safe and mine. In the way that thoughts and memories move, I imagined 38 years earlier, to the day I was born and taken away from my mother immediately. How awful that first night must have been for her and how empty her arms must have felt. For the first time ever, I felt as if I knew her in some way, perhaps knew a small amount of her suffering.

The bigger question, "do I belong?" has haunted me and been re-asked in many different relationships throughout my life. That is, when I've had the most difficulty with boyfriends, girlfriends or family, I fall back into this idea that I don't really belong, after all, my own mother gave me away. Finding my "birth parents" isn't going to change this element of my personality. The fact is, I was adopted and in my search for place, I've come to realize most of us feel orphaned in some way, even those with living parents and siblings. I'm not as interested in finding my birth parents as I am in finding a way to feel truly connected with people.

7. *Still Waters* covers about 25 years of your life. Was there a particular period during that time span that was the most difficult for you? Which was the happiest?

The best time of my life is right now and I can chart that back to beginning when my son was born. I love my children and I am very lucky to have a good friend in my husband.

The most difficult has to go back to childhood and being a witness to my mother's dark struggle with her body that ended so tragically. Her death marked the beginning of a long period of deep unhappiness that lasted until the day I moved out of Dick and Peggy's house.

8. You've described yourself as a "survivor." Yet you not only survived, you wrote two acclaimed books based on your experiences and managed to harness a painful past into incredible personal strength. Do you think you would be the person you are today if you hadn't gone through such adversity?

I feel that I am here, that we all are here, to learn. Life is like a big compost pile with layers and layers of rotten junk that really stinks but, if used properly, can grow the very best fruits and vegetables and grains. You can turn the cycle of compost over and over again and that is the harnessing of energy that creates intense personal growth. I am the person that I am today because I pay very close attention to what my life has to teach.

9. Both of your memoirs read very much like novels. Do you ever plan to write fiction?

I wrote both books first person present tense in order to tell the story through the moment of experience. I wanted to hear the purity of a little kid's voice and that's why it feels like a novel. Also, with first person, you are right there with the narrator, which I think is very powerful. I am working on a fiction-based story right now, using that same technique. It just feels very honest.

10. Do you feel that you've resolved the issues of your past, or do you expect that you'll have to keep working on them for some time?

The idea that we ever resolve issues of the past is appealing but not realistic. We are the product of our experiences; everything we believe and know comes from them. Unless we are truly enlightened, we can't have real "freedom." I see my journey is to keep looking at my life and digging for layers of understanding.